Dear Friend

Dear Friend

Reports from the Unconscious

by

Sally Levison

OPEN GATE PRESS

LONDON

This book is a true account of a patient's experiences of psychoanalytic depth therapy. As it is a case history, we have followed normal psychoanalytic practice in altering names (including that of the author) and some minor details in order to protect the privacy of the individuals concerned.

First published in 1990 by Open Gate Press
51 Achilles Road, London NW6 1DZ

Copyright © 1990 Open Gate Press

British Library Cataloguing in Publication Data
Levison, Sally, *1955–*
  Dear Friend.
  1. Psychoanalysis – Biographies
  I. Title
  150.195192

  ISBN 1-871871-02-6

Photoset in 11 on 13pt Bembo

Printed in Great Britain by
Halstan & Co Ltd., Amersham, Bucks.

Contents

Preface

I have always been fascinated by the idea that there are thoughts and feelings in our minds of which we know nothing – a second world of reality, as it were, which holds sway beneath our conscious world. My studies of philosophy led me to assume that mind was synonymous with consciousness and that the study of our conceptions, judgements and values was the ultimate concern of our intellect. In addition, my reading of books on psychoanalysis and my conversations with friends who had undergone psychoanalytic treatment caused me to believe that what was called the unconscious was something that could only be glimpsed from free associations and from the interpretations of the analyst.

But then an agonising and very frightening neurotic disturbance led me to seek professional help. It soon became clear to me that in the treatment I underwent, I encountered an experience quite different from that which I had come to expect, either from my reading of psychoanalytic literature or from reports from those who had undergone or were still undergoing conventional analysis. I was transported into a world so strange and yet so real – a completely unexpected continent of the mind – and even at a quite early stage of the treatment I decided that I would eventually want to write about it. Indeed, I soon developed the habit of writing down everything that happened during the analytic session as soon as I got home. As the notes I made multiplied, a story emerged which not only charted the progress and transformation of my psyche, but also revealed to me the extraordinary world of my unconscious mind. Surely, I thought, this must be an important area of the mind which lives in everybody.

When my notes became a book, I addressed them to my analyst, whom I call my friend – for that's what he became, as I could share my innermost secrets with him without shame or embarrassment. Indeed, it was just because he helped me to overcome my fears and my inhibitions and gave me the confidence to reveal to him and to myself things which I could not believe could he shared with anyone, but which I feared had to be hidden away in the secret chambers of my soul, that he became my real friend. I also want to show my gratitude to him and my deep appreciation of the method of psychoanalysis which he has developed, which I believe to be quite new – a method of depth therapy which is not restricted to the often rigid conventions of traditional psychoanalysis.

My reasons for publishing these notes are essentially twofold: first because I want to share the quite extraordinary insights into the unconscious mind, and secondly because they may contribute something to a better understanding of the human mind generally. For I must assume that I am not the only person in whom this largely undiscovered world of the mind exists, or the only person who wants to explore it.

I am grateful to the publishers for their advice on the etiquette of publishing case histories: they have suggested that I change names and certain minor details of what is otherwise a true story, and that I myself write under a *nom de plume*. These suggestions I am pleased to accept.

London, 1990

1
What's Going On Around Here?

My dear friend,

The single most courageous thing I have done in my life is to acknowledge that I needed your help.

One morning, I woke up, and realised that I could see nothing left to live for. Put that way, it sounds terribly dramatic – but in fact, there was nothing dramatic or exciting about it; it was a tragedy of nothingness. From the outside, no one would ever have guessed that anything could be wrong; I seemed to have an enviably happy and fulfilled life. I had achieved everything I had striven for: I was a popular and presentable young woman; I was married to a kind and considerate man who loved me; I had somewhere nice to live; I'd been to one of the best universities in the country; I was considered one of the rising stars at work; and it was difficult to conceive of any reason why I shouldn't be entirely contented with my lot.

But the reality which I lived was quite different; I was desperately miserable, filled only with an aching emptiness. I felt that I couldn't make my marriage work; I didn't really care where I lived; my experience at university had been devastatingly disappointing; and I hated every moment of my job. It seemed to me that all the paths which had until then forked out in front of me, inviting me to choose my way to happiness and a worthwhile life, had suddenly arrived at a dead end. I'd made all the choices. This was it – and I still wasn't happy. And now there was nowhere else to go, and nothing else to do, except to wait for death. Or was there?

★   ★   ★

It is difficult for me now, even with the benefit of so much hindsight, to pinpoint exactly how I came to realise that there might be another way forward. For many years I had been aware of a groping after a wonderful Something which was going to rescue me from the pendulum of peaks and troughs which had characterised my life. I had hoped that I had found that Something in philosophy, and my passion for the pleasures of the mind had brought me, still at well under thirty years of age, to a senior academic position.

I must have known that things weren't quite right with a life of peaks and troughs – and yet at one time, I had actually liked the manic ups and the depressive downs, and had seen them as an interlocking whole, in which the pleasures – the heady intoxication of power, passion and danger – far outweighed the pains of helplessness and melancholy which filled the troughs. There had even been pleasure in helplessness and melancholy when they were seen as the necessary and inevitable foreplay to the orgastic delights of the soul's flood tide!

As I became older, the balance between the peaks and troughs gradually shifted. The rot was slow, but deadly. Almost imperceptibly, the peaks became episodes of frantic grasping after pleasures which always receded in front of me. The pleasures of riding the mind's surf and experiencing its power increasingly became the impotence of being dashed onto the shingle by the force of a passion which was no longer benevolent. I began to feel not pleasure, but panic and terror. I would lie awake at night, willing sleep to release me from the torment of my soul .. but was unable to achieve this peace before I had completed several hours of mental self-flagellation. Only then could I experience the release of slumber.

It seems to me now that one of the causes of this was my total lack of adjustment to my job. The work itself was very stimulating, but I was in profound disagreement with most of the political and educational initiatives being implemented and promulgated in my college. Although I agreed with what they purported to be striving towards, I considered the *methods* being used to 'promote' them both totalitarian and counter-productive. I could not accept the prevailing ideologies of feminism, equal opportunities and anti-racism, not because I didn't believe that all people were equal, but because I felt that the tenets which underlay the policies undermined all the ideas of individual responsibility for action; they assumed that people were just pawns in a system, and that by changing the system, you could change people. This seemed to me to miss the essential point.

But what made this so traumatic for me was finding that my training in philosophy, which I had valued so much, did nothing to help me stand up against the moral blackmail which I felt at the core of totalitarian ideologies. I was so dependent on the approval of the establishment within which I worked, so dependent on the opinion of others for my picture of myself, that when I found myself at odds with it, my brain quite literally could not find the right questions to ask and to answer. Yet, I felt, if philosophy was not able to understand the fundamental issues of contemporary morality, and to point the way towards a better world, what was it? Not only did my emotional world break down under the external pressures of political indoctrination, but my intellectual world crumbled in front of me, leaving me with neither an outer nor an inner Self.

All the trappings of adulthood fell away from me as I found myself back again in the helplessness of childhood. I was ashamed of and frustrated by my inability to speak out against the totalitarianism I saw around me. I was afraid both of the opprobrium I would have to tolerate, and of being out-argued on matters of dogma by people whom I didn't respect. And yet, I could not remain silent. Almost without my being aware of it, I found myself introducing 'contemporary' issues into my moral philosophy classes, so that I could encourage my students to think the matters through properly, and help them to see, at the least, that there was more than one side to the question.

My Self approved of this course of action; maybe it wasn't as good as speaking out publicly would be, but at least it wasn't as bad as just pretending I didn't see what was going on. Unfortunately, however, the plan didn't work as well as it might have done. I would find myself in the middle of my classes, sweating with fear, and completely losing my sense of perspective on the present. Every lesson, I would say something which somehow broke through a taboo, and would experience the terrors of hot flushes, ringing ears and blurring vision. I was afraid.

At night, I would lie in bed, remembering all the things I'd said, and I would tremble at what would happen to me if Anyone Found Out. What would happen if my students told one of my colleagues that I'd been spreading seditious counter-revolutionary propaganda? I'd deny it, of course! But how could I, when I believed in what I'd said? I would justify it all by saying to myself that actually, I hadn't said anything, really; I'd just encouraged my students to see how many different ways there were to look at issues.

My mind tortured me with images of being hauled before the Principal and the Board of Governors, and being unceremoniously dismissed for corrupting the young and leading them into reactionary ways. I would defend myself staunchly in the court of my tortured mind: I wasn't a reactionary; I was a sensitive intellectual; I was standing up for goodness and truth and human dignity. My judges didn't believe me: I was beyond the pale, and the only punishment worthy of me was total extirpation, root and branch. I would be thrown out and cut off without even a reference to get me a new job. How could I stand it?

In reality, there was no way that my colleagues could have been in any doubt as to my political opinions; I never hid them, even though I didn't go out of my way to seek out conflict. My students enjoyed and were stimulated by my classes, and their examination results brought credit to the college. Although my colleagues didn't agree with the positions I took up, they didn't regard me as a threat to them; in a curious way, they regarded it as an enjoyable challenge to test the strength of their opinions against my intellect. I was a valued and popular member of the common room. But I couldn't see any of this; my mind was populated by demons and dragons and life-threatening monsters, which gradually became so powerful that even getting up in the morning to go to work became an event to be dreaded and feared. I was, quite literally, falling apart.

One day, a kindly fate introduced me to you. My soul leapt with joy as it recognised in you someone I could trust – a man who understood the Truth. I wanted, quite suddenly, to be your friend, and to learn from you all the wonderful things my soul had forgotten – to learn to live again. The history of my analysis with you is quite simply summed up: I gained the courage to believe that you really were .. my friend.

★ ★ ★

In retrospect, the thing that most fascinates me about the time I spent in analysis is the way the course of the analysis itself so clearly reflects the development of the soul in a human child. For the first many months, all that existed for me was you, and the experience of myself that I gained through you. I had no self of my own; I didn't know who I was; I didn't believe in the existence of myself except on your couch; and my interest in the outside world shrank almost to vanishing point. I was interested only in feelings, in smells, in being with you, in absorbing the life-energy which seemed to flow from you. While outwardly, I continued to play a normal role in society, inwardly I became a baby again, or a small child, for whom all existence is centred in the person who feeds her. For what you did for me was to feed my soul.

MEETING MYSELF

My first visits to you were really traumatic. My overwhelming feeling each time was one of fear; my knees would shake and my vitals turn to water as I walked down the road towards your consulting room. Yet underneath the fear was the excitement and pleasure of the conviction that this time, at last, I was on the road to milk and honey.

The fact that I'd plucked up the courage to do something about things, though, didn't mean that the voyage to normalcy was going to be all milk and honey! The conflicts I used to feel as I walked from the tube station to your office were quite overwhelming. Ideas – not yet even ideas, but merely formless anxieties – would crowd into my brain, clamouring for attention. But could I tell you about them? Dared I tell you? I so much wanted to tell you everything – yet I was afraid you wouldn't listen. But equally, I was afraid that if I didn't tell you, I would still be angry with you for not listening to me and understanding me. That, I supposed, was what projection was.

In the real world, though, you never gave any hint that you wanted to do anything but listen to me, help me and "cure" me. But it was so difficult for me to believe and trust in you. One part of me – would you call it my ego? – recognised you as a wise, strong man and wanted you to love me; yet another part of me would whisper seditiously in my ear,

"You're hurting him, you know; he'll be angry with you. You're going to kill him by all the demands you make on him. Then what will you have done?"

I couldn't bear it. And yet .. was it really possible that you could give me what I wanted? Or that I could actually *ask* you for it?

I sat opposite you in your consulting room on many occasions, desperately looking through my mind for what I really wanted to say and trying to summon the courage to say it. For to ask you to help me, to look at me, to acknowledge me, seemed to be equivalent to asking you to let me kill you with the overwhelming power of my demands. Dared I try it? My whole being became concentrated – and paralysed – into this struggle for action. I often used to sit for minutes at a time, quite silent, struggling with the words I both wanted and feared to say.

You never let my inner struggle go on until it was terminal; you always intervened after a decent interval, making it all right for me to speak.

"What is it thinking?" you would ask me.

I loved that term "it". It enabled me to detach myself from the me that was going to kill you, and refer to her in an impersonal manner. But, more importantly still, it also helped me to acknowledge the nice me. There was me, and there was it. Which was the nice one, I didn't really know; I didn't know much about myself at all in those days. All I did know was that one of them was nice – and that was what counted. Because, for all that I knew that I liked myself really, I found it terribly difficult to believe that I was nice; I could not conceive of acknowledging the side of me which deserved to be loved, without then exploding from the power of a pleasure which I didn't know how to handle. By calling her (or me) "it", you allowed me to look at her, too, in a kind of 'objective' manner which was far enough removed from ME for me to cope with it. And as we talked about these two people – the nice me and the horrid me, I was able gradually to accept the one and reject the other. Yet within the framework of each session, I could take back to myself as much or as little as I could handle.

"Tell me all about it," you said to me. And on my first visit, I talked to you for a long time. I believed that the whole point of psychoanalysis was that I had to recognise that there was something the matter with me and present it to you for healing. I told you the story of my life, as you had asked; but I was careful to make it clear to you that I realised that it was all my fault. It was I who was lacking in compassion and understanding and it was this that had caused me to be in such a mess, with a life which seemed so unworth living. What was I doing here? The best thing I could do was to lie down in the path of an oncoming bus. I wanted to confess my sins to you and you to cast them out. That meant that you would punish me – cast me out. But then, that was what I deserved.

You asked me about my family, and I told you what I could about my husband Eddie, my brother David and my parents – and especially about my mother. I explained to you that she only wanted the best for me, but that I was only able to construe her help and assistance in my life as destructive interference. I didn't appreciate any of her ambitions for me and her desires that I should be great and powerful, and her bulwark against the nasty outside world. I was an unappreciative daughter who wasn't prepared to repay all the sacrifices my mother had made for me over the years, so that I could have all the successes which had been denied her. What I wanted was for you to make me into a good girl, so that I could appreciate her better and stop being so angry with her all the time. I don't know what I would have done if you *had* .. but in the event, the question didn't arise!

For when I had finished, you exploded with rage. I quaked into the back of my chair. Now it was going to happen. I prepared myself to leave with dignity, before you threw me out. Yet as I listened, I heard what you were actually saying. "What a monster your mother is!" you exclaimed. Gradually, I realised that you believed that there was nothing wrong with me, but only with her.

My brain reeled. One part of me was singing and dancing; "Fall at his feet and worship him," it said. "Be his slave. At last you've found someone who understands." After all, anyone who realised that it was her and not me had to be a god. But another part of me howled with anguish:

"Oh dear, is he going to ignore what is the matter with me? Is he going to ignore my wretchedness, and lavish all his attentions on punishing *her*?"

I could not bear it! What about me? Yet at the same time, I was absolutely terrified; I had obviously hidden from you the fact that I was a monster. You were prepared, in all good faith, to listen to me and acknowledge me. What might I do to you as you offered yourself to me in this innocent way? Should I not warn you against me? But I didn't want to. I liked you liking me; I wanted to take the risk that you wouldn't ever find out! So I remained silent about all the terrible things I hoped you wouldn't have to know.

Before I went home from that first ever session, you lay me on your couch and hypnotised me.

"Say hello to yourself," you said.

An extraordinary pleasure of wholeness crept in a blissful warmth through my body. For the first time – it seemed, ever – I felt myself as a unity rather than as a concatenation of separate parts. It was wonderful. Like being a baby again, I thought. You came and sat on the edge of the couch, like a daddy coming to kiss his little girl goodnight.

"How does it feel?" you asked.

It took me some time to work out what I ought to say in answer to this question. For all I could think was that you had come to lie on top of me and put your penis inside me. It was such a wonderful thought! But I was overwhelmed by fear; how could I think such a thing? You'd be so shocked with me if you knew. I erased the thought and talked to you about daddy instead. You smiled; and something inside me whispered that you knew about the other thought too. But we hadn't said it. Could we?

COMING TO TERMS WITH MYSELF

Something I found particularly wonderful was the fact that you offered yourself to me as a friend, and let me feel and know you; you weren't afraid to touch me, or to talk to me about yourself. You weren't frightened; you didn't hide yourself in a box of theory or sit behind me as I lay on your couch. You were real.

This was quite overwhelming for me, as I had been afraid that I was going to have to be real all on my own. Other people I knew, who were in analysis, seemed not to know their analysts at all; there was no real relationship between analyst and patient, but only something they called 'transference'. This seemed to mean that the analyst had no personality except that 'determined' by the patient. It was a looking-glass world, in which my friends' deepest and most sacred essence was understood only through reflections – and because the reflections were so difficult to interpret, the quest for truth took on a merciless and ruthless character. But surely, I thought, if the analyst refuses to be a person, the patient's soul is deprived of all sustenance.

You didn't want to have power over me by knowing all about me without giving anything of yourself. Better still was what followed from this: for the fact that you were prepared to be a whole person meant that you weren't afraid of me .. and this filled my soul with intense relief.

You used to talk to me about the difference between my superego, my ego and my id. I loved listening to you .. but it was a long time before I started to be able to make any certain distinctions for myself. For my superego held sway, paralysing my brain .. and it didn't like me. Nor did I like it. Yet it WAS me .. and I did like me, even though I didn't like it. But because it was me, I didn't like me. Oh dear. Who did I like? And who didn't I like? And who was this "I" anyway? It all felt terribly complicated, because I couldn't separate the I who judged from the I who was judged. I wanted to rip out this terrible monster who sapped my strength and lived on my pleasures .. but I was afraid that if I did that, I'd kill myself too.

A negative superego, you called it. Yet as you talked, I only half understood what you were saying. All I knew was that I hated her, and wanted her gone; she drove me mad with despair and misery. "Take it away!" I would scream. But you always said that we couldn't yet.

"We have to strengthen the ego first," you would say to me.

This was terrible; I didn't hear you talking about me – for, although I was my ego, I didn't recognise myself. All I could hear was you telling me that I was stuck with the superego for now. And now meant forever; I couldn't distinguish NOW from any other time. It was like being locked in hell.

You were right, though, to go slowly and respect me; for it was as if my ego had been fed upon for many years by a destructive parasite with which it had, almost inevitably, entered into a symbiotic relationship. If we had killed the parasite without ensuring that my ego knew how to survive on its own, then all we'd actually have achieved would have been the death of them both, and that would have been appalling.

But how it hurt! For the first thing that had to happen was that my ego needed to wake up and realise that it was being squeezed. It hadn't wanted to know, and so had numbed itself, because the pain of acknowledging its bondage, without the prospect of freedom, had been too terrible. Now, though, it was safe to experience the pain, because the way was open to removing its cause. However, it wasn't easy; for the first few months of my analysis, our – or do I mean your? – major task was to contain and acknowledge the rage, the fury, the outrage that had been stored up in the silent world of my unconscious, but which now came flying out, demanding attention and restitution for the evils perpetrated upon my Self. Only then would we be able to proceed to neutralising it.

I was immensely grateful to you, and at the same time, absolutely terrified. For one part of me loved the anger, loved the opportunity at last to speak of all the terrible things and to gain much-desired revenge for all those years of oppression. And you acknowledged it. You listened to me as I cried and screamed and raged. I hated everything and everybody; I couldn't have believed that so much hatred could exist in a person without destroying them, or their family, totally. But another part of me was deeply shocked by it all; I didn't want to talk to you about it, because bringing it into the open so that it could be acknowledged, and showing myself in such a light, actually reinforced my anxiety that I was totally unworthy of anything except punishment and contempt. Somehow – I still don't really understand how – you managed to tread the delicate line between acknowledging that I was right to be angry and encouraging me to discharge the anger and put it behind me. Only then I could start again without the permanent shadow in my soul.

*　　*　　*

Each week, I found myself with a seemingly new concern or preoccupation, which revealed itself as an anxiety, or even as a physical symptom. Sometimes, I was able to guess at the cause, but on other occasions, I just floundered in a sea of searing uncertainty, waiting for it to be time to come and see you, to tell you about it. You always seemed to understand what the REAL problem was, and you used to ask me questions I didn't know how to ask myself. We often reached a point, however, where my conscious self didn't know the answer to any more questions; then you often decided that we should talk to my unconscious directly. By hypnotising me, you put me back in touch with all kinds of ideas and feelings that I had completely forgotten.

The first few times I came to you, you taught me how to use the hypnotic experience to relive emotions and episodes from my past – and sometimes even from my present. You showed me how to create pictures for myself of how things looked – and the pictures would contain in them all the feelings which I had long forgotten, or of whose causes I had become unaware. Like all truly brilliant ideas, this was the epitome of simplicity. After all, art, literature and poetry create images which elicit emotions; and it is from the unconscious that these deep impulses come.

At the beginning, you used hypnosis to help me remember painful experiences from my childhood so that I could come to terms with them as an adult. Children make decisions based on little experience, and in any case, they are too dependent on their parents to be truly independent in the ways they look at the world. To reinterpret things that had happened to me with the benefit of twenty-five years' more experience was a most liberating experience. But as we went on, you began to put more emphasis on bringing the real me out of hiding. As I came to be freer of the terrible thoughts and ideas which had tyrannised me up to this point, my soul found the space to develop ideas about how IT wanted to be, and I realised that there was more to life than being free of my past.

I soon came to understand that my unconscious was an exciting, dynamic place. Sometimes, lying on your couch, I would draw up from my memory pictures of things which had really happened to me and which had hurt; sometimes, the feelings associated with an experience would create pictures of how the unconscious side of it had looked (and seeing these pictures was a powerful aid to interpreting the scene); and sometimes, the pictures would be a wonderful mix of memory and interpretation.

But that wasn't all; you entered into my pictures yourself.

"See me there; see how I react," was a frequent encouragement of yours as I lay on your couch.

The effect that such an episode would have on my soul was quite revolutionary. Often, when I had relived a scene from my childhood – perhaps a memory of something that really happened, or perhaps a memory of how I felt about something and what pictures this had created in my unconscious – I would find that, along with my relief at having understood it, would go a sadness that this was how things had to be. After all, no matter how much I resented it, my parents were my parents and didn't always know how to behave nicely towards their daughter. The patterns of response which I had developed towards them were deeply etched into my soul, and understanding HOW things had happened was only the first step in learning new ways of doing things. By entering into my unconscious world as Uncle George, you helped me to create another model of how things could be nice; by letting me see how it felt to have some-one else other than my parents or my brother watching what I was doing, you enabled me actually to replace old assumptions about myself with new ones.

What was particularly extraordinary to me, in the early days although as time went on, I couldn't imagine how I could ever have not known about it – was the effect the pictures had on my body. Unpleasant pictures would make me purse my lips, or arch my back, or pull in my bottom .. and the constant presence of these pictures in my unconscious had an effect on the way I stood, the positions in which I felt comfortable, and the attitudes I would strike. As I came to understand the pictures, and to replace nasty pictures with nice ones, the shape of my body changed! The changes were scarcely perceptible week by week – but over a period of months or years, they added up to something quite dramatic. And that was terribly exciting, not just because I came to feel better about my body, but at an intellectual level as well: we are as we look!

GETTING DOWN TO BUSINESS

The first few months of my analysis are rather hazy in my mind; I had so many new experiences that it was difficult for me to compre-hend them all at once. A whole new world of symbols and fantasies was opening out in front of me, and it took a while before I started to make sense of it. Gradually, however, I began to become more aware of what kinds of things my unconscious mind was pre-occupied with, and to be less alarmed when strange thoughts popped, unbidden, into my head. For as time went on, I learned to trust you, and to believe that you would know how to respect my bizarre thoughts for their real worth.

It wasn't always easy, though, incubating a new idea. One of the first such episodes I remember took place in the middle of a cold, dark night. I had been feeling particularly depressed that week, without really knowing why, and I was sleeping only fitfully at nights. Suddenly, I leapt into wakefulness, horrified by the thought I found in my brain:

"My God; my vagina has teeth in it!"

My first reaction was one of total despair. I was so upset; how could I live with myself? For just a moment, I hoped that it might not really be true .. yet deep down, I was certain that it was, so there didn't seem any point in denying it. Yet as the panic subsided, I found room for a new thought:

"Do I want to have teeth in my vagina or not?"

I really didn't know the answer to this question. I could see that teeth could be extremely useful, and there were many times – when I was feeling angry or frustrated – when I was very pleased they were there. Yet another part of me was truly horrified at the idea that I might have such teeth; somehow it seemed to me that this would mean that I had to behave like my aggressive mother, which was the last thing I wanted.

Perhaps, I thought, I could prove that I wasn't really like her by smashing my teeth up. Now that was real pleasure. But what a terrible thing to have pleasure in! In horror, I asked myself why I should think breaking things was so pleasurable. Back came an answer with which I was satisfied: that it was my way of asserting that I was really a moral and good person, even if it meant that I had sometimes to do things which I wasn't proud of. Yet that's what all totalitarian regimes through the ages have said: that the end justifies the means. So what did that imply for my morals?

I spent most of the rest of that night awake, as my mind whirled with the new ideas and associations that poured into it and raced around inside it. I was amazed by the images it created for me, and the (not always pleasant) light it shed on aspects of my everyday life. In the starkness which the small hours create, I grappled with what felt like the fundamentals of the universe.

It seemed to me that one of the reasons why I had to smash my teeth before I could become a 'good' person was that if I didn't, there would always be the risk that if I lost control, I'd bite. This realisation certainly made a lot of sense of some of my more inexplicable behaviour: during lovemaking, I would lie in bed rolling my eyes back and clenching my teeth. Anything not to lose control; I didn't want to bite the penis. The pleasure of making love was always outweighed by the feeling that something terrible was going to happen, and by knowing that I had to hold on tight. No wonder I found the unconditional release of orgasm so difficult to achieve!

I looked at this strange behaviour of mine and wondered how I could solve the problem. The trouble was that I could only see a solution in terms which involved destruction: I felt that I had to let the penis smash through my teeth and break them and show me who was boss.

One part of me was pleased with this 'solution' and considered me to be a good and moral person; after all, I was declaring that I wasn't on the side of vaginas which ate penises and that in order to prove my innocence of evil intent towards the penis, I was prepared even to let it break me and to attain total mastery over me.

Unfortunately, though, the 'solution' didn't solve the problem, because I wouldn't be able to love or respect a penis which was prepared to violate me in that way – so I wasn't paving the way for love and harmony! What could I do? My brain reeled with the effort of making sense of all these possibilities, and I wondered whether perhaps it was better just not to show anyone my vagina and then they'd never find out. But that wouldn't do the trick either, for you had said that you wanted me to learn to love my vagina, and denying its existence was clearly no way to do that.

Eventually, I dropped into the deep slumber which follows such nocturnal tussles, and resolved that I would discuss the whole knotty problem with you at our next session.

When I told you about it all, you were pleased. After some preliminary questioning, you let me lie down on your couch and hypnotised me. By this time, I was used to the kinds of pictures which my unconscious mind produced under hypnosis, and to the extraordinary heightening of all sensations which is a characteristic of your 'method', so my mind responded quite quickly.

"What do you feel like?" you asked.

My body was enormously tense; I felt like a violin with the strings too tight, or as if I was saving something up so that I could run away.

This tension brought images to my mind; there were so many

strands to the feeling. I found myself thinking about the 'real' world, and how I didn't ever like working hard at anything, because it was somehow always too terrifying. And now I became aware that one part of me never really respected myself being unable to do anything properly. I'd always been clever enough to get away with it, even if only by the skin of my teeth .. but I knew always that there were things I wasn't doing, or knowing, or finding out about, because I was scared. Unless someone was standing over me, threatening me with punishment, I wouldn't do it.

My attention came back to the more immediate feelings which my unconscious was trying to show me. I could see the pictures which my mind created from the feelings, and experienced the sensation of both BEING and SEEING myself. By now, I was used to this phenomenon – but the first time it had happened, I had been very confused. After all, I wondered, should I tell you about the pictures I could see of myself by calling myself "me" or by referring to myself as "her"? It didn't really seem to matter, though, and I used whichever term seemed more appropriate to the occasion!

On this occasion, I saw myself feeling that I was stamping my feet and being angry. I didn't know why I should be feeling that; I only knew that it was somehow a familiar pattern, which I recognised.

"Just look," you said, "and your unconscious will tell you."

Suddenly, there in front of me were mummy's breasts. I tried to tell you about them, but my brain was overwhelmed by a terrible, whirling confusion.

"Don't worry," you said, "just keep looking."

As I did so, I found myself terribly upset: it seemed to me that she didn't want to give them to me when I wanted them, but only when she wanted to. But I didn't want to take them and suck them when *she* was ready. The whole point was that I wanted her to let me suck her because she was pleased that I wanted her. My brain seized up: did I want to suck mummy's breasts or not? She could feel me not knowing; then she was cross and thrust them at me:

"You said you wanted them; well, here they are. Have them."

I was so confused. She was right; I did want them. Yet at the same time, I didn't want them, because what I really wanted was to have them *because* I wanted them; the point was that I wanted her to respond to my desire. Actually *having* the breasts was somehow only secondary. What was important was that they should like to come to me when I invited them. But this was not happening, and I found myself tied up in a knot of what seemed like total sophistry.

Then I began to understand; I felt the pain. I thought of it as "the pain" – because it was so familiar to me. What I'd never done was associate it consciously with this picture. It was a prickling sensation, a tightness. But where did it come from, and what was it? I stayed with it for a while, and suddenly, everything became clear; I realised that it was the pain in mummy's vagina when I sucked her breasts! I could see and feel that she was upset by the pain, and that she didn't know whether she liked feeding me or not. In a way she did like it; I could feel that, too .. but she somehow drew back from me and didn't give herself to me properly.

Then I was afraid. I wept as I looked at the hopelessness of the situation. I couldn't bear not getting the good libido from her, and this made me angry and upset. But I was worried that I would lose my temper with her and bite her and stamp my feet, or kick my legs; I was frightened of being aggressive; after all, what would happen if I made her angry and she never came to me again? So I took the breast she offered me and tightened myself against the tantrums. But then ... it was extraordinary: it was *my* vagina that became prickly! I had to take on the feeling for her, in order somehow to protect us both from the consequences of her feeling it. But it was quite dreadful; I hated it. Yet what else could I do?

As I whirled round in a state of total confusion, you came to my rescue.

"Tell it to stop prickling," you told me.

And to my unutterable relief, I felt it relax. The danger was past.

It was not only a relief to my feelings – it was fascinating at an intellectual level as well. I realised that when I had taken on my mother's feelings in order to protect myself against having my own authentic feelings which were somehow unacceptable to her, I had felt that what was hers became mine. And unfortunately, the fact that

I never really accepted it didn't alter the fact that having it made me a different person. No wonder I got depressed!

My brain began to work again; I spent many pleasurable hours thinking that this must be how cultures are transmitted from generation to generation – without anyone seeing what goes on. A mystery began to unfold itself in front of me ... There was an intellectual dimension to this as well. What pleasure!

As I brought to you problem after problem which was caused by my having taken on my mother's characteristics, I found it almost incredible that you still thought that she and I were different in some fundamental way. You told me (though in all honesty, I didn't really understand what you said at the time) that the very fact that I came to see you and she didn't, proved that I had rejected all that side of myself, and found it alien to my true self .. while she, even if she didn't like everything in herself, had nonetheless compromised with it and was quite prepared to live with it, moan about it, and justify it as not her fault if it came to the crunch. By taking responsibility for what I didn't like, I was able to rid myself of it. Or something like that.

I WANT TO BE A GIRL!

At this stage in my analysis, it happened quite frequently that I became aware that something was the matter, but I didn't know what it was. One week, I came to see you in a most terrible state: everything was wrong with the universe; nothing worked; and I was in a frenzy of chaotic anxiety about sex and men and women. And what it turned out to be about was a revelation! After some preliminary explorations at a conscious level, you let me lie down on your couch, and suggested that I might look at my mother and my brother.

But I couldn't do that, because all I could think about was how I needed a pee.

"Why is that?" you asked.

I could see myself in my cot .. and gradually, I became aware of that moment of extreme pleasure just before the pee comes out. It was wonderful – such an exquisite kind of pleasure. The trouble was that mummy didn't like it. This changed everything: I felt that I couldn't enjoy it with her there; I didn't want to pee in front of her and have her spoil it. I was upset, and the urge to pee became a tense pain.

"Where can you pee with pleasure?" you asked.

The pictures weren't terribly clear at first, and the sensations which went with them didn't feel as direct as usual. But a story emerged nonetheless. I saw myself peeing in my bed. That was very nice indeed; not only was it a good way of getting revenge on mummy for not appreciating my peeing, but it was also a good place to be sure of getting some privacy to enjoy it myself.

But I still didn't really know what all this had to do with mummy and David.

"Look at them and see what they're doing," you told me.

I looked, and the pictures began to emerge more freely and distinctly, bringing the full range of feelings with them. I saw an un-circumcised penis, with mummy pulling its foreskin and stretching it. Then I saw her big hand covering David's little penis, and felt his confusion about whether to enjoy it or not. It was difficult for him not to enjoy having his penis played with; the way she did it was perverse – but at least it was sexual. Then mummy smiled at him, and showed him all her love and protection – and I was jealous. I watched all her ploys to give him attention: how she pretended to worry that he was stupid so that she could draw attention to how clever he was really; and how she then enlisted my support in teaching him and looking after him. My cleverness was all used for him, and in competition with him – and then it had to be a phallic cleverness, not a vaginal cleverness. I felt an outrage, a tension, because I had to be clever *or* be a little girl; I couldn't do both, because it was the penis which was important. David's penis was the only thing that counted.

Pictures from my childhood unrolled in front of me. I was hor-rid, because I was so unhappy. All I wanted was for someone to tell me that it was all right to be a little girl .. but no one did. I became hugely fat and my body became rigid, so that instead of walking, I strutted. I wouldn't wear a skirt, and I pulled my vagina so far up into my body that it almost disappeared. I felt that I was vulgar and obscene .. but I tried desperately hard to smile and be happy and make jokes so that people would like me. But they didn't; they hated me because I hated myself. I was angry, though, because the self-hatred was unnecessary: if mummy had valued me and daddy had known how to show what he really thought, then none of this would ever have needed to happen. Yet as things were, the only way I knew to obtain love was to be clever – in a phallic way .. and I couldn't even be proud of that because I didn't really have a penis. I was a fraud.

Suddenly, a realisation dawned on me: the uncircumcised penis that I had seen right at the beginning wasn't a penis at all, but my clitoris. I wasn't interested in what mummy got up to with David, but only in what happened to me. And I wanted to be nice. But I couldn't. I could feel a pain in my clitoris, and my legs shook. I realised my reason for wetting the bed was that boys pee out of their penises, and I wanted to assert my penis so that mummy would love me too. And yet, it suddenly dawned on me, as if for the first time, that it was no wonder I was anxious; I didn't want to be a little boy and have a penis; I wanted to be a little girl! Yet even this simple desire was fraught with difficulties; quite apart from the fact that mummy seemed only to appreciate penises, I was afraid that it was dirty to be a little girl. I didn't know what it might involve. After all, I might become a penis-eater like I had always felt mummy to be – and I certainly didn't want that. But what else could vaginas do?

You knew that I knew.

"Feel your vagina," you suggested.

And to my unutterable relief, I realised that actually I *did* know what vaginas were for and what they did. And that I liked mine! I could feel it good and warm and blossoming and tumescent and juicy. It was a wonderful fulfilling sensation, spreading right through my body. But there was still a problem: I couldn't connect the clitoral sensations with the vaginal ones. I wanted them to hold hands, as it were, and cooperate in loving harmony, and allow me to release my orgastic tensions.

"Let them do just that," you said.

But I couldn't.

"All right, then," you went on. "Allow yourself to feel that you have a penis .. and then feel that you have a vagina."

I was rather nervous about this .. but I did what you suggested. And it was the most extraordinary sensation! I really felt that I had a penis. I could feel it all big and heavy and real, lying against the top of my legs. Then .. it didn't get bitten off, or ripped out, or any of the other dreadful things I'd been afraid of. As I lay on your couch, I felt 'my' penis becoming absorbed into my vagina, merging into it to provide it with extra warmth and body – and existence. It was as if my vagina suddenly had a corporeal existence instead of just a psychological one. I could feel it, and recognise its sexuality and its size – just as one can feel the size of a penis.

Then – and this was the real breakthrough – I realised that the reason I'd always been so afraid of showing it, or feeling it, or whatever, was that I'd been frightened that it WASN'T THERE. That was the most tremendous feeling, bringing such waves of warmth and recognition and catharsis. I didn't have any idea in my conscious life that I didn't believe in the existence of my vagina and that this was the cause of a lot of my troubles. But now I saw – and the very acknowledgement of the fear made it possible for me to understand – that of course I did have a vagina after all. I felt suddenly that it would be possible for me to seduce a man, because I had something that didn't rely on him. He wasn't pushing a hole into me, through which I would try to feel things; I had an organ of my own which could feel things, and I could offer him the richness of my vagina because I loved it. I had something to offer! That was amazing.

Suddenly then, I felt my breasts. I hadn't ever really known what to do with them. They had always puzzled me, because I knew that they were sexual things, and that if they were touched nicely, then I could feel sensations in my genital area – yet it was as if the connections between the two somehow fizzled out half way there. But now, as if by magic, I suddenly felt my breasts organically connected to my vagina and my womb, as if they were feeding each other. And that was wonderful. I was so pleased. I woke up feeling like a different person, relaxed and unafraid. I was whole!

THE BAD BREAST

Unfortunately, I always used to discover that whatever we'd done just opened the path for something else to pop out. I was very worried about this. I always felt that you expected me to be entirely better and not to have any more problems because we'd done such a lot of work the time before. I felt like such an ungrateful bitch because I was always complaining about there being something new the matter and not being happy about the things we'd already sorted out. It was a very long time indeed before we'd dealt with enough of the problems for me to be left in a reasonable degree of peace between sessions; it was as if I was reading a book which contained all the secrets of my soul – a kind of Pandora's box – and all these terrible things kept leaping out. Yet I couldn't ignore them. And you were so kind to me then; you kept assuring me that it was all right that I was still upset. You told me that I was right and justified to be upset, because terrible things had happened to me .. and you stood by me while I relived them all and hated them all and was angry with the world. You didn't hurry me through the anger and refuse to look at the me who was unhappy. And that really was a relief.

One of the things we discussed often was my fear of my own aggression, and my anxiety every time things didn't go right that it was the fault of my destructive nature. I particularly experienced this anxiety with Eddie. If I wanted to hug him, or go to bed with him, or talk to him, and he wasn't in the mood, I used to go completely crazy with anxiety and aggression. And if he came to me, but wasn't as assertive or demanding or intense as I thought he ought to be, I was quite unable to look at what he was like and say to myself that he had a nice gentle libido which I liked – I had to go crazy then too, and felt myself rejecting him and hating him .. and then hating myself for being such a monster. I wanted to love him – but I simply didn't know how. In retrospect, that's not really surprising; I didn't have people around me when I was a little girl who knew how to love each other and from whom I could learn how it was done .. but at the time, I was torn between my righteous indignation that Eddie didn't know how to love me, which "justified" my anger with him, and my feeling that if only I had known how to give or receive love, we wouldn't have been in this mess in the first place.

I remember the first time that we ever tackled this problem head on under hypnosis.

"Go back to the time when you were a little baby," you said. "Now see your mother's breast approaching. What is happening?"

I could feel her nipple in my mouth. It was small and hard and blue – cold and lifeless – and horribly rough on my tongue.

"What is the milk like?" you asked.

I was rather puzzled by this question. I wasn't sure that the breast gave me milk; you seemed to be making assumptions about it that I couldn't myself take for granted. But in fact, as I waited, I found that the breast *did* give me milk. The trouble was that it didn't let it flow out properly so that my mouth could become full with milk; it let it out in squirts. I had to hold the milk in my mouth to make it feel as if it was full, before swallowing it and having the next suck. I tried to play with the breast and enjoy it – but then mummy just couldn't cope and dissociated herself from her breast. This meant that as soon as she felt me not sucking "properly" but trying to play, to get the feel of her breast and to get to know it, she put me back in my cot. But I hadn't finished! So I cried. And she picked me up again .. and so we went on. In the end, I just didn't want to suck any more, because it was too much effort for nothing and only produced frustration and misery.

"Suck properly, and see what happens," you told me.

I didn't want to. I couldn't bear to; I could feel a tightness in my upper lip which reminded me of her, and I didn't want to be like her. So instead of using my lips to suck, I used my tongue, but that made me terribly tired and angry. It wasn't a real solution to the difficulty.

"I'd like you to go back to the time when you were about two months old," you said. "Feel your teeth just starting to develop in your gums."

I didn't know what you meant. How could I feel my teeth when

I was only two months old? After all, they weren't going to come through for some time yet – so they didn't exist yet. But such is hypnosis that I did what you said. And, to my utter amazement, I found that I *could* feel them; I didn't know that babies were aware of such things .. but there were the little teeth inside my gums, waiting to grow and come out. Even though they were still inside me, I could feel them and feel their power. They were lovely!

"What does your mother's breast feel like?" you asked.

I was terrified. After all, my teeth were coming alive inside me .. but if she didn't like sucking and detached herself from that, what the hell was she going to do if I bit her?

"See how she reacts when you suck her," you insisted.

There was nothing for it. I took my courage in both hands and pressed her breasts with my gums with the teeth inside.

"I'm biting her! What will happen now?"

I waited for her to cast me away. BUT .. she didn't; she *loved* it! She didn't like my lovely sucking, but she did like being bitten and forced to give things! I was so angry. I was quite overwhelmed by a desire to raze her breast to a bloody pulp with my new teeth. I didn't know that such strong feelings existed; feelings that just swamped me with their imperative and their extraordinary power. I was furious with her.

But then, just as suddenly, I became terrified. I didn't know what to do at all. My fingers wanted to attack her as well .. but I didn't *want* to attack her breast. Or, rather, I did! I was swamped by the desire to do two completely contradictory things, and my mind and my body became paralysed with the strain. I couldn't do anything.

"Of course you're angry," you said. "Your mother won't let you enjoy the sucking, so you're furious about the biting."

I didn't really understand what you meant at the time; all I could understand was that everything was dreadful, because what would solve the problem was somehow worse than the problem itself. I didn't want to kill mummy. Or did I?

You tried to intervene at this point.

"Imagine a happy smiling mother," you said, "and feel good about your lips and about sucking."

But I couldn't. I couldn't make sense – or didn't want to make sense – of the term 'good' next to mummy. I knew that she wasn't, and I didn't want to capitulate to her. I didn't believe it was possible to imagine a new mummy; we'd just be telling lies about the old mummy and denying that I'd really suffered any injustice or horridness at her hands (or breasts!). So you said,

"If that's how you feel, then what we have to do is to help you feel good about yourself. Feel that you are nice, and enjoy that."

My anger and anxiety subsided, and I felt a sense of greater peace and acceptance inside. However, I wasn't totally satisfied with this outcome; I suppose that nothing short of killing my mother would really have satisfied me .. but I didn't want to do that. What I didn't realise at the time, and what was really important, was that I would, in fact, never come to terms with my feelings about my mother if I didn't first like and acknowledge the me who felt them. This was a possibility which had quite literally never occurred to me.

* * *

In the short term, my fear of my mother dominated everything. I desperately wanted to be free from her influence, and yet I didn't believe that I had the strength to liberate myself; you often talked to me at the beginning of a session, and I would find myself trembling with anxiety because you were asking me to face things I didn't know how to handle. I don't think I really knew that I had a Self at all – or if I did, I was so afraid that it would be overwhelmed with nastiness that I couldn't sustain my confidence in it. I didn't believe that things could change at all unless you hypnotised me so that I could think as I wanted to think, in safety, with you there to protect me. But you made me face the fear and stand up to it; you used to push me, until I nearly went mad. Then, just as the pain and the distress got to a point where I couldn't stand it any more, you would nod towards the couch and ask me if I'd like to lie down. Would I? You bet! The sensation of lying on your couch and knowing that whatever happened, it would be safe and it would get better, was just wonderful. It was almost like having an orgasm .. the tension would build up and up .. and suddenly, almost out of the blue, recognition and understanding would dawn, and my body, which had been strung up to an intolerable pitch of tension, would relax at last into peace and quiet.

I was always a little ashamed of this, as I was vaguely worried that something sadistic was going on in my mind. But I never really knew what it was .. and the relief was so palpable that I didn't really care! I had faith that if you said it was all right, then it was all right. But I didn't dare ask you to hypnotise me. One reason was perfectly straightforward – it was your job to be psychoanalysing me and I didn't want to tell you how to do your job. But the other reason was darker; I was afraid that I was harming you by letting you see all the terrible things in my soul and burdening you with them. An even more alarming possibility was that when you saw what I was really like underneath, you wouldn't love me any more. But that was a risk I had to take.

2

Some Uncomfortable Truths

CAN YOU COPE WITH ME?

For a year or so, I lived in a state of uncertainty which was at the same time profoundly exciting and horrendously alarming, as the pleasures of resolution and the idea that one day I would be a stable, contented person contrasted starkly with my fear of rejection and the anxiety I felt at having my deepest secrets uncovered.

The trouble was, I think, that I didn't really know who I was. I was nervous even about asking the question; I didn't know whether I had a right to an independent existence, or a right to ask for what I wanted when I wanted it. Nothing worked, I felt; I was haunted by the feeling that trying to be myself, trying to be independent, or asking for what I wanted, had always ended in catastrophe in the past. I didn't really know what I meant by this – and that itself was part of the problem. It also made it difficult for me to be straightforward in asking you to help me. If you didn't know what I needed or wanted, then I didn't want to have to tell you; I thought that only a man who could intuit my every need was going to be powerful enough to liberate me from my mother. What I didn't realise, though, was that by asking for what I wanted, I could help myself to take control of my world.

One day, at last, I plucked up the courage to ask you if you would hypnotise me and show me those wonderful pictures which brought freedom and pleasure. I learned two things from the experience: the first was that you would, in fact, grant my request .. but the second was that if I didn't know how to ask nicely, then I wouldn't always get quite what I expected!

You tended not to plunge straight in to hypnosis; you often

started sessions by talking about real life – psychoanalysis only had a meaning within a 'real' context – and on this particular occasion, I'd been telling you, with some enthusiasm, about how brave I'd been that week. There had been quite an infiltration of my college common room by the hard left, and 'equal opportunities' was the flavour of the month. Not that I could see anything equal about any opportunities being proposed: the hidden message was,

"Let's give the oppressed an equal opportunity to exploit and hurt the oppressors, equal to that of the years and years of exploitation that they have suffered."

This seemed to me to be wrong for two reasons; firstly because I couldn't see how answering violence with violence would solve any fundamental problems, and secondly because the overt message of 'equal opportunities' was one of kindness and brotherly (and sisterly) love, which ran counter to the hidden message. I felt very strongly that this was a perversion of justice, and I wanted to speak out. Gradually, I was amassing the courage to do so – yet every time I did, the hard left amongst my colleagues heckled and insulted me, hissing in meetings and whispering, "fascist, racist, reactionary". I found this very hard to take, but I was becoming increasingly unable to sit back and watch such travesties of morality take place under the guise of goodness.

It was hard to work out how to counter their arguments, especially as many of the problems they identified really existed. For example, the education department were teaching their students on teaching practice that it was immoral to set homework, because it disadvantaged the underprivileged even more, as they had nowhere to do it. Yet, I felt, identifying the problem that some people's homes weren't conducive to homework wasn't at all the same thing as knowing how to solve it – and it didn't seem right to deprive children of the opportunities to test their own power, away from the classroom. But I was still desperately afraid of my colleagues. I would now speak out when I could, but at the cost of much sweating and trembling; in fact, I used frequently to vomit on arriving home after such an episode. But my courage was growing, and I found myself able to think more clearly even under intimidation. I knew that I could never have done this with such success before knowing you, and doing with you the work on my soul which had affirmed my self, so I was very pleased about it all.

You too were very pleased with me for speaking out, and my adult as well as my infantile self felt approved of. I basked in this pleasure for a while. But time slipped away as we talked, and I suddenly realised that there wasn't going to be any time to do what I had hoped for — to look at mummy's nipple again. I couldn't bear it! You faded away as I surged off into a vortex of emptiness and terror. I couldn't hear what you were saying any more. I felt that you were ignoring what I really wanted; that you knew that I liked lying on your couch, but were avoiding the issue. Heaven alone knows why I should have interpreted things in that way; all I knew at the time was that I was angry with you. Yet I couldn't express that anger because you were really being very nice to me and I felt dreadful and ungrateful and horrid because I couldn't appreciate it. I became completely paralysed. What could I do? If I didn't speak, I'd be angry all week with you, and I'd hate myself .. but if I did say anything, then you'd be angry with me. My mind span round, but eventually, desire conquered fear, and I just blurted out what I wanted — to lie on your couch again.

I didn't realise that my fear was hiding a desire to test you. I wanted to know if you would just know what I wanted and give it to me. But you wanted me to learn how to ask — which was a possibility which I had never thought of! And on this occasion, you explained to me what was going on. You didn't pretend that I wasn't testing you, or tell me off for doing it; you told me that if I needed to test you, then I also needed (within reason) to find out that you wouldn't respond in the way I feared. I gradually learned that this was a major part of the way you worked: that you considered that it was important that I should learn that you actually *didn't* behave in the way my parents had behaved.

Suffice it to say that you let me lie on your couch. But by this time, I was so afraid of having asked that I couldn't do or feel anything. I remember you looking at me as if to say, "Well, if you won't see any pictures, I'd better wake you up," — and I was so terrified that you would do just that that I tore out of my soul the request to see mummy's nipple again.

"See it, then," you told me. "Feel it with your teeth."

I could certainly feel it .. but instantaneously I felt also the tight withdrawal in mummy communicate itself to my vagina; my whole pelvis and vaginal region between my legs hollowed out in distaste, trying to keep away from her – and the hollow emptiness gave a feeling that there was nothing there! Then there followed a terrible, overwhelming, obliterating frenzy of chewing mummy's breast to pulp and sieving the pulp through my teeth to get out the liquid – which was, after all, what I expected. It was awful. But you stayed with me.

"It's all right to bite," you told me. "But see if you can do it in a non-frenzied way."

My panic subsided somewhat, and instead of pulling my vagina in, I suddenly found that I could push down around my vulva .. and there was an enormous – and quite unexpected – pleasure in my teeth, an almost sweet sensation of potency.

Then you said, "The pleasure in your teeth is because you have sadistic impulses towards your mother and feel pleasure in those impulses."

But I absolutely wouldn't accept this; I denied it quite categorically. No matter that I'd just spent the last few minutes mincing mummy's breast into a pulp; I couldn't accept that I was a sadist – and certainly not that I might have any pleasure in any of it. I could only conceive of myself as entirely the innocent victim of circumstances. It was nothing to do with me.

You didn't push it. After all, in one very important sense, it *didn't* have anything to do with me. It wasn't my fault that mummy didn't know how to give things nicely, so that I had to attack her to get what I needed. But I couldn't face the responsibility for what I'd done, and still less could I face the fact that I might actually have had some pleasure out of it. All I was aware of at the time was a feeling of desperation: it was *her* fault. I was prepared to acknowledge that maybe I had a momentary pleasure at the moment the teeth made contact with the nipple .. but I absolutely could not acknowledge that I might have enjoyed the total devastation. Me? Surely not. The guilt was too great for me to take it all in. It seemed to me that I was the one who had been subjected to sadistic attack and humiliation, and that I didn't want that. So I couldn't possibly be a sado-masochist.

"I can't be having any pleasure in this," I said. "Surely the fact that I'm so afraid of what I might do proves that I don't like it."

Anything rather than have to look things squarely in the face; and not surprisingly, I went home with this matter unresolved.

Yet for as long as I wouldn't acknowledge what I'd done as real, I couldn't feel myself as real. It was a very delicate balancing act that you helped me perform. You had to make me feel good enough about myself and safe enough to acknowledge my own sadism; then I could start 'curing' it; then I wouldn't need to feel bad about myself any more. What a complex business!

AGGRESSION

I felt really terrible for the entire week after this episode. I was depressed and exhausted, and felt dreadfully anxious in case you were cross with me. In reality, I suppose, I was cross with *you*. Goodness knows why – but it all seemed very reasonable to me at the time. It wasn't long, though, before I started to feel remorse at having not listened to what you said about my being a sadist. All the sadistic pleasure suddenly loomed up in my mind and tortured me; every time I didn't get exactly what I wanted, my mind filled with pictures of myself gouging people's eyes out and biting them until they were a lifeless but screaming pulp. I really shocked myself. I couldn't bear it – and I kept feeling that if only I'd done what you said and acknowledged the sadism when I was last at your office, then we'd have been able to discharge it all under hypnosis, and I wouldn't now be suffering all this torture. For it really was torture, having to come to terms with the totally unacceptable side of myself. I began to understand why it is that we repress things; if I had had to live with this degree of self-awareness and self-hatred, then I would not have been able to bear living. It was only possible to bear it now because I knew that in a few days' time I would see you again and you would make it better – whatever that meant. But the waiting was sheer purgatory.

You weren't very pleased with me the next time I came to see you. You said that you'd known all that would happen to me if you hypnotised me, because I hadn't been ready to acknowledge the sadism, and so wouldn't be able to bring it out as a picture for you. It was I who had insisted that I should lie on your couch, not you. I could see what you meant, but even so, I understood why I had done it; it had been difficult for me to wait patiently for it to be the right time, because something terrible was going on inside my head, and I wanted most desperately to do something about it – even at the risk of trying to bring it out too early. I hated it. Even if I had to violate myself to get it out so that we could make it go away, I didn't care. I knew this feeling well from the 'real' world as well .. and it made me very glad that you were still there ...

We talked about my mother again. You asked me what she was like, what her breast was like. My mind filled with images of pus-filled breasts; even if you cracked her open to get at the goodness, there was no goodness there, but only sourness and bitterness, the sort of thing that makes you want to wipe the taste out of your mouth. As we talked, I remembered seeing a programme on the television where they interviewed prostitutes about their lives. One of them was a very prim and proper lady who dressed up in a black dress and white apron and whipped her clients. The interviewer had asked her if she had ever had an orgasm while she was with one of her clients. She had replied, with obvious unease, that it had happened to her once, quite against her will, and that she had been so ashamed of herself that she hadn't known what to do. Much to my embarrassment, I found as I talked to you that it was exactly that same shame that I felt at the idea of having an orgasm of sadistic pleasure as I launched my teeth into mummy's breast. Although I was deeply embarrassed and ashamed, I knew it would happen and that I would be powerless to control it. In a sense, I even liked it – but that was something that I was still not really willing to admit, even to myself.

You let me lie down again on your couch. But before you hypnotised me, you put your finger in my mouth and told me to bite it. This gave me enormous pleasure .. but I was absolutely terrified and wanted you to take it away.

"You're frightened in case I'm a masochist and you're hurting me; then, you think, you will have to despise me for being such a weak creature," you told me. "But I'm not a masochist. Now, bite my finger again."

God, it was awful and wonderful at the same time, until I didn't know how I'd cope with the confusion of emotions whirling round inside me! But then you put me to sleep.

An extraordinary, cathartic realisation dawned on me: I thought that I was bad, and that mummy was bad, and that nothing good could come out of me because I was her. That seemed a bit curious; logically it didn't make sense .. but it was nonetheless what I meant. My thoughts rolled on: I so much wanted to give things to people, but I was afraid to do so. Yet it was precisely this fear which made me horrid-aggressive rather than nice-aggressive. It was all very well things being good when you made them good for me, but they didn't come nicely out of the inside of me. I was so upset; I knew that I was nice really, but how could I believe in the goodness inside me?

"I'll count to three and then the goodness will be inside you," you told me.

What a wonderful feeling that was! I felt it coming into me, creeping with a blissful warmth through my body and my flesh, filling me with relaxation and pleasure. And feeling it made me recognise a new truth: that I had something to give, and that I was no longer so dependent on there being nice things around for me to take. That was an immense relief to me, because, for as long as I was dependent on mummy and she was so unpredictable and couldn't be trusted to give me nice things, I had no store on which to draw, and that made me most terribly dependent on the outside world – a state of affairs which I didn't like at all.

As I talked to you about all this, a picture started to create itself in my head: I saw mummy coming to me; I opened my mouth for what she was bringing me – and then she was gone before I had had time to take what she gave me. She hadn't really given it to me properly; just as I relaxed and started to expect it and anticipate it .. it was gone! I felt myself trembling with shock.

"Relax your breasts," you said, "and see what you are doing with them unconsciously."

I could feel the tension under my arms as if I was ready to withdraw my breasts at any moment. I suppose that's why I was so worried that I was mummy – because unconsciously I'd adopted her mannerisms and ways of doing things. Yet I'd known that it wasn't right; I'd always been upset at the way my breasts became almost concave where they joined my arms.

"OK, then," you said, "stand in front of a mirror and look at yourself and see your breasts how you want them to be."

It was wonderful! I could see them tilted upwards, with the nipple aloft; they were rounded underneath – and they were smiling. The nipples somehow had little faces on them which smiled. And as I felt them smiling, I could suddenly smile too, and my hips relaxed, and my vagina moved down and forward, and my bottom fell into a more relaxed position as well. It was still all a little apprehensive – but it was there.

Then you woke me up. As we chatted afterwards, you told me that I wouldn't worry so much about giving and taking now, because I would be more confident that I knew what it was all about, so I wouldn't feel so responsible every time something went wrong.

THE UBIQUITOUS TEETH

And indeed, things were much better. I suddenly became aware of a whole new dimension of pleasure that I had never really been aware of before. That was enormously exciting, and gave me a feeling of real joy. I wasn't, though, fully able to appreciate it yet, and that created a dynamic tension in my soul; for as my sense of what pleasure really WAS increased, I also became more concerned to be able to experience it to the full. For as long as I hadn't known about it, such thoughts had been impossible for me to frame.

For some reason which I didn't really understand, I became at this time very preoccupied with the anxiety that you wouldn't love me any more .. and it seemed that the worry about pleasure and the worry about being loved were connected in some way. The twofold nature of my concern presented itself to my mind as a dilemma which I had to confront: it seemed to me that there was a whole great wonderful reservoir of goodness inside me, which I was hugely pleased about, but which I couldn't get at or communicate with – and the only way I could see to achieve peace was to mutilate myself or beat myself so hard that I lost consciousness. But that certainly didn't have anything to do with pleasure, and I couldn't understand why I should represent it to myself as the way to peace. This caused me a lot of anxiety and a lot of guilt.

*   *   *

One day, you cured my vagina of thrush. I used to get thrush quite often, and the doctors didn't seem to be able to do much about it in the long term, even if they could alleviate the symptoms of each separate outbreak. I dreaded developing thrush again after each bout, as it made me feel dirty and smelly and unacceptable. At last, it dawned on me that you might be able to help!

When I told you about it, you asked me to tell you what I thought about it all. As we talked, my mind gradually brought up all kinds of ideas which I felt to be connected with the thrush, but had never before recognised as such: for example, how I found it so difficult to have orgasms, and how ashamed that made me, too. The emotions seemed to be the same ones as I associated with the thrush. So you let me lie down.

"What does the thrush feel like?" you asked.

I could feel it as lots of little teeth in my vagina. I was quite upset to think that I had teeth in my vagina. But as I stayed with the picture, I found myself asking what was so terrible about having teeth; what was wrong with them?

"Quite right," you said. "You have a good tooth-libido, so you shouldn't be upset with your teeth. Now, I'd like you to imagine a penis entering your vagina and tell me what's happening to the teeth."

It was wonderful; I felt them retracting like cats' claws, and then I felt that they could grip safely and firmly but without hurting. That was very nice.

"Now," you told me, "tell the thrush to go away."

I felt it dissolving! And as it dissolved, my vagina sucked it into its walls, with pleasure and a quiet excitement. It was almost as if the thrush had been living on the moisture in my vagina like dry rot lives on wood-sap – and having the same effect: drying it out. But now it was gone. It was extraordinary!

"Now, relax the muscles which inhibit orgasm," you told me.

I was amazed to find that my unconscious knew where the muscles were, down the front of my pelvic wall – but I couldn't let them go. I tingled nicely, but I was too afraid to relax fully. I was rather distressed about this, as I didn't know why I couldn't do it.

"Look into the blank," you said, "and then see what's going on."

There was mummy's breast – and I was picking off the protection over her milk-ducts just in the same way as one might pick off a scab. The texture of her nipples underneath was just like the texture of the thrush I found in my vagina! It was quite incredible.

Then you made me squeeze your leg with my fingernails.

"You needn't be afraid," you reassured me.

As if by magic, I felt it all warm in my vagina, as if a rush of energy had surged into its walls. It wasn't quite an orgasm, but it was very nice all the same. I was rather upset that it wasn't an orgasm, but you seemed quite optimistic:

"It might just work now," you said .. so I left your office quite hopeful – and thrush-free!

The week after that, I felt terribly happy inside. I didn't remember being so happy for a long time. But interestingly enough, the very happiness made me nervous. I was afraid that it would cause me to choke, or burst, or vomit; I didn't know how to believe that happiness could really culminate in melting – I was still afraid that it had to be violent and terrible and destructive. No wonder I was afraid of orgasms. But that fear made me very ashamed. It took me a long time to admit even to myself that I didn't have orgasms. I was worried that there was something very seriously wrong with me .. and I couldn't bear that idea; it made me angry and desperate. Eventually, I plucked up the courage to talk to you about it, and just sharing it with you was a relief. You asked me what was so terrible about not having an orgasm; maybe it was frustrating, but why was it so horrendously dreadful? I didn't know .. yet at the same time, I felt that what you said cast a whole new light on the matter, setting in train a new way of thinking which ultimately would release me from my obsession.

My new courage to face things squarely revealed itself in the 'real' world, too. By now, I was regularly speaking up at work, and imposing my will on situations. This gave me an almost intoxicating feeling of potency, which resulted in the most exquisite pleasure. But I still didn't know how to control it; if I let it go, and experienced the power and pleasure to the full, then it wouldn't be long before I would, as it were, roll over the crest of the wave into the most dreadful, black episode of self-doubt, self-hatred and self-destruction. It was most puzzling; I liked the manic episodes, but the depressive episodes were not worth it! What should I do? This was a problem which we tackled gradually over the very long term indeed.

GOOD BREAST: GOOD BABY

I took the first opportunity which presented itself to talk to you about the desire to vomit, and about the anguish my vagina felt at not being satisfiable.

"Why don't you imagine a good breast and see what happens," you suggested.

I remember sitting in my chair, facing you, trying to think what on earth I should do with a good breast; my conscious mind just had no idea. It was clearly a case which required hypnosis.

"Now see the breast," you told me again.

It was curious how I could do under hypnosis things that I couldn't do consciously; it never ceased to puzzle me what it was that happened when you hypnotised me. It was as if there was a kind of block which was removed by the hypnosis. After all, I could *see* the good breast when I wasn't hypnotised .. but I was locked into a certain way and certain habits of thinking about things and relating to breasts, so I couldn't make the picture move and live in any positive way; for the only way I knew how to relate to breasts was as if they were bad. I still don't know how you knew that I knew inside how to relate to good breasts if only I was given the chance. Perhaps everyone does, given the chance. But how did you know I was ready? That was the real miracle.

Suffice it to say that under hypnosis I could see it.

"Take the nipple in your mouth," you said.

I could feel the nice breast all relaxed around its base, and I could taste the good, sweet milk that it gave out, and my throat opened all wide and eager to receive it. But the picture kept being blotted out by the picture of the bad breast. It came to me and looked as if it was going to come into my mouth .. but in fact it didn't; it reared away, pulling upwards in an aggressive manner, and I developed quite a pain in my neck trying to catch it in my mouth. I couldn't get hold of it, but it wouldn't go away – and while it was there, I found it quite impossible to swallow anything or feel anything properly.

"It's the sadism that you can't take and that you want to vomit up," you told me.

Quite suddenly I saw that this was true. I realised, with an intense relief, that I'd always thought that it was my fault that the breast didn't come to me, and that this made me frightened of asking. But a baby has to ask – and I had learned how to ask for things in a way that a bad breast would understand. Yet that presupposed a sadistic infrastructure, and so created a vicious spiral of demand and rejection. Now I understood, though, that I was not the one who started all this, and that made me feel good about myself. Then, once I felt that I was nice, all sorts of possibilities revealed themselves, of which the best was learning how to ask for things nicely. This in turn made me feel that I could relate to the good breast without being afraid of destroying it by my nastiness. For I was not nasty! I felt so much better; everything opened up inside me and I felt good.

THE PENIS AS BREAST

At this point, I still had only a tenuous relationship with the outside world .. although I was, at least, beginning to recognise that this was the case. It was like being a baby again, where all the most important things happen inside. Although I went through the motions of going to work, preparing meals, being sociable, making love, and so on, the vast majority of my energy was concentrated on the exciting discoveries inside my soul. Understanding the outside world fully was still some way away.

For example, after the previous session, I didn't immediately rush out to experiment with asking nicely; I turned my attention inwards to see what else was going on in there – and I found myself with a problem I hadn't expected: how was I supposed to relate to penises? Did I have to bite them? Was I supposed to have a penis really? Was my vagina as good as a penis? One part of me was sure that it was, but somehow I still felt upset; I didn't know why. You said that it was because once I'd relinquished my desires and fears about the penis and having to bite it, then I didn't know what to do with my teeth. After all, if they weren't for biting and being aggressive, then what were they for? And if I couldn't use my teeth, then life was just boring, wasn't it? Nothing to get hold of.

"Actually, you still feel guilty about your teeth, and that's what the matter is," you told me.

And you let me lie down to see how it all really worked.

"How do you feel?" you asked me.

The first thing I noticed was that my vagina felt free, and accepted itself for what it was.

"Feel the libido in your lips," you said.

I couldn't do that very well, which was most puzzling.

"It's all to do with your teeth," you said. "Feel the libido in your teeth and nails."

It was a lovely feeling, if rather anxiety-making, all that energy and pleasure pouring into the ends of my teeth and my nails. But I still felt terribly inhibited. So you ran your fingernails up my arm .. and I felt a wonderful warmth inside me; it wasn't terrible and damaging, but an exciting and almost melting sensation. And suddenly, I wanted to take daddy's penis in my mouth!

"Yes, do that, and see what happens," you said.

I was a bit frightened, and I approached daddy with my teeth bared in anxiety. He could feel the anxiety I exuded, and he wasn't very inviting. I didn't know what to do now.

"Try again," you suggested, "but this time, without anxiety."

Then, there I was, resting between his legs and with his penis in my mouth. And he lay back and laughed with pleasure and love. I was so happy! I caressed and squeezed his penis with my teeth and it didn't hurt him; it just provided more intense pleasure, like the waves of sensation when a penis enters a vagina, in and out. And then I was warm and tingling – and daddy's penis got small again – but he wasn't destroyed, he was happy. I sucked some more, and he didn't pull his penis away, even though it was soft and little again. He wasn't castrated! It wasn't very exciting sucking the little soft penis – but it wasn't excitement that I was now looking for, but only the reassurance that it was still there. Oh, it was lovely, daddy being so happy with me and getting so much pleasure from me.

But the weak look of total surrender and total giving frightened me; it was so close to the look of total self-giving-up and sacrifice to mummy – the weakness of destruction rather than the weakness of love. It was the difference between giving the penis and giving up the penis.

"Your mother wanted the actual penis, not just what it could give her," you observed.

That was what was terrible; it frightened me and it frightened daddy.

"I'd like you now to start being confident to want and to enjoy the self-expression and enjoyment of wanting – even if feasting on penis-libido is not immediately available," you told me.

I experienced then a marvellous feeling of self-acceptance, which gave me a glimpse of what might be in the future. Even though I wasn't, at that stage, able to sustain the confidence for long, it provided a vision of where I was going.

But in the real world, at this time, my major preoccupation was with libido and how I would react if it was withdrawn. It was all very well learning what to do with it when it was there .. but supposing it wasn't? Would I still attack and destroy the source? Dared I do anything, or would I find myself attacking against my will? This, of course, was THE great challenge.

⋆   ⋆   ⋆

Many different kind of things emerged under hypnosis: sometimes I would see things which had actually happened, but which I had forgotten about. Sometimes I would relive these happenings and find ways of dealing with the feelings. But sometimes you would tell me to look again, and I'd find that in fact I'd misinterpreted what was going on, and that I'd based my entire adult behaviour on mistaken assumptions. However, on other occasions still, I would bring out of my unconscious pictures of things which had never happened, like the episode with my father. But somehow you always seemed to know when my perceptions were authentic and when they were not. It was that wisdom which made me trust you so implicitly; I knew that I would always be safe in your hands.

TIME STARTS TO BECOME CONTINUOUS

One week, I was myself for seven consecutive days; the first week that had ever been all mine. That sounds a rather curious thing to say – but it was true nonetheless. I hadn't actually realised until that point that I wasn't in control of myself all the time. What I had always done seemed to me to be normal .. and I had never noticed that I split off into different parts – or, rather, that the 'I' that I knew as myself wasn't there all the time.

I suppose that at some level, I was aware of this; I remember reading a book about a woman with 16 personalities and recognising that she and I shared certain characteristics. I didn't ever think that I was schizophrenic, in the sense of doing things that I wasn't aware of afterwards, or anything like that .. but I *did* always feel that my personality was under siege and that if I wasn't careful, it would be overwhelmed by something or someone who somehow wasn't quite me.

Sometimes, this could be quite pleasant; at concerts, I would fidget for the first 10 minutes or so, and then, under the influence of the music, I would go drifting off into another world; I wouldn't hear the concert through from beginning to end, but only in snatches. If the music became very dramatic, or romantic, or arresting in some other way, then I would resurface and find myself hearing it .. but for the rest of the time, it was like being in a different world.

The phenomenon of losing myself wasn't always pleasant, though; in fact, it could be very threatening. If I had to spend an evening at, say, a boring party, I just didn't know what to do with myself. I would fragment up, not wanting to have anything to do with it. Then I would find myself panicking; I could not understand that three or four hours would soon be over, or indeed even comprehend what three or four hours meant. I would be lost in an eternal present, and one which I didn't like, doomed to an eternity of non-existence. It sounds ridiculous now, but it was quite terrifying at the time.

I never knew whether anyone in the outside world noticed that this was going on. This would have been the least of my problems, though; I was terrified by it myself. Yet I didn't even dare look at what it was that was going to happen. What I do remember, though, is that I felt an overwhelming urge to hang on for dear life. It was like holding on to reality with my fingernails quite literally. I felt like a sadist, scratching and tearing the world, just in order to remain in semi-control. I became unable to hear what the other person was saying; they faded away into the world of terrors – and I felt that I had to shout and shout, and keep talking, if the world of monsters were not completely to overwhelm me.

The feelings that went with this syndrome were most odd. I would feel suddenly as if I had become enormously large, as if I was surrounded by an aura into which my physical self had expanded. I would feel and hear my voice echoing from far off as I spoke, and bouncing from one side to the other of the cavity in which I dwelt, and which was my extended self, as I lost the sense of myself as a whole person.

So when I remained intact for a whole week, it was fantastic; I regarded it as a real sign that I was truly getting better. For as I didn't have an overall view of my Self, it was extremely difficult for me to evaluate my 'progress'. I was at this stage only able to see that small things changed from week to week after visiting you, and didn't yet have a firm grasp of what was happening to Me. This was the first time I glimpsed what it must be like to be 'cured'. If I didn't disintegrate, then I really existed – and that was extremely exciting.

TIME – RHYTHM .. PEEING!

You were very pleased to hear that this had happened, and offered without further ado to let me lie down and do some work (as I always thought of it!).

"Look at whatever you want," you said.

I was very proud that you were trusting me – this new, whole self – rather than telling me what to do .. and what I saw was a shadowy picture of a little baby standing next to a big fat lady with huge breasts and saying,

"I don't want my mummy any more. I hate her. Will you be my mummy, please, and let me suck your breasts?"

The fat lady didn't say anything at all, but I knew that it would be all right to take her breast. But I didn't do it. For as I thought of taking it in my mouth, I realised that I would need a pee – yet somehow that was unacceptable.

"That's wonderful!" you said. "Very important. Let's look at this some more. Feel your urethra and enjoy the sensations."

I was very pleased about this; I loved my urethra and all the pleasures it gave me, but the anxiety over the years had been so great that I'd actually forgotten where it was! It sounds odd, but it's true. And suddenly I could feel it all the way up, pulsing and giving out a life-giving warmth, tingling and exquisitely sensitive and pleasurable.

"Can I lie or sit on mummy's tummy and pee on her?" I asked you. I felt that this would be the ultimate expression of my love. I could see the pictures of me on mummy's tummy, and feel myself almost sucking her with my urethra, making her all wet and luscious. It was the most wonderful feeling of acceptance.

"Peeing is a kind of infantile orgasm," you said. "It's particularly important to you, because musical people have the most urethral libido."

That gave me great pleasure. Although I didn't really understand what you meant, I knew it was right. And sure enough, my unconscious understood. For suddenly I could feel a penis thrusting in and out of me .. and the rhythms were strong and beautiful and like a symphony of feeling. It was like walking in a wood and watching all the trees and flowers coming out into bloom ... lovely. I was so contented.

"Why did you repress all these wonderful sensations?" you asked me.

Inevitably, there was mummy. I was having a pee, and she was holding me at arm's length in total disgust. Her face was all wrinkled up as if she was shocked .. and I could feel my urethra puckering up at the end in just the same way as her mouth. No wonder it didn't come out right! But then you said,

"It's all right, you can pee nicely; do it now and be pleased."

It was difficult, because I was still rather ashamed .. but you were pleased that I'd noticed that.

"It's natural that you should feel ashamed," you said, "because repressed urethral libido causes shame. But I'd like you to learn that it's nice."

That was something that we had to leave for another time, though; the session had run out. The unconscious fits only with difficulty into tidy time-boxes .. but that in itself was something which over the years I came to love about my unconscious. It quite literally had a mind of its own!

However, the frustration of waiting for 'another time' could be extremely hard to bear; it was as if I split into two people, one who understood that I had to wait, and another who would brook no

delays. In the second world, there was no room for 'later, darling' –
no, it had to be NOW. And it had to be perfect. If not, then I would
throw the most monumental tantrums. Because it was always
everyone else's fault. Never anything to do with me. Part of me
knew that this was ridiculous, and that I behaved perfectly
abominably on many occasions, and that I asked for what I wanted
in such a way that it became a challenge. But deep down, I knew that
I knew how to ask nicely. How could I actually do it in the real
world? That was the problem.

UNDERSTANDING THE SADISTIC SYNDROME

For a good while, I continued to feel that life was a bit of a tightrope,
and that I might fall off into death or insanity or oblivion at any
moment. I didn't really understand this, as one part of me was
happier and more contented than I had ever known it. Perhaps it was
precisely this that made me even more anxious about losing my new-
found contentment. After all, for as long as I'd been miserable, there
had been nothing to worry about in going mad and losing it! Now,
though, I became aware of feeling permanently on guard against
something terrible. And one week, you let me descend right into the
pit to see what it was that I was afraid of.

I can't remember how the hypnotic pictures arrived at the scene,
because the horror of where we ended up was so gruesome that it
rather cast everything else out of my mind! There I was, watching
my parents making love – if that is an appropriate way of describing
it – and instead of doing what one might expect a loving couple to
do, they were up to the most terrible things. Mummy was whipping
daddy's penis, shredding it, almost, with a kind of cat o'nine tails.
She had tied him up so that he didn't run away. What seems
remarkable in retrospect was that I didn't think to ask why he was
there in the first place; to me, the whole scene was so clearly showing
what I knew to be the case, and to be inevitable, that I was blinded
to such obvious questions. Then I saw her peeling his penis like a
banana – and telling him,

"I'm only doing this because I love you."

Poor daddy – he so much wanted to be loved, yet was so confused about what it entailed, that he actually believed her! I wept for
him as I saw this happening, and his humiliation and impotence. I felt
that it was unutterably tragic. The scene played itself out in agonies
of pain and pleasure, filled with the most extraordinarily powerful
feelings and emotions – until at last, his penis burst! It ejaculated
violently, splattering everywhere and simply ceasing to exist, and he
lay defeated and helpless on the ground.

"What is your mother doing now?" you asked.

I didn't know; I couldn't concentrate on the picture any more.
My attention was all absorbed by a terrible pain in my groin, just
above where the pubic crack begins.

"What do you do next?" you asked.

Then .. I saw myself on a horse; I was bringing my little penis
to rescue daddy! I was so proud of myself – and yet I could still feel
the pain – because I had taken into myself the pain in daddy's penis.
My clitoris was standing up and wanting to ejaculate at mummy –
to spit in her eye.

This thought confused me immensely, as I actually caught it in
its entirety. After all, my clitoris didn't have a hole in it like penises
did – so how should I do it?

"Actually, you would have spat out of your urethra," you told
me.

Then suddenly, with a flash of illumination, I realised why I
needed a pee every time I got upset; that was fascinating!

I didn't want things to be violent and horrid like they were with
mummy and daddy, and my mind started thinking about giving and
receiving; it seemed to me that it ought to be a lovely unbroken circle
of pleasure and reciprocation .. but it wasn't; the circle always got
broken.

"It's sadism that short-circuits the circle," you told me.

That was a new thought for me. But what really amazed me,
now that I thought about it, was that I hadn't even registered that
the scene I'd just witnessed with mummy and daddy was sadistic; I
had been so drawn in to the emotions which it generated that there
had been no time or energy left for judgements of any kind.

"It's important for you to feel the sadistic syndrome so that you know what it is that we are talking about," you told me. "Feel it."

I didn't know what you were asking me to do .. but as I lay there, the most extraordinary thing happened. I felt my top teeth grow big and move forward; then my fingers grew long and sharp and bony. All these sensations were heightened so that it was as if they were the whole world. Then I felt a tension down my neck, into the small of my back and down my legs, until my toes curled. My clitoris was erect and apprehensive. My whole body was, as it were, on the alert for attack – or do I mean defence? The two somehow became inextricably linked. Whatever it was, I didn't like it. But the feeling was familiar; before knowing you, I had felt like that ALL the time!

You sat there, not passing judgement, nor making me feel that I was an unworthy person because I had these terrible feelings, but just being there, sitting quietly. Then you said,

"We're going to dismiss these awful feelings for ever now."

And I felt my body enveloped in a most wonderful relaxation, as if there was nothing else to worry about. What else could anyone ever want? The world was perfect!

"What does your vagina want now?" you asked.

It wanted something round and soft to suck.

"OK, then," you said. "Let it have just such a thing."

I felt a wonderful, reponsive, alive sensation in my vagina. Then I felt my eyes and shoulders relaxing and becoming straight, rather than pulled back and somehow curved inwards. It was very nice; I was *so* grateful to you. And I went home happy.

That week, I noticed something I hadn't expected: I no longer needed to wear sunglasses all the time. I'd been a bit puzzled about how my eyes couldn't seem to tolerate intensities of light which were not excessive .. and suddenly here they were, not afraid of the sun any more.

But there were plenty more battles to fight. I had no idea how complex the unconscious world was, and I always expected that each session with you would cure all my problems and that paradise on earth would come immediately. Then, of course, it didn't, and I became desperately angry. But the very anger frightened me; it was the most unequivocal indicator to me that I wasn't yet 'cured'. You often said that there was nothing wrong with anger in itself. Yet I felt that I still didn't know how to discharge the anger in a way which would be safe – or, indeed, whether if I were a different person, maybe I actually wouldn't be angry. Anyway, there wasn't any point in protesting about wanting things, my infantile mind would tell me, because someone (I didn't know who) would only set out to prove to me that I was the one in the wrong. And then all that would be open to me would be to collapse in a helpless heap and cry like a baby. It was better to swallow the anger. Or was it?

URETHRAL FEARS

At this point in my 'analysis', the whole business of peeing became particularly interesting to me. I began to realise how much of my orgastic libido was tied up with it; peeing wasn't allowed, and then, somehow, nor were orgasms. And if I didn't have an orgasm during lovemaking, my fingers would swell up and tingle, and my wrists would feel as if they had electricity running through them. During the day, my heart sometimes started to palpitate for no immediately apparent reason; I'd be walking down the street minding my own business, and suddenly off it would go, until I had to sit down if I were not to faint. It was all very curious.

You let me lie down one week and do some work on it. But before hypnotising me, you ran your hands over me and felt how tense all my muscles were. This was something you did quite often, and which I didn't really like, because I felt guilty if my muscles were tight when you wanted them to be all relaxed. Why guilty, I didn't know. Embarrassing – yes, I could understand that – but guilty! Why? I often felt that I ought to say something .. yet I couldn't even talk about it; I just had to let you get on with it. I suppose that if you hadn't found out which muscles were tense, then you'd never have known what was the matter with me. For I certainly wasn't coming to you each week complaining that my muscles were tight. I didn't even know that the state of my soul had any effect on my muscles!

In fact, I didn't even know that there was anything the matter with them until you pointed it out.

On this occasion, you massaged my muscles until they eased a bit and then hypnotised me. Then you told me to relax and see what was going on.

I saw myself as a baby, lying on my back. Mummy was changing my nappy and I was lying there with it dirty but open, waving my legs in the air.

"You're inviting people to look," you told me.

That was interesting; I hadn't realised that for myself. But mummy certainly wasn't looking. In fact, she absolutely *wouldn't* look. She was embarrassed and kept casting sidelong glances out of the edges of her eyes before looking away again. I felt the most terrible sense of embarrassment myself because she wouldn't look; it ran all through me and made me feel terribly uncomfortable, lying there exposed but with no one looking.

"I think that we should go back to the stage at which the urethral libido was at its peak," you said. "Focus on it now."

I didn't know what you meant; I was sure that I wasn't going to be able to do what you wanted .. but then I suddenly felt my whole self concentrated into a long thin area which, there was no doubt, was indeed my urethra. The sensations were all of peeing so it had to be right. Yet it was a terrible disappointment: it wasn't nice. But that was all wrong – it should have been a supreme pleasure. This made me furious. I couldn't even THINK about the possible niceness; my urethra felt as if someone had cauterised it with a cigarette end. I was terrified of showing it.

Then I saw mummy. She was stroking me up the genital crack and seemed to be pinching it at the top, as if to nip it off. I was sure that she didn't actually do this, but there was something about the expression on her face and the feeling in her fingers that made me think that it was what she really wanted to do. Her face wore a look of sly pleasure and anxiety mixed together, and I could feel her desire.

Then, quite suddenly, I had the impression that I had a penis. I didn't know where this thought came from, for of course, I didn't have one. But when I felt my clitoris all sore and cauterised, and at the same time saw mummy's face with that expression of wanting to nip it off, I thought that she must have cut off something bigger than what was left; and what was that if not a penis? The thoughts rolled on, and I found myself thinking that it must be because I had peed that it had been cut off. After all, that was where all the evidence seemed to my infantile mind to lead.

It was such a relief to my adult self to realise all this .. because once I was aware of what I was really afraid of, I was able to judge clearly that this had not actually been how things had happened, after all. The short circuit of unknowingness had been broken!

And, like a miracle, once my brain was free, I found that I was able to have thoughts about what I'd like to do, rather than just closing off in an uncontrolled spasm of fear and not thinking anything at all. Not only that, but I was actually able to tell you about them. I lay on your couch, with the pictures streaming through my brain: I wanted desperately to be able to pee into someone's mouth and have them accept it and not spit it out in disgust. After all, if mummy gave me milk into my mouth, then it was right that I should pee into her mouth, and that we should both have pleasure from this reciprocity. But mummy thought that peeing was dirty.

You were going to show me that she was wrong. You listened to what I wanted, and then said,

"Go on then. Let it go, and show it."

Well ... I nearly blew a head gasket. I was afraid that I would actually wet myself. How could I let it go? You wouldn't love me any more if I made a mess. It was terrible; I was so afraid. I lay on your couch shaking and trembling with terror. After all, you loved me; that was why you were being so nice to me and helping me find my soul. But now you wouldn't love me any more.

"It's all right," you reassured me. "I'm there with my straw hat on. It will be perfectly all right."

I couldn't see how it could possibly be all right; I was still frightened. Yet now the fear was tinged with the anger I felt at myself for not doing what you wanted. The hypnosis world magnified all these feelings until they became intense enough to fill the whole universe; everything hung on whether or not I would pee for you and whether or not you would receive it nicely.

This must be what it's really like, being a baby; there is nothing else except what it feels; that is the whole world and the only truth. Fortunately, I wasn't a baby any more, but an adult with years of other experience to help me evaluate what I was now feeling again – and there was you to guide me through it all.

You gave me a while just to feel, and then you started to rescue me from the terror:

"Don't worry; it doesn't matter if you don't make the picture of peeing, but just feel what it feels like."

That certainly helped ease the panic. But it was all still blocked, as if it was frightened. You stayed with me for a while, helping me to come to terms with the idea .. and then you told me again,

"Let it go."

And at last, I saw what I was afraid would happen. Mummy was being sucked into my urethra, feet first, and she was screaming, her hair standing on end and her teeth bared in horror. She was terrified of drowning, and screaming for her life! It was awful.

I lay there, shaking with fear and anguish. What could I do? I just had no idea. Fortunately, you knew; as my brain reeled in shock and horror, you changed the scenery!

"What *should* have happened?" you asked.

I knew the answer to that question! Quite spontaneously, a whole different world emerged from the depths of my mind. What I wanted was for her to enjoy it and to feel that the sucking was nice, not that it would kill her. But she couldn't. No wonder she wanted to stop me .. it was a matter of life and death to her! Yet now that I knew what I was afraid of, and had dismissed it, I was free to relax the muscle that caused the cauterised pain in my clitoris; it was no longer a matter of life and death to me if mummy looked at it.

The pain in my clitoris was much better after that session. Yet it still felt under threat, and my unconscious mind was frenzied with a nameless anxiety. What I didn't know at the time, though, was that my mind was preparing for a final assault.

BREAKING FREE

For there came the day when we really got down to fundamentals.
You hypnotised me, and asked me what I saw. There I was with a
penis .. with a set of disembodied teeth chewing it off. God, it was
awful!

"Stay with it," you encouraged me.

And suddenly, there were mummy's breasts. I felt a quite overwhelming urge to sink my teeth into them.

"Go on, then," you said.

So I bit off her nipples at the base .. and sucked all the blood out.
I can't begin to tell you what an exquisite pleasure that was – just
wonderful. The trouble was that I felt rather ashamed of it, and kept
closing my eyes.

"Let your eyes share in the sadism, and acknowledge it," you
told me.

And this time, I didn't hesitate to do what I wanted, and I set
to with gusto and pleasure.

A deadly feast took place – no holds barred! First I concentrated
on one nipple and chewed it thoroughly off. Then I turned my attentions to the other, and tore it with my teeth until there was nothing
of it left. And as I gorged my desire and my fury, I watched her
before my eyes becoming all twisted up and bony and evil, and I was
seized by the most powerful urges to destruction that I ever
remember. I attacked every stiff, unyielding muscle in her body with
my teeth, until she lay helpless and lifeless on the ground – just a
heap of dead bones on the floor. What next?

I felt the most extraordinary desire to pee.

"Do that," you told me.

And I peed long and with a sense of refreshment, all over
mummy's charred remains on the ground. I could feel the pee coming from right deep within me, deeper than I ever knew before ..
from the neck of my womb at the back of my vagina .. welling out
from realms of passion and truth. It was wonderful. Then .. you said,

"Your mother is truly dead and your libido can be free of hers,
and you don't have to be like her any more."

I was so pleased that I wept.

But then you still wanted to go on further. Hadn't I finished? I wondered. I didn't realise at the time that you didn't much like (or do I impute motives to you that you don't really have?) finishing a session on a destructive note, but always want to do something constructive and ego-affirming. Unfortunately, though, I was so enjoying lying back with bloody, satisfied jaws, that I wasn't able to do much that was very constructive. I was a bit upset by this, because one part of me thought that as I'd killed mummy and so I wasn't like her any more, I should be able to do whatever I wanted without any inhibitions or worries. I didn't understand that this was all only the first stage, and that only now that I was free of mummy, was I also free to start developing in a way that was good and positive and gentle.

*   *   *

I never ceased to feel a sense of excitement and wonder that my unconscious had a life of its own; it changed and grew and made decisions about things; it was a living and dynamic organism. All right, it had got stuck in some rather strange habits and assumptions .. but the fact that it was stuck didn't mean that it was dead. All the books I'd ever read on psychoanalysis talked about the unconscious as if it was somehow fossilised – that its useful life was over and that it was just rather a nuisance because some of its habits prevented people from living a normal and fulfilled life. So all that remained to a person who wanted to be free of its rather strange dictates was to kill it, or break it open to understand it. There was no question of having a dialogue with the unconscious, or asking it how it felt or why it behaved as it did, or made the assumptions it did about the universe. The only thing to do was to attack it, to come upon it unawares, as it were, in the hope of tricking it, or deceiving it, into spilling the beans. Then one would be in a position to undermine its power-base.

But you never talked about my unconscious like that. You always respected it and understood, without being patronising, that it must have had very good reasons for being as it was. Yet, equally,

I never felt that you fell into the trap of saying that because we must respect it, we had to accept it without judging it. You seemed able to say: "Yes, you have become sadistic because you needed to attack things to get the goodness out of them. That was very reasonable at the time, and we can ask sensible and reasonable questions which will provide us with the answers to exactly why you did it. But nonetheless, it's no way to live and we don't have to accept that you can't help it. We don't have to prove that we understand you by accepting a world based on sadistic assumptions. We don't need to justify your decision to become a sadist by saying that it's all right for you to remain a sadist for ever." It was that ability to draw a distinction between the actual and the universal which seemed to me to be where your genius lay.

At this point in my analysis I felt that I didn't want always to be dependent on you. After eighteen months of preoccupation with the inner world – almost to the exclusion of the outer world – I felt strong enough to deal with the problems of relating with the world on my own, and I wanted to stop having to come to you every week to have my soul 'cured'. What I really wanted was an adult relationship with you, where we were equals rather than pupil and expert. You had taught me that I didn't have to be a woman like my mother – and I wanted to try it out.

"If you're able to frame such desires, then the fundamental problem is solved," you said. "I hereby declare you better."

You told me that I would be quite able to cope on my own in the big outside world. But you also made it quite clear to me that you weren't abandoning me, that you were still there as my friend, and that you would be happy to help me again whenever I asked you. And so I took the first step in my adult life.

3
Loving and Hating

THE PROBLEMS OF BEING ME

It was intensely satisfying being my own mistress, and not being so reliant on you all the time – but after a year or so, I began to find the responsibility of being me a bit too much to bear. I remembered the pleasures of lying on your couch and feeling myself .. and felt that I had not really succeeded in incorporating the confidence of wholeness into my everyday life. Although I was far better at asserting myself, and enjoyed it far more, I was still plagued by doubts and anxieties, and I gradually came to realise that what I wanted was to ask you again for your professional help. This time, I felt, I would be seeking your advice as an adult and not as a child – and that opened the door to all kinds of discoveries at new, previously unsuspected levels.

The precipitating factor in my decision to reopen my dialogue with my unconscious was my realisation that I was unable to sustain my creative enthusiasm. I had all sorts of ideas about things to do and brilliant schemes for showing my wonderfulness to the world .. but when it actually came to it, I found it very difficult to DO anything other than sit around twiddling my hair. Something else which was intensely puzzling to me was that I still didn't really know how to have an orgasm. After all, I thought, surely it's natural to have orgasms; all the books I had read – like a good child of the seventies – said that once you reached the plateau phase, then the orgasm followed inevitably. This was not my experience. Time after time, I would get stuck at the plateau phase, and would finish lovemaking deeply depressed and insanely angry.

Yet I didn't know why I inhibited the orgasm .. for there was no doubt in my mind that it was I who did it, and not someone else who inhibited it for me. It was a perpetual cause for concern; I didn't feel worthy to call myself a woman for as long as I couldn't have orgasms with a man. Masturbation was all very well, but it wasn't the same .. especially as I was afraid that it was all there was, and that I wasn't even doing it to remind myself of nice things I had once known. This fear made masturbation a fleeting pleasure .. followed by devastating misery. Yet, somehow, I felt compelled to do it; my soul left me no peace until I had satisfied myself – regardless of the wretchedness which came in its wake. But what was this depression which ensued after masturbation? I didn't know – but I wanted to find out.

It used to drive me mad to read in magazines for "progressive" women that masturbation was the real thing, and that orgasms were just the same however they were achieved; the main thing was that women were entitled to them. At one level, of course, there was something in that. This was why the "progressive" women had so many followers. But at another level, it was pernicious rubbish. All orgasms are not the same, and if a woman's vagina won't give an orgasm to her man, this is something to take seriously, not a matter for papering over the cracks by self-induced orgasm.

THE CLITORIS AND THE SELF

Still, at least there was now you to discuss this all with. You said that it was all to do with my clitoral primacy.

"That's very important for you," you told me "It's connected with your teeth and nails, and it stands for independence."

Then you told me that if I couldn't love my clitoris, then I wouldn't be able to love penises either. I knew that you were right, although I would never have had access to the thought in my own soul; I was suddenly swept back into the world in which I understood things you said without knowing why! So I knew all was well .. my unconscious was working again.

You let me lie down.

"Feel your clitoris," you told me.

I could feel it big and round, and I could feel my back arching. Then I stopped – just where I always stopped! – because I was afraid that my clitoris would burst. I expected that it would have an orgasm like a penis did. But as I didn't have a hole in my clitoris, the only way for anything to get out was for it to burst. I was terrified; I didn't know what to do next.

"Look at little boys peeing," you suggested.

That was very nice; I saw how proud they were, and how they held their penises aloft and sprayed everywhere.

"Now, look at your little self in the mirror," you said.

I could see her bending down to look at her clitoris. But she couldn't see it from above, so she had to squat down to have a look. She was upset that it was little, and she started pulling at it to make it come out .. then she started attacking it because it was little and she was angry with it .. and she didn't know whether to accept that it was little and be upset, or to pay attention to it and risk attacking it because she was angry with it.

But as I realised all this, and told you what was going on in my mind, I found that I felt better. I had understood the conflict in the little me.

"Feel it again," you told me.

This time, I felt it all warm between my legs; I could feel my clitoris blossoming out like a flower. Then I became aware that I didn't have to thrust it forward for it to be seen – and that was nice. I'd always felt that it would be invisible unless I pushed it forward. But now it was just there.

"You need someone to acknowledge and accept it," you said. "I would be really pleased if you were to ask me to do it for you."

I was quite sure that I didn't need you to do that because I knew that you liked it.

"Ask me," you insisted.

Then I realised that I was still really nervous. I found myself having to ask you if you were sure you wanted me to; that was very curious, because I also knew that you'd never have let me see all these lovely pictures unless you did like it. It took some courage, but eventually I asked you quite directly if you would come into my unconscious and look at it and acknowledge it.

"Of course I will," you said.

I experienced a whoosh of pleasure as the pictures in my mind moved to show me you looking at it. Everything felt wonderful; there was no hurry and no urgency about anything, and since I was me, I felt that I could be submissive and gentle and not have to thrust myself forward at you – or anyone else, for that matter. Everything was all right. The best thing, though, was that my clitoris stopped hurting; it could be quiet.

LOSS AND RECONCILIATION

After this first session of the new phase, my soul needed to adjust again to the rhythms of emerging from its wrapper. Curious fantasies swept through my mind: at one level, I was calm in a way which was quite new to me, but at another level, I found myself really upset. I felt that I'd given you my soul back again; and although I felt a sense of profound relief that you were going to look after it again for a while, I also felt a sense of total helplessness; a feeling that you had my soul in thrall. I was consumed by a searing anxiety that you'd die before I ever saw you again, taking my soul with you to the underworld. It was all most odd.

I talked with you about it at our next meeting, and in the course of conversation, all kinds of unexpected things emerged. I found myself remembering a former boyfriend, who used to masturbate in front of me. I had found this exciting in a way I didn't expect – but I had been insanely jealous when he had an orgasm. We had both been rather inhibited about sex, and hadn't been sure at that stage whether or not we were going to sleep with each other. It was the first time for both of us. Even so, he didn't feel embarrassed to masturbate in front of me, while I would have died of shame before masturbating in front of him. But paradoxically, I was jealous because he could do it and I couldn't.

"That is a classic complex," you said, "feeling that everyone else can do something, but you can't."

But what really amazed me was that you knew what I didn't know: that was, why it was that it had upset me so much.

"What did he do when he ejaculated?" you asked.

My mind brought back a memory that I hadn't even known was important – of him covering his penis carefully with a handkerchief, so that I couldn't see it. Presumably, he did this to stop it making a mess, but all I could see was that it was hidden.

"What would you have liked to have happened?" you asked next.

And to my amazement – for I was fully conscious – I saw myself taking it in my mouth.

You let me lie down, and told me to go back to where we had been the session before.

"Feel your clitoris," you told me.

I was so happy that it was there! I had a conviction that my clitoris was the spokesman for something, and that we'd shut it away on the previous occasion before we'd sorted out what it was trying to tell us about. And so I had feared that its message would never be heard, and therefore, that my soul would die.

Now I felt what the message was about: it was the water which I could feel rising up and falling again inside me – only to be stopped, sending shock waves back through the torrent. It was like all those poems in which rivers flow backwards in shock. It was terrible. But you told me:

"Let the feeling through, and then you'll see a picture which will show you what's behind it."

My first thought was that I wanted to touch a penis, but I was afraid that it would be all hard and unyielding, and that it wouldn't come to me properly. But then came a picture of mummy; she was a big black witch with long fingernails, cutting the hood off my clitoris and leaving it all exposed. And I wasn't sure whether I was pleased it was out, and so visible and real, or sad that it had been cut.

"All this fear is hiding a pleasure," you said. "Feel it."

I didn't know what this pleasure was that you were talking about .. but suddenly I felt it! It was all warm and pulsing in my genital area, as if I was sucking something – big, strong rhythms of sucking. And I could feel my upper lip filling out in the centre, getting big and fat, and not holding itself back from resting gently against my teeth. I hadn't realised until that point that my lip was tense and felt afraid of the teeth .. and it was lovely to find that it was relaxed and happy.

"Now, see your little brother," you told me.

As I looked, I found that I wanted to take his little penis in my mouth. I could feel it all soft and alive, resting gently on my tongue and between my lips. But the best thing was that I had no desire to bite it off; not until that moment did I realise how afraid I had been that this would be what I would do. The picture was rather confused, because I didn't know whether he was a year old or I was – I had made a total identification between penis and clitoris. But it didn't really matter; what was important to me was that I could make penises happy. That meant that I didn't have to be frightened of asking them to come to me.

Then I found myself thinking that if I sucked, things would come out. That thought – which seemed a new one to me – made me feel a sense of power, as if I was in control of my world. I suddenly realised that we *didn't* have to break my soul to reveal what was inside it, and I was overwhelmed by the pleasure of the thought which followed: that I wanted to cooperate with you in revealing what was in my soul – for this would make me your partner in the quest for wholeness.

LOVING MY BROTHER

One day I came to you having had a very interesting dream. I was helping backstage in an operatic production, in which there were lots of trapdoors through which props moved up and down. I wanted a pee, but was too embarrassed to say so. So I went to the wings of the stage and peed long and enjoyably into one of the holes, which had lengths of material wrapped round planks of wood in it. I felt foolish for not having said what I wanted and done it openly.

You were very interested in my dream.

"Peeing is connected with shame, but also with creativity," you told me.

I suppose that that's why I was at a theatre, but also why I had to hide. But I wasn't going to need to hide that day, because you let me lie down and have a look at what was going on.

I could feel my bladder really full and my urethra tingling to let it out. The trouble was that I was afraid to let it out, because I felt that there was too much of it. I didn't understand this; but before I had time to consider why, my unconscious showed me the reason. The scene moved and I found myself terrified: I was certain that a hot sharp needle was going to come and make a hole to let it all out. I was doubled up with fear and pain, and torn between two equally dreadful consequences: the pain of keeping it in, and the pain of having it let out.

But then I saw a baby.

"Who is it?" you asked.

I didn't know; it was very puzzling. After a while, you helped me out:

"It's your brother," you told me.

I was very surprised – but you were right; it was. He was a little red baby with a big navel. I wasn't sure why his navel seemed so important to me, until I realised that looking at his navel was a way of not looking at his penis.

"Go on, then, look at his penis," you urged.

So I looked. And as I looked, he had an erection! I was so surprised; I didn't know babies had erections. But my attention was soon distracted by the fact that I could feel my fingernails tingling.

"What do you want to do with them?" you asked.

I didn't really want to answer this question. I felt that I wanted to cut off his penis and have it for myself. But I didn't really know whether I did or not.

"That's the censor not letting you know," you said. "Do it."

Well, I did it .. but I didn't really feel anything; I didn't feel better for having it. In fact, I didn't really want it. But the very fact of having tried made me aware of what I DID want. I found myself wanting to take his little penis in my mouth and to run my fingernails up and down his body. It was such an exciting feeling which filled me with waves of pleasure – but pleasure mingled with anxiety. As I watched and felt myself doing it, I was afraid .. but, much to my amazement and delight, he liked it! That was wonderful.

Then I wanted to take his penis in my hands – but I was still afraid in case my fingernails punctured it. I didn't want to puncture it; I loved it. I caressed it in my hands – and as I looked, he peed for me. I took it into my mouth, and it was lovely.

I could feel my clitoris erecting as well as I looked at his little penis peeing. You told me that little boys have an erection in order to pee. I didn't know that. But as I digested this fact, I found myself thinking,

"Oh dear, mummy won't like that!"

Then I felt a terrible pain in my breasts – her pain – and my brain threw up all kinds of pictures of her fantasies: of cutting things off, because she felt cut up and bitten and punctured .. because she hurt. And, as I saw these pictures, then like magic, all the pain went away; my breasts, my vulva, my skin DIDN'T HURT. I was so surprised; the problem was solved! But that wasn't all; when you woke me up and I put my feet to the ground off the couch, I found that they could rest better on the floor, not recoiling from it in fear, but embracing it better. Very interesting.

MAKING A NICE MUMMY

In the early days of my 'analysis', just finding out what had happened and realising that it didn't need to be like that was highly therapeutic. But as we went on, you placed more and more emphasis on drawing out the me who was hidden underneath and who wanted to emerge from the shadows of the superego. I remember one particular session when we'd looked at mummy's breasts and seen how horrid they were, and how they didn't know how to come to me, and how they wanted me to make everything safe and all right for them, and how angry they were when I didn't, or couldn't. I felt that I had angry breasts, too, and I didn't want to be like her.

You must have known that if I was expressing overt desires not to be like her, then I knew what I *did* want. So you asked me, "What do you want?"

I wanted a wet vagina, and a mummy who gave me things because she liked to; a mummy whose milk was ready to fall out just because I wanted it, so that we could have pleasure together. I didn't find it easy to say all this; I felt a terrible guilt at wanting something I hadn't worked for, and so deserved. I felt as if it wasn't mine by right unless I'd worked for it. That was an interesting thought; how outrageous, I thought, in retrospect, that even a little baby can't expect something unconditionally. What a terrible mummy!

"Imagine a nice mother and a nice breast," you told me. "Think of them as yours, and see what they are like."

I could see a lovely round breast, with all its curves and angles different from the breast of my real mummy. This nipple didn't poke into the air away from me, but bent down towards me, so that the whole way the nipple fitted into my mouth was more comfortable and didn't involve me straining myself to get it. Then I sucked it .. and the milk came flooding out. No more fighting! I was really pleased about this – yet at the same time, I was a bit worried that at this rate I would empty the breast before I'd satisfied my desire to suck.

"Think about how you're sucking," you suggested.

Suddenly, I found that I was sucking in a completely different way. It was the most extraordinary experience: instead of having to use all the muscles round my jaws in order to get enough power to pull the milk out of a reluctant breast, I was using the muscles round my lips; it was much more relaxed and far easier to control the flow of milk that way, and now that I had a willing breast, I didn't have to worry about getting all the milk out in a hurry before it ran away, so I could take my time and relate to it nicely. And it would like it too! That was wonderful. Life became less urgent.

"What does the milk taste like?" you asked.

I ran it over my tongue, feeling it. The words 'milk and honey'

came into my head. It wasn't so much that it was sweet as that it had
a real taste – like milk! – and it was real and solid and I could feel
it in my mouth.

"Feel it going into your stomach," you told me.

I wasn't sure that I knew where my stomach was .. but, sure
enough, my unconscious knew. I could feel the lovely milk lining my
stomach. I couldn't imagine why this should feel so special .. but suddenly I had a memory of the other milk; it didn't line my stomach,
or want anything to do with me, but cowered in a little ball in the
middle of my stomach. This new milk liked me, though, and was
happy to touch me. I had no idea before this point that babies made
a relationship with the milk they drank as well as with their
mummies. But the new relationship was truly heavenly. The old
mummy ebbed gently away, and the new mummy took her place.
The world became interesting again.

*   *   *

After this, sex was different, too. My vagina knew how to suck with
its lips and not its jaws, and all the feelings became more sensitive.
Unfortunately, the old mother still had quite a lot of power, but at
least we'd broken her complete stranglehold.

I was very excited by all this reconstructive work. I often used
to ask you about it while I was under hypnosis:

"George, is this real, or am I just fantasising about it?"

And you would answer,

"Yes, it's real, because it represents the perceptions and
knowledge of your authentic self."

I gradually came to realise that when you said we made our own
reality, that this was genuinely true. If I have a horrid mother, then
I will feel that everyone is attacking me, and have no energy left to
assess whether this is really true or not; if I have a nice mother, then
I won't think that everyone is attacking me, but if anyone really *is*
doing so, my brain will have enough space in it to make an assessment. I suppose that I would still be making reality – but the amount
of brain I have available to do the job is that much the greater, so I'll
do it better.

RELATING TO MEN

By now, I was developing more confidence that things were getting better. But I still felt a powerful taboo on orgastic fulfilment. This represented itself, at this time, as a fear that daddy's penis was bent or deformed, which made it very difficult for me to know how to relate to it. This, in turn, made sex with any man fraught with difficulties, as I would always carry an image of a bent penis. Should I pretend that everything was perfectly OK, or should I tell him the truth and risk him being upset? I didn't know. But it was very interesting to see all this coming out of my mind, because I had always been very puzzled about what exactly it was that men wanted from me – and, indeed, what I wanted to give them. I never really knew whether they loved me, or whether I loved them; relationships always felt so complicated that I used to wonder whether it was all worth it. Yet, at the same time, I was very ashamed of my ambivalence partly because I thought it insulted the men, but partly because my estimate of my own worth was based on my ability to attract a man. But it was such hard work!

At this stage, I was too embarrassed to tell you much about all this. I tried to maintain a position which said that I loved men really, but it was just that I was worried that they would be frightened of me. No doubt you knew the rest, too, but you never pushed me faster than I could cope with, and it was very important to my self-image that I should retain the fantasy of being a totally loving woman. You were certainly very sympathetic about my lack of fulfilment, and let me lie down to find out what was going on.

"How did your father's penis get bent?" you asked me.

Well, I believed, mummy bit it, and it broke. Then it set wrongly!

"Where does your mother have her sexual focus?" you asked.

It was in her teeth, of course, and her clitoris.

"What is her vagina like"?

I saw it like a mouth which was firmly and adamantly closed; nothing was to open it. Yet there was a great pressure inside it of something trying to get out. All I could think was that it was blood in there, and I was afraid – but I didn't know why. Her genital area looked like a bomb-site, all chewed-up and regurgitated. It was awful!

"Look at your mother as a little girl, masturbating," you told me.

The most dreadful pictures passed across my mind. There she was, standing up, tearing at her clitoris with her nails, ripping it apart, until it bled. But she was getting such enormous pleasure from this! I couldn't believe it.

"Of course she is," you commented. "She's a sadist, and the only way she knows how to get pleasure is by drawing blood. She doesn't care whether it's her own or other people's."

As I looked at the little girl, I found myself terribly happy and relaxed. This seemed most curious, and I didn't know why such horrors should be causing me such pleasure. Then I realised: it was because my unconscious had seen the picture before, and I had been afraid that the little girl was me! But she wasn't – and I was *so* glad about it.

You held up your finger, in the shape of the deformed penis.

"Your mother projects her own sadism onto the penis," you told me, "and thinks that she is being attacked by it."

That was quite right, and as I looked at the picture again, I noticed that she held her finger in just the bent shape as she attacked her own clitoris with it. What an extraordinary business.

Then you told me to focus on my own clitoris.

"What does it feel like?" you asked.

It felt like it was retracting. I put out my fingers and made them into a retracting claw shape. Just like that.

"Make it come forward and just let it feel itself."

I did .. and I felt as if the claw-fingers were pushing out like a flower opening, rather than pulling in. It was the same movement of back and forth, but somehow it was like sucking and not like pushing away. Then I found my clitoris feeling big, and saw it moving out to rub noses with a penis; it could relate to it without eating it up!

"What does it want?" you asked. "Let it do whatever it likes."

And as I watched, I saw it let my vagina open and take in a penis and suck it. It didn't suck it so that it disappeared and was destroyed, as I had feared it would; on the contrary, it made it come alive and rejuvenated it. And that was quite wonderful.

⋆   ⋆   ⋆

Over the years, we worked a lot on my fear of my teeth. It was a long time before I could believe either that they were nice or that anyone could like them. Before I came to see you, I didn't know anything about my teeth at all; I only knew that I harboured fears that people were shying away from me when I spoke – especially if I spoke forcibly or with conviction. I had been aware for a long time that there was something wrong .. but that it should turn out to be my feelings about my teeth was a real revelation to me! It was an enormous relief to me that you were open about them, and that you reassured me so often that you liked them. There was a difference between good biting and bad biting, you used to tell me – and I knew how to bite nicely.

It was a long time before I could really believe you, though. What I thought was that analysis would help me get rid of my teeth, so that at last I could be a good girl and men would love me. But my clitoris didn't like this at all; it kept standing up and demanding attention. I could make it lie down, which was equivalent to pulling my teeth, but then I felt empty and dreadful. As time went on, though, I slowly came to realise that I didn't *need* to pull my teeth; that they could both exist and be nice. This was a real revelation.

THE IDEAL SELF – FIRST ENCOUNTER

One day we looked for the first time at my ideal self under hypnosis. You told me to look into a crystal ball and see her. I looked, and saw that she was exceptionally beautiful. She had slim legs (especially at the tops) and broad shoulders and high, well-hung breasts. She was frolicking around, dancing, doing head-over-heels .. but what was most amazing to me was that she was doing all this without having

to stop and think about it first. I could see all the fat from the lumps
at the top of my thighs melting off and running down my legs.

"What is the fat?" you asked.

I didn't know; I could feel that somehow it was an obstruction
and a covering – but I didn't know what it was for. You told me that
it was undischarged energy.

Well, that made sense; I'd often felt that I didn't know what to
do with all my feelings and emotions – libido. It certainly explained
why in the ideal world all the fat was disappearing. And it explained
the real-world phenomenon of people not liking being fat. That I
found fascinating.

We didn't get too far with that ideal picture that day, though.
You asked me what she wanted .. and I could see that she wanted a
man. The trouble was that she didn't really know what to do with
him. I had a terrible pain in my clitoris, because I didn't know how
it related with a man; would he respond to the assertive side of me,
or did I have to deny that and just let my vagina have pleasure? And
if I did this, how *could* my vagina have pleasure without my clitoris?

"This lady can manage with just her vagina," you said. "Stop
worrying about the clitoris and pulling at it and thinking about it.
For as long as you do that you'll continue to be afraid of castrating
or being castrated, and that will make everything hurt or feel
devastated. This ideal lady's vagina can manage on its own."

It wasn't really convinced, though, and after I went home, I still
felt angry and sick, with a persistent headache. Things were a little
better, though; I did notice, for example, that when I ate, I could
chew better and didn't throw the food down my throat in such a way
that it didn't touch my teeth. Yet something was still angry.

MY SADISM – THE CASE FOR THE DEFENCE!

You soon let me look in the crystal ball again.

"Look at all the angry parts," you told me.

At first, I couldn't see them at all, but gradually, my whole body
relaxed and the area between my legs tingled with pleasure at the idea

that the angry bits were going to be looked at and acknowledged. Then I saw a set of teeth – disembodied teeth!

"Just so," you said. "That's all part of the primary splitting process."

I was very puzzled by not knowing whose teeth they were, but that puzzlement was soon overridden by another phenomenon: I felt my skin split off from me, too. Often in the 'real' world I would feel immensely ticklish, and I now found myself wondering whether ticklishness and split-off skin were different sides of the same coin.

"Give the teeth a face," you told me. "And some eyes. Now what do they want to do?"

I could see the teeth chewing, and blood everywhere .. then I saw them grinning in a kind of exultant triumph-pleasure .. and *then* I saw that they weren't my teeth, but mummy's. The trouble was that I didn't know the difference – or, rather, I did, but I didn't believe in it. She made me feel her feelings and have her pleasures, and so, it seemed to me, there was now no difference between us. God, I was miserable.

"Your sadism is good," you explained, "because it wants to get things out of her reluctant breast, but her sadism is bad and destructive. The trouble is that she's taken your sadism and projected hers onto you, so that you think it's yours."

As you talked, I remembered episodes from my childhood. I used to feel absolutely impelled to tell her things, even though I knew she'd chew them up and make them horrid. In fact, she'd deprived me so much of my own personhood that it was almost as if I *had* to tell her everything so that she would make it real for me. Yet *her* reality was a bloody sadistic mess, and that made me sad. Telling her everything wasn't the solution to my difficulties either, as I found out; as life went on, I began to feel that I'd capitulated to her, and that made me very depressed about myself.

But now, lying on your couch, I gradually came to see why I had pulled at my clitoris. It *wasn't* because I was a nasty sadistic person; it was because I could see daddy there. He was worried about whether mummy was going to cut off his penis in revenge for all the terrible things that she believed had been done to her. In fact, he was

SO worried that he actually believed that it had really happened. Then I saw myself pulling at my clitoris to try and make it longer; I was trying to make it become a proper penis so that I could offer it to daddy. Then, I believed, he would have a penis again and we would all be happy.

I was so relieved. The angry bits were suddenly happy. They were so delighted that we had looked at them; for now we could see that the case for their defence was self-evident and proven; they weren't nasty and sadistic, but had just been confused by mummy into thinking that they were. And as I had all these wonderful, liberating thoughts, the pain went away, leaving a wonderful feeling of sucking. A freedom in peeing rushed through me; I wouldn't squirt it out through the barrier of a reluctant clitoris. I liked being looked at!

AND THE CASE FOR THE PROSECUTION.

But unfortunately, things didn't improve unconditionally after this! I was subject to the most terrible temper tantrums. This had always been a bit of a problem for me, but it was one which, consciously, at least, I had solved as a child. I had decided that I was going to be nice, and that at all costs, I wasn't going to risk losing friends and the love of my family by shouting and being an old misery. At the time, I was immensely proud of this decision, as it represented a victory over a part of myself which I no longer wanted to align myself with. But what I didn't realise was that by suppressing the symptoms, I wasn't curing the problem.

And, my heavens, now that we were investigating inner causes, the little one inside me saw her opportunity to let me know how she felt about having been so tidily disposed of! The moment I didn't get what I wanted, off she went, screaming and shouting, leaving me shaking with fury and seemingly powerless to shut her up. I used to shout at Eddie, and be furious with you, and generally behave like an ungrateful bitch all round. Yet the little one was quite adamant that she was right and that it was quite unfair and outrageous that she should not have what she demanded – now.

When I told you about it, you said that actually, it was my temper tantrums which were outrageous. I was really put out by this; I didn't like you telling me that I was in the wrong, but wanted you to sympathise with me because I was right but misunderstood! You weren't taking that line on this occasion, though.

"The little girl deserves a good spanking," you said, "and if it proves necessary, I'll administer it myself."

I was thrown into a frenzy of confusion; I didn't know whether I was pleased that you were going to control the little monster inside me or whether I was angry because she was me, so you were going to reject me too. But you intervened in the conflict.

"We must have a look at her," you told me, "and see if we can do anything about her."

That meant that you were going to hypnotise me – and that meant, as far as I understood things, that everything was going to be all right after all.

RESOLUTION

"Look into the crystal ball," you said, "and see the little girl."

There she was; she was about seven months old and in the bath. I could see her teeth, and feel her anxiety about what to do with them. But I liked her; she was a nice little girl. That was a source of great relief to me, because I had been afraid that I would hate her and spank her myself.

"What is she doing?" you asked.

She was thinking how nice it would be to pee in the bath. But would it be acceptable if she did? She didn't know – but she tried it anyway. The trouble, though, was that the uncertainty about whether or not it was allowed spoilt the pleasure, and then she became furiously resentful.

"What does she want to do?" you asked.

"She wants to lie on her back and pee into the air to make a fountain," was the only answer that popped into my head. I didn't want her to have to hide it in the bath – I wanted it to be visible and accepted. But as I looked at her, I could feel her clenching her fists and sweating and getting angry at not being able to let it out.

"I think that we should go further back in the life of this little girl," you said.

I felt her become very little indeed.

"Feel it all over again," you encouraged me.

I wanted to lie on mummy's tummy and pee all over it, and rub my sex up and down against her and show her that it was nice. But as I conceived these thoughts, I felt the little girl start back, unable to cope, just like the older little girl in the bath. My mouth chewed and sucked itself to make saliva – wetness, comfort, lubrication – and I wanted to suck mummy and make her wet and share it. But she didn't want it. I was so upset.

Then you arrived in the picture.

"Here I come, me, Uncle George," you said. "I like it. Pee for me; it can be seen."

I was very anxious – but I saw myself do it .. and it was very nice. Then you told me to lie on my back and make a fountain for you. And as I did, you sat there and smiled and smiled and were pleased. I lay there and felt my eyes relaxing into their sockets with pleasure and relief..

"What do you want me to do now?" you asked.

I thought for a moment – and then I wanted you take the pee into your mouth, and kiss me and make me wet with your mouth as a response; a sharing, a reciprocation, a loving. And, telling you what I wanted, I could see you in my mind, doing it – and it felt wonderful, full and sweet.

When you first entered my unconscious as Uncle George, I was very nervous. I felt that by fantasising about you, I was involving you in me and in my life, and making you do what I wanted – perhaps against your will. But as I spent longer in analysis, I came to realise that this was just a fallacy born of my wrongly held assumption of the omnipotence of thought. Presumably, you were pleased if I wanted you to participate in my newly-found freedom and to share in my pleasures – but the point was that by lying on your couch and making pictures, I wasn't forcing you to do anything. That took a long time for me to realise. I remember thanking you once for what you'd done – and you said that you hadn't done anything; I had. And that was quite a revelation to me.

But this session wasn't over yet. Next, you took me forward to when I was about four or five, when the first genital sensations arose.

"What's this little girl like?"

Well, this one certainly was bad-tempered, and with the most dreadful self-destructive urges towards her genital region. I could see and feel it all chewed-up.

"What does she want?"

That was difficult. Did she want a penis? I asked myself. No – but she did want a sex organ – a proper one. As the thought entered my head, I felt my vagina as real, inside me; that was wonderful.

"Tell her to take her knickers down and pee for me and make a puddle."

I did. She took her knickers off .. and, much to my amazement, the pee fell out at her feet. I had expected that it would shoot forward in a kind of parabolic curve. I had had the most terrible backache that week .. and I suddenly realised that it was from the effort of trying to push the pee out forwards when it really wanted to fall out downwards, as it would out of a little girl and not out of a little boy. But the best thing of all was the exquisite pleasure in being watched by Uncle George. You were pleased with me.

"What does she want next?"

My brain filled with desires. I wanted to see you kissing it again, and putting your tongue inside me.

"No," you said, "that isn't really what you want. What you would really like is for me to take down my trousers and pee for you, and to let you take my penis in your mouth."

The earth moved under me as this picture unfurled in my soul. I had had no idea that this was what I wanted, or how much I wanted it, so the intensity of the pleasure came almost as a shock. It *was* what I wanted .. and the depth of feeling which pulsed through me as I watched the pictures in my unconscious was quite extraordinary.

The consequences of that session were wonderful; I felt such a pleasure in myself and in my beauty afterwards. It was like being more me.

RESTORING MY CLITORIS

This was not the end of the matter, though; my clitoris wasn't yet fully content, and we looked at it under hypnosis again the next time I came to see you.

"Feel your whole body and see what it feels like," you told me.

It felt very nice indeed .. but there was a persistent throbbing between my legs, all round the big genital lips.

"Let it throb, and then ask your clitoris what it's doing."

I looked, and, to my enormous pleasure, it was having a nose-around, enjoying itself stretching out and burrowing into things. I felt that it was like an excited and stimulated penis when it raises itself into the air and sniffs about. Yet although it was very nice, I kept feeling that I was pulling it back in anxiety.

"Feel it some more first," you said, "and then we'll find out why."

I lay back and felt it .. and all the hollows in my body, where it had been tense and held itself back, filled in like a balloon being filled with air. I felt my anus and the back of my neck especially relaxing and getting filled out.

"Now," you told me, "look and see what made it all pull back in the first place."

There was daddy; he was ashamed of his penis. And suddenly, there was mummy too – and she was laughing at it! I was so upset that I couldn't even talk; I just lay there and cried and cried, and gasped and heaved, all abandoned like a little child in total grief. It was so terrible, I couldn't bear it.

You put your hands on my head.

"Feel that your brain has room to move," you encouraged me.

I didn't know quite what you meant – but as I felt my brain expanding into the space, I realised that it had indeed felt hemmed in

by all the anguish until it couldn't think straight. It was nice to feel
it expanding into your hands; very comforting.

It was all very confusing, this business of mummy laughing at
daddy's penis. On the one hand, she was sneering to protect herself
from her fear of his penis .. and when it all shrivelled up and died,
she was relieved. But she was contemptuous of it at the same time,
because it wasn't right that he should let it die like that. Yet the fact
that he was able and willing to let it die was not only mummy's
responsibility, because he was a bit like that about his penis. He did
think that it wasn't going to be able to do anything.

"What's all this got to do with your clitoris?" you asked me.

I thought for a moment, and then I realised that it was imitating
daddy.

"OK, then, but you've got sounder instincts than your father.
How are you going to handle the situation now?"

I could feel my teeth and nails wanting to tear at mummy and
kill her.

"You want your father to kill your mother," you said.

I did indeed. *Then* I realised that if daddy was such a coward and
wouldn't stand up to mummy, I wanted to kill *him*. But as I felt the
cathartic relaxation induced by this realisation, and waited in trepidation for the inevitable guilt which would follow it, you went on,

"But the tearing is two-sided; if you tear at a penis, it can be to
stimulate it, or it can be to destroy it."

And I suddenly realised that actually, I'd wanted to make
daddy's penis come alive .. but felt that in reality, I'd only succeeded
in killing it.

"The best thing you can do for your father is to stop imitating
him and to get on and show him that you aren't afraid to do things,"
you told me. "Now, teach your clitoris how to act."

I felt it getting more confident .. and I wasn't afraid to wake up,
because the activity of the penis was mine and the stimulation and
stimulating were mine for ever. I found myself thinking how I'd
always hated women who thought that all sex lay in the clitoris .. and
realised that in order to defend the proper role of my clitoris and to

assert that it was not the only seat of my sexuality, I'd overdone things and tried to deny it altogether. I was so glad not to have to do that any more.

AND STARTING TO UNDERSTAND THE PENIS

Then, at last, came the day when I had a real orgasm. I was so surprised that I didn't know what to think. But there it was, all warm and bringing this wonderful feeling of gratitude towards Eddie and the world in general. I had been afraid that I would feel disloyal towards you, or daddy – but I didn't; I just felt wonderful.

I had been certain that if I was able to have real orgasms, everything would be all right for ever – but I now found, to my great puzzlement, that this was, in fact, not the case. I had invested such a lot of almost mystical energy into the whole business of the orgasm, and elevated it into the only thing worth having or doing, and the only thing that justified my existence. But even though I had now 'done' it, I was still not right. So what *was* the universe, if not an orgasm?

On the morning of my next appointment with you after the orgasm, I woke up and found that I couldn't see. Or, rather, I could see, but it was as if a piece of gauze had been placed in front of my eyes. I kept blinking and blinking, trying to clear my vision .. but nothing worked. Thereafter, things went from bad to worse; I sat in your waiting room, waiting for you, and became angrier and angrier. I was sure, for some reason, that you weren't going to have time for me, and that I would kill you. But in fact, you asked me nicely why I couldn't see. And all I could think about was that you were going to be too busy for me.

"Ah, I see; you mean that if you can't have what you desire, then you won't look at it, either," you said. "Why is that?"

Well, I got more and more anxious and more and more angry with you; I felt that you weren't looking at me properly, and that made me furious. Yet I didn't know what to do at all.

Much to my relief, though, you let me lie down, and told me to look.

"What do you see?" you asked.

I could see an erect penis. But that wasn't the end of the story. The fact was that it was erect because I was looking at it. I didn't know what to do or what to feel.

"Look at your brother," you suggested.

I saw him about 2 years old; he seemed to me to be infuriatingly smug and self-satisfied. He had what I didn't have, and I couldn't have it.

But, much to my surprise, the thing it was that he had and I didn't *wasn't* his penis; it was the relationship that he had with mummy because he had a penis.

"Look at his penis," you said.

I looked, and I had the distinct impression that it was erect in a kind of 'up yours' gesture. This made me absolutely furious; I could feel my nails and my clitoris seething.

"What do you want to do?"

I *had* thought that I wanted to bite it off .. but in fact, I couldn't see myself doing it. That was very puzzling. What *did* I want? I looked again, and I found that what I *really* wanted to do was to take it in my mouth and love it and suck it and give it pleasure – better pleasure than mummy could give it.

Then I remembered how I'd wanted David to love me, and how I'd grovelled to him and been his slave, and read him stories and done for him all the things no one did for me. And how I got fat because I ate because he had things and I didn't, and how I beat him up out of frustration because he wouldn't love me. Yet I hadn't beaten him up because I hated him; it was a kind of invitation gone wrong. I suppose it was a bit perverse, but I was at least trying. The trouble was that people took me at my face value; I was only being horrid because I wanted them to know about the nice me underneath .. but then they didn't understand and I felt locked into the horrid me. Yet, I felt, it wouldn't go away until people said, "Ah yes, we see that you're only being horrid because no one understands you and responds to you nicely." But no one ever said that, so I was doomed to remain awful.

You brought me back to the matter in hand.

"What does your brother's penis do when you want to love it?" you asked.

I saw it sneering at me! I was furious; I wanted to bite it off and spit it out. I didn't even want to keep such a penis in my mouth, and certainly didn't want to chew it up. I was quite beside myself.

You released me from the spasm of rage.

"Think of a nice vagina that will eat it nicely," you said.

I could see a nice friendly, open, relaxed vagina .. but I was still terribly worried about the not-nice me, and felt that we hadn't really acknowledged her properly before trying to change her. I didn't realise that she only existed because the nice me was not recognised, so the way to solve the problem was to acknowledge the nice me. At the time, all I felt was that no one would love me. That wasn't very nice.

"It will come," you reassured me. "If you eat nicely, it's like loving."

I understood; that was the garden of Eden for which I was striving. And the particular pleasure was that I really believed that one day my journey would be over.

4
Intimations of Happiness

INNER WORLD: OUTER WORLD

One morning I woke up and found that I was happy inside myself.
I looked at some sweet peas growing in the garden, and saw the
colours shading and blending; I actually SAW them – as if for the
first time ever. Everything I did felt quiet, relaxed and voluptuous;
unhurried and luxurious. I looked at people and tried to speak to
them with my eyes:

"I love you. Do you love me? Shall we love each other?"

Yet this was, for me, a very difficult sensation to bring into the
outside world. I felt almost guilty for having expressed it, because I
feared that by bringing it out, I had made it into a challenge, and not
into a desire.

I felt my breasts and loved them, how they lay on my body, all
soft, and yet firm and upright. I felt how they responded with such
pleasure to being fondled and caressed; they belonged to me, and to
my body. I snuggled down inside myself, into that quiet and gentle
world where no one could see me, so everyone loved me. For
'everyone' was the population inside my head; I knew that they were
all there, and I could feel that they loved me.

The only problem was the transition between the inside and the
outside world; for the inside world didn't fully satisfy my body, and
I wanted it, too, to have pleasure and satisfaction. Yet just as two sets
of ripples cause discord where they meet, so I felt torn-up and out-
of-tune when I tried to navigate between the two worlds.

It was as if the inner world, for all its peace and beauty, was a
world of shadows. I had to *have* a shadow, but I didn't want to *be*

one. I wanted to live in the real world, with my shadow tucked securely and lovingly in behind my eyes. Music, I felt, was an inarticulate yet public expression of the shadow world. In it, what is hidden can be expressed. And yet, paradoxically, you have to be able to see before you can hear.

I loved you with every atom of my soul. The only thing I could not contemplate was that you should not love me. I wanted you to take me in your arms, and to caress and fondle you, and to smell you. And I wanted to wrap myself round you and love you, and laugh with you, and exult in you, and feel you having pleasure because I loved. I wanted there to be time for love, for feeling, for joy. I wanted you to be mine. And by wanting it, I made it true for me. Of course it wasn't the real world, in which we both lived our normal lives – but I didn't care; the world of dreams was also real.

All this was a real breakthrough for me. I had never really given rein to my fantasy world, because I had always been paralysed by the realisation that it was different from the real world – and that didn't just go for things concerning you. I had felt almost embarrassed by myself for being so naive as to think that fantasies had any value, yet at the same time, I was rather envious of the romantic movement who talked at such length about things which could never be true, but which they wanted. Yet suddenly, here I was, also able to create my own fantasies. Surely this was the first step towards bringing my own will to bear on the outside world. After all, I needed to know what I wanted to achieve before I could know how I wanted to act! And here I was, acknowledging my desires. I was happy.

TAKING THE OUTSIDE WORLD IN

Not long after this, we did some more constructive work on the good mother. I had become aware of various inhibitions in my body which prevented me from moving easily; I found it difficult to walk naturally, without feeling stiff or self-conscious especially if people were watching. I was also bothered by the conflicting emotions which assailed me when I went swimming; although I loved it, I was unable to give myself properly to the water, and feel the full, exquisite pleasure. So you let me lie down.

"Look at the good mother," you told me, "and feel your lips and suck her."

But when I tried, I found myself somehow puzzled, only without having any idea what was causing this. My teeth tingled, and felt as if they were filled with a huge amount of energy. I didn't know what to do.

"You're afraid of destroying the nice mother," you said.

You were quite right – I was. Destroying the bad mummy was bad enough, but at least I could justify that by realising that it was all she deserved .. but destroying the nice mummy – God forbid!

"Ask the nice mother what you should do with your teeth."

I didn't want her to go away, so I asked her. And she said that I wasn't the only one to like my teeth and to have big powerful ones; she had nice teeth, too, and was proud of and pleased with their power, so that she could give as good as she got, and then we'd both have lots of pleasure.

I was so pleased! I felt my teeth in her breast, and her nails in my back, and we didn't hurt each other; we just had a pleasurable and constructive tussle, back and forth. There was such a lot of energy passing between us – it was wonderful. Then, suddenly, I felt that my teeth had become part of my lips. They didn't need to separate off any more to go out and attack things; I felt them become pullers-in rather than rampagers-out.

Then I saw the nice mummy's whole breast going into my mouth – but it wasn't all ripped up and destroyed; it was whole, and went, nipple first, all down me into my stomach. It was lovely. And as I looked, the whole of mummy followed it! She wasn't shouting and screaming and struggling; she was pleased to be going into me. She curled up happily and cuddlesomely inside my tummy .. and wriggled around so that I thought I'd give birth to her. Yet even her wriggling was constructive; she wasn't kicking and screaming. I liked feeling her alive inside me and wanting to come out, and I liked knowing that I would let her out because she wasn't a monster, so I didn't have to be afraid of opening my vagina and letting her out.

My pelvis was alive instead of dead. It was alive because there was a nice mummy in there .. and because she was a nice mummy, I didn't have to kill her, so I could open up and be alive myself.

Then you said,

"Stand on the grass and feel your feet, and see what they are saying."

I felt my feet standing flat – not curled up – on the ground, caressing it; my ankles relaxed, and the grass said,

"Hello, can I creep all the way up the back of your legs into your shoulder-blades, please?"

I felt that it wanted to relate to me.

"That's very nice," you said. "Now go swimming. Take off all your clothes and look at yourself."

I looked .. and I saw a long thing coming out of my vagina. Was it a snake? No. Was it a penis? No again. I was so relieved; I had felt a huge compulsion to have a baby just to prove that I wouldn't give birth to a penis. This thing was like a tongue. And it got longer and longer until it went into my mouth – and then I was a self-sufficient circle of love and nourishment. It was lovely – almost like an umbilical cord. Then I jumped into the pool .. and it was warm and soft .. and my vagina melted as if it was going to have an orgasm; there was a kind of total relaxation.

You were very pleased with me that day. After you'd woken me up, you told me that what I'd seen was an uroboros. I was fascinated; I'd read about the uroboros in the works of Plato and of Jung – but I'd never really known what it was. Imagine me with eternal symbols in my soul! But I was pleased with how it all felt, too. All that positive introjection was a fantastic recipe for contentment and self-esteem and self-love.

INSIDE THE NICE MUMMY

Yet there was still a feeling of non-continuity about my sexual identity. Although it was fine in episodes, it somehow didn't fill up the bits in between! I found myself very puzzled about what my vagina was and how it worked and what it wanted. Indeed, I was even puzzled about what a woman was. After all, there weren't many role models about. There were the feminists – but I didn't feel that they had any real answers. It seemed to me that they were the biggest haters of women around; why else should they want to be like men all the time? They didn't have any original ideas about what women were; although they were always moaning about how men held all the positions of power and made all the rules about how societies should be run, when it came to the crunch, the feminists wanted to have all the positions of power in a world which had been created by the men they purported to hate so much. My reason couldn't understand that. But I was rather afraid that my emotions could. This tension of reason and emotion bothered me enormously, and was something which I brought to discuss with you quite often.

The trouble was that although I didn't want to be an aggressive man-hater, I didn't really see myself in the role of the passive, sub-missive woman, either, yielding at all times and in all places to the will of a man, never doing or thinking anything for myself. I wanted very much to be more able to do that than I actually was – but I didn't see it as my métier full-time and essentially. I remember being very anxious that this might be what I had to do if I wanted satisfac-tion as a woman – but I didn't want to swallow patriarchy hook, line and sinker, either! Yet the alternative seemed to be becoming a witch. Oh dear. I talked to you about this, and you let me do some more work looking at the happy mummy. I looked at her breasts, and that was very nice. Yet curiously, I found that I couldn't see her face above her teeth; nor could I see her eyes.

"Think about your own eyes," you said.

But that was difficult. I felt my vagina pulling right up, and couldn't think about eyes at all, but only vaginas.

"That's all right," you told me. "Let your eyes see through your vagina, and become a part of it."

Well, that was amazing. It was like proof that the person is a unity and that different parts of the person relate to each other, and

take on the habits and characteristics of each other. Who would ever
have thought that the eyes and the genital system were in sympathy
with one another, and behaved in the same way as each other, and
had an effect on each other? But here I was proving that they did! I
looked, and sucked .. and everything was all liquid and soft, and my
vagina salivated like my mouth, and went out and enveloped things
and drew them in; it was just like embracing things. I felt like a *good*
witch, with a supply of good and benevolent magic; I could see a
penis – the 'essential' penis - wanting to come inside me, because I
drew it to me and it wanted to come. It didn't want to attack me,
because I didn't have a nasty closed and dried-up vagina like my real-
life mother had; on the contrary, it wanted to come in because I was
nice.

Then I wanted to look at the nice mummy's eyes after all. But
I was afraid. I could see flashes of lightning like swords coming out
of evil green eyes.

"You can stop seeing that," you said. "Your eyes are the centre
of libido now, and so you won't see the tooth-symbolism any more."

So I looked .. and I didn't see the horrifying flashes any more.
The nice mummy had big liquid brown eyes which drew me suc-
culently in – or was it my eyes that drew her in? – it didn't seem to
matter; they were both the same thing really. And I felt everything
open up.

Suddenly, all I could think about was the nice mummy's vagina.
I went down and looked at it and sucked it and played with her
clitoris. THEN .. I started to crawl up it .. and it was soft and elastic
and flexible and wanted me. I crawled right back into her womb and
settled down in there. And there was a tube – was it an umbilical
cord? – in there, which I sucked, and nice things came out, and I was
happy. There were all sorts of knobs and bumps and passageways in
there .. and because she was happy, that gave me the freedom to explore them all, and to give us both pleasure.

After that session with you, things changed; I felt as if the world
was very close to me, and embracing and intimate. Seeing was not
just a matter of focusing; it was a question of relating - and I felt that
I could suck the world in through my eyes .. and that was wonderful!

THE MAN COMES IN

The next week, though, my soul threw up some more things it wanted to investigate. I was constantly amazed by how complex and difficult a business it was, getting through to all the parts of my unconscious and helping them to realise that everything was all right really. For although at a deep level, I felt very much better, one part of me continued to feel that I couldn't do anything really, that I wasn't sexually attractive, I wasn't clever, I was just a nothing. I hated this feeling, since ultimately, I didn't believe it – but nothing was going to persuade the stubborn part of me that it wasn't true. I would be in the middle of doing something: hugging Eddie, talking at work, reading a philosophy book .. and suddenly I would find that I couldn't concentrate any more, because I'd become so anxious. And however much I tried to muster the confidence to keep going, I couldn't; the fun had all gone out of it.

"That is a castration-anxiety," you told me, "and you can't even get angry about it, because that makes it worse, as then you really would have reason to be anxious about what would happen next."

Then you let me lie down.

"Feel your lips," you said.

I could feel them; they were saying "I am nice; it's not fair."

"Go into a room," you told me, "and see yourself making love with a man in just the way you've always wanted to."

I went into the room, but I got such a pain in my neck that I couldn't do anything at all.

"Just look," you told me.

But every time I concentrated on seeing the scene, I cried and cried until I didn't know what to do with myself.

"That's because you're feeling an orgastic sensation that you're not letting out," you said. "Keep looking."

I didn't really know what you meant by the orgastic sensation, but I kept looking anyway. I saw the man kissing the woman who was me, and playing with her breasts. Then he opened her legs and had a look. I was afraid, but you made him keep looking. He kissed her and loved her, and I could feel the muscle down at the bottom of his back all flexing and elastic and desirous of entering. But I didn't know what to do. Suddenly, I saw him crawling inside me, and I could feel him excited inside my womb, licking me out. It was wonderfully exciting for me, too!

"Watch him enter you with his penis," you said.

But I couldn't! I was afraid I'd chew him up. And when I looked, I saw that my vagina was all held up and sewn up so that he couldn't get in. I was so upset! But *then* I realised that the emphasis in this picture was wrong: I wasn't so much concerned with the state of my vagina as with the fear that he would have to tear me up in order to pull my vagina down far enough for the entrance to it to be visible and accessible. This fear represented itself in a pictorial form which somehow made it all my fault. Yet it wasn't as simple as that!

Once I'd seen that, I felt better. I felt my vagina fall down, and I could see the flaps all funnel-like between my legs. I had something between my legs! I was so pleased. And there were little teeth all up my vagina which caressed the penis. Then I felt my clitoris fall into my vagina; they were all one; it was like the day when my teeth joined my lips .. and I sucked the penis just like sucking a breast – just the same.

When I woke up, I found that my arms and legs were all woolly and relaxed. I could walk better; my hips swayed and my feet felt more secure on the ground. But the most extraordinary thing of all was that in the course of the next few days, the lumps of fat at the top of my thighs became smaller, because my pelvis had moved forward. And that was quite incredible.

AM I DEAD OR ALIVE?

Everything went very well for a while; but then came a terrible week, during which I felt totally dead. I wasn't absolutely incapacitated by this, as at one level, it was possible to snap out of the deadness, and to pull myself together and be normal .. but at another level, I was quite unable to come alive. And with the deadness went the most desperate rage, a total inability to think or to plan, and a terrible, insistent headache. I kept telling myself that it wasn't long until I could come and see you and you would make everything all right .. but in this frame of mind, that was of little consolation to me, because I couldn't tolerate any kind of suspense; it had to be all right NOW, or else my clitoris developed such a dreadful pain that I didn't know what to do with myself.

I remember that the night before I was (at last!) going to come and see you, I had a dream, in which I was coming to see you. You lived at the top of a staircase in a bright, airy room with big windows, a comfortable easy-chair, and books. I looked, and the staircase was filthy dirty and dusty. I knew that you wouldn't mind if I was a bit late, so I decided that I had to sweep the stairs before I went up. You were, meanwhile, sleeping peacefully in your chair. When I eventually got to the top of the stairs, you gave me a big hug, and then started to think about making some phone calls because the rest of your appointments wouldn't be running on time.

You asked me what this dream was about. I had been thinking about this, but I hadn't reached any very satisfactory conclusions. I often found that I didn't really know what a dream was about until I actually talked to you about it; then there was something about being with you, and about the way you framed your questions, that suddenly made everything seem obvious. I realised that the dream said that you had arrived, while I was still on the journey; you were sleeping peacefully, the sleep of one who knows pleasure and satisfaction and peace .. and I wanted that too. I also wanted you – but felt that I could only have you after I had cleaned out my soul.

"I'd like you to notice, though," you said, "that I'm happy to wait; also that sweeping the floor is not just a means to an end, but a productive activity in its own right."

I was very pleased by your comments on my interpretation. If I fantasised about you, you never said, "What an outrageous thing for you to be thinking; how inappropriate!" Nor did you become pompous and arrogant and self-conscious because I loved you. You just accepted my feelings towards you as if they were good, and the most natural thing in the world. On this occasion, for example, you pointed out that the dream wasn't pessimistic, as I had thought, but optimistic because you weren't going to run away while I swept out my soul. And I felt that what I desired was accepted by you.

I was fiercely proud of my wonderful soul and all the things that came out of it, and all the things it had thought and organised in its fight for survival in the face of my superego. I really thought that I was extraordinary, and that no one else's soul had ever yielded such treasures, and I wanted to show them to you and you to be pleased with them, and me to be proud of myself. But the paradox was that I was so upset by the fact that I seemed unable to get any pleasure in my soul except through you, that I began to feel that my soul was really yours and you were the only person able to do anything with it. It was all most puzzling – like having lost something.

The next time I saw you after the dream episode, you let me lie down and see what it was that had been making me feel dead.

"Focus on your body," you said.

It felt like a corpse; it was quite dead.

"Feel the pain."

I didn't understand what you meant: there wasn't any pain; I was dead. But, as I mustered the strength to tell you this, I felt it. There was an enormous anger in my clitoris, and a desire to make a huge pee and be seen. Then I found myself locked into a confusion: how did I know whether and when I had had an orgasm?

"Look in the mirror," you told me, "and see the pain of orgasm."

I was rather frightened. There was a crazy woman in my head, who kept her back to me and tore her hair and attacked herself. I had seen her once before, and I didn't want to see her again; I certainly didn't want to have to *be* her.

What I actually saw was the front view of a woman with blood between her legs. I didn't know whether she'd been injured, or whether the blood was in a huge mouth all over the pubic region. I could see a snake coming out of her, and I wanted to be nice to it – or do I mean, to her? – but I couldn't.

"That's the front view of the crazy woman," you said. "But women like that don't let you see their fronts."

I could see why not – I wouldn't have wanted anyone to see me like that!

"How does your clitoris feel?" you asked me.

It was thirsty. Yet it was wounded.

"Be a surgeon," you said. "Investigate it and see what's going on."

I touched my clitoris .. and as I laid my fingers on it, it healed up. All it wanted was to be touched. Yet it didn't trust me; it wasn't going to be fooled. And then, there were mummy and daddy; she was looking furtively away from me because my clitoris was insignificant and unlovely, and he wanted to look and smile, but was intimidated by her. It was terrible! I shrivelled up, and my shoulders hunched, and I was furious and cringing at the same time. The only thing that seemed open to me was to throw the most monumental tantrum.

But you had another solution.

"What would make the anger and the teeth better?" you asked.

I saw a tongue coming out of my vagina to lick my clitoris; then my clitoris became a breast-like figure and there was a mouth sucking it and making it wet and responsive and lovely. I felt that my clitoris lived in my mouth and then in my vagina.

"Feel it move to where it can show itself," you told me.

I felt it move to a relaxed position between my legs .. and I felt it, and looked at it opening. It was wonderful; it was just like a flower coming out, and it was so pretty. I liked it. Then suddenly I felt that it was safe to have an orgasm without closing my throat, and without hurting afterwards. I felt that it would just happen because that was the way things happened. I didn't have to be puzzled about what an orgasm was and whether what had happened was one .. I could just do it! And I was happy; I had it. I could think clearly again; no more forcing my brain through narrow spaces. That was nice.

"That's right," you said. "First the clitoris has to have its primacy, and then it can let go."

I didn't really know what you meant at that time; I only knew that I was pleased with what had happened.

IS THE MAN MINE?

One morning I woke up – and I could see! I couldn't quite believe it, but it was true. No more focusing at 3 inches from my nose .. I could see right across the road. It wasn't quite as sharp as I could achieve through wearing glasses or contact lenses .. but it really wasn't at all bad. I could distinguish the mortar from the bricks in the house across the road, and could read the labels on packets in the kitchen from the other side of the room. It was such an exciting feeling; it had never crossed my mind until that point that there might be a psychosomatic component in short sight – so not only did I have the thrill of being able to see; there was also the intellectual excitement of realising that there was a new dimension to the perceived universe! The I who could see was a different I from the short-sighted model; I felt potent and powerful and able to take things in .. it was fantastic.

Unfortunately, it didn't last. We were going that day to the wedding of a friend who was a pillar of the local church. Everything at this wedding service was about God, and about how you mustn't love each other but only Christ in each other. I felt as if there was going to be a third person in their bed, watching them, telling them what was allowed and what was not allowed .. and telling them that they weren't allowed to look straight at anyone (as opposed to looking at Christ in them) in case they wanted to have sex with them.

Yet, ran the unspoken message, the sin was committed just by the looking: looking at someone was precisely having sex with them .. but that wasn't allowed, because the only person who was allowed to have sex with anyone was God .. but he hadn't got a body so he couldn't have sex .. and anyway, sex was bad .. and so on and so on. Suffice it to say that by the end of the day, I couldn't see at all. I was so disappointed. No more power. No more pleasure. Only submissive passivity. It was terrible.

I talked to you about the dreadful guilt and depression which resulted from all this. You were very sympathetic and let me lie down almost immediately.

"Feel the part of your brain that has to do with seeing," you told me.

My conscious mind had no idea which part of my brain had to do with seeing. But my unconscious mind knew exactly what you wanted. I felt a pain just above where my head joins my neck, on both sides of the vertebrae. It felt like a set of membranes, or strings, or cords being pulled and squeezed – like a frayed rope. Then I felt a numbness in my forehead over my eyes, and a complete vacancy in the top of my head between the sites of the two previous sensations.

"I'd like you to go back in time and see what some of the causes of this were," you said.

I knew immediately where I wanted to go. There were mummy's breasts, and there I was, a little baby, wanting to ask her if it was all right, yet knowing that it wasn't, and so not wanting to ask .. yet wanting to ask. Anyway, her breast sort of wasn't there .. and so I wasn't there .. and it was all very confusing. But then I realised that there was a solution to this problem: if I bit her, everything would be all right.

Then, without warning, the scene moved to daddy. I was a lot older – about four; I was thinking about his penis and wondering whether it was worth trying again and seeing if it worked better with a penis than with a breast. But he put his hand over his penis. That was puzzling: at least if he had to hide it, that meant that it was really there – unlike the breast – but it didn't bring it any closer to me, and it was that that I wanted to achieve. I wanted to ask him for it .. but I was afraid. I didn't want to bite it, as I had wanted to bite the breast; I felt that although that had been the right solution for mummy, it wouldn't be for daddy. Deep down, he didn't like being bitten. I could see blood everywhere, and his penis bursting. It was horrible.

I could feel myself wanting a pee, but holding it in – like daddy was.

"What do you really want?" you asked me.

I watched daddy as he did what I really desired. He got up and came towards me, and I lay on the floor with my legs in the air, and he peed into me. Then I made a fountain for him. It was really wonderful – just like having sex – but in a certain way, even better!

But the trouble was that I didn't really believe in all this pleasure, yet I was at a complete loss to know why not.

"Have a look," you suggested.

There was daddy's penis with a rein around it, which pulled it up and back like a horse's neck. It was yoked to mummy, and I couldn't have it; that made me jealous. But the extraordinary thing was that as I saw his penis being reined back, all the nerves in my head going down from the back to the front also reared back .. and I lost touch with my eyes. It was like the empty sensation in the top of my head that I'd started with.

"See what you really want," you told me.

I could feel it, but I couldn't see it.

"Just keep looking," you insisted.

Very gradually, I saw the picture of a penis standing up for me. But it was soft and yielding even though it was erect. Then it came towards me; I didn't have to do anything. I just yielded to it. Then it came right into me through my eyes and my mouth, down my throat and into my stomach. And once it was there I found that I could also feel and believe in my vagina.

"Let the penis look and let your vagina look at it," you said.

That was all much more difficult. I tried very hard, but I couldn't muster any confidence in it. I was rather upset by that, as I would have liked it to work. Still, I did feel an underlying sense of contentment and me-ness, and a feeling that I was in charge of me. I felt my head whole, and my shoulders joined up with my body, and the gap I'd always been aware of in my abdomen filled up with contentment.

Although I couldn't see any better after this session, I was not as disappointed by that as I might have been. IT had decided that it wasn't going to see, and I had no control over it. Still, there was always another time, and I was becoming better at controlling my disappointment. In any case, I felt more anchored inside, so something good had happened – even if it wasn't quite what I had hoped for!

PLEASURE ANXIETY – THE EXISTENTIAL VOID

One week, I had a particularly wretched time at work; I felt that my colleagues didn't like me and value me, and this made me feel worthless – as if the world might as well come to an end. It wasn't clear to me even at the time whether this state of affairs was real, or whether I was imagining the slights and lack of regard. But whether it was real or not, the feelings that went with it were pretty strong: I felt humiliated and upset at the idea that I should have thought they loved me, and now had discovered that they didn't care about me at all. All I could think about was putting myself under a bus – the ultimate act of self-directed aggression. But it suddenly occurred to me that I was angry with *them* – so why should I turn other-directed aggression against myself? Although this made sense at one level, another part of me rebelled violently against its logic. Why did I have to kill myself?

You took this all very seriously, and let me lie on your couch.

"See what's going on in your mind," you suggested.

I could feel only a sensation of nothingness. Yet I couldn't quite take it seriously; I knew that it wasn't nothingness really, but was just pretending because it didn't want to look at something.

"Look what's going on," you repeated.

My jaw and nose and eyes were all tight and somehow swollen up from tension.

"That's a basic oral aggression," you said. "But it's not really anger – or at least, not primarily so – it's more a kind of hanging on to something."

I knew what you meant, but I didn't know what I was hanging on to; in fact, the precise problem was that I feared that what I was trying to hang on to wasn't really there, and that was what was so terrible about the whole situation.

"Have another look."

Suddenly, I saw me and mummy in the hospital ward where I was born. I could feel the frustration of not knowing whether I could have what I wanted or not, or whether it would be satisfying or not if I did have it, and therefore whether I really wanted it or not anyway. I could see myself thinking about mummy's breast, and snuggling up to it – and then a picture that I blotted out of my mind because it was too terrible to look at. Yet, although I blotted it out, it was still there, and it was precisely the fact that it didn't go away when I didn't look at it that made it so frightening; after all, that meant that it could jump out at me any time when I wasn't expecting it.

"Do you want to look at it?" you asked.

I did, but I also wanted desperately for you to want me to look, and not to disapprove. I wanted you to tell me that you wanted me to look.

"Ask me," you said.

"George, do you want me to look at this picture?"

"Yes."

The relief was unspeakable. The very wanting had become taboo and not allowed. Yet even now, I wasn't sure whether I really wanted it or not. I could get the picture as far as getting the nipple in my mouth, but then I felt that it was inviting me to bite it. But I didn't want to have to bite it; I felt that I'd already done that enough times to satisfy myself, and it didn't work. Did I have to do some more work building myself a new breast?

"I don't think that's quite the right thing for today," you answered.

So I looked again, and saw myself sucking the breast as I would really want to. It was wonderful; just for a split second, I felt the breast soft and responsive, just like I wanted it and how I would really make it if I could .. but then the earlier picture returned, now in more detail: the breast retreated from me and I felt it all hard, with the nipple standing up inviting me to bite it. I couldn't quite believe my eyes. But yes, it was actually an invitation. What the hell was going on here?

"What does it feel like when your mother withdraws the libido from her breast?" you asked.

I could feel all the muscles leading from the nipple, across the breast and under the arm, tighten up; that was what drew the nipple into the upright position. But what I was really aware of was the withdrawal of her vagina, and the pulling back of her hips to facilitate this.

"That's absolutely right," you said. "That's the most important thing of all. Your mother suffers from a pleasure-anxiety which causes her to behave like this."

Well, if my mother was anxious about pleasure, then it figured that she would have desires to attack the person – me – who might break down her defences and make her feel it. She wouldn't even really know that pleasure was nice, so she would view anyone – me again – trying to make her feel it as an enemy. Of course she would attack them, unconsciously, at least. This wasn't something which I projected onto her when I felt aggressive urges towards her; it was REALLY like that!

"Look again at the picture where you sucked the breast as you really wanted to," you said.

And as I looked, I felt the pleasure and the anxiety become separate. There *was* pleasure for her in my sucking, she *did* respond, and it was *her* problem that she then became anxious. It was nothing to do with me; I didn't set out to hurt her; she hurt herself.

I had never before realised that the two elements, pleasure and anxiety, were separate; I had only ever experienced them, in the sucking context, as a single phenomenon – but now I could affirm the pleasure without having to accept the anxiety. What I hadn't ever understood before, either, was that the bad breast appeared to me actually not to exist. The withdrawal of the libido had felt like a destruction of the breast – and that had been very worrying for me. Now, though, I felt such relief; I could suddenly feel all the parts of my body, like my vagina, that I'd never felt properly before, because they, too, had disappeared with her withdrawal. Yet now I realised that it was the *libido* that had been withdrawn, and not the *object*, I could understand how all the parts of my body which had felt that they didn't exist either, because the breast didn't exist, could actually be real, after all. That was wonderful.

I was sorry that the libido, the colouring, the fullness, should not be there .. but that wasn't the same thing as existential nothingness. That was nice. I could suddenly understand all sorts of things that I hadn't known about, like what pleasure really was .. and as I thought more about sex and love and pleasure, and realised that I could have these things as of right, so to speak, I felt my vagina fill up – with libido? – almost like a balloon which someone has filled with water. And I believed that it wouldn't ever go away because it was mine.

Then I thought that to have an orgasm, I didn't need to do anything; the balloon wouldn't explode, but would just open up to let the water flow out. The libido would stream naturally by the force of its own energy. And at last this energy was being freed. I was so relieved!

"When a baby sucks at its mother, the sensations in the breast are felt in the vagina, and remind the mother of her love of, and yielding to, her husband," you told me. "But if the woman cannot yield, all kinds of problems materialise."

That I could well understand ...

What was *so* amazing about all this was that if anyone had asked me if I thought I had a vagina, or breasts, I'd have thought they were mad. Of course I had these things; all women had them, and they were important. Yet, at an unconscious level, the existence of these essential parts of my femininity was not established beyond doubt, and was permanently under threat; either they would cease to exist, or they would, in some way, be not nice, so that I wouldn't be proud of them. And then I'd want them not to exist. But who would ever have guessed this? And especially, who would ever have thought that matters like having arguments with colleagues at work could have anything to do with the existence or qualities of vaginas? But they do!

RECONSTRUCTION .. AND DESTRUCTION

I experienced a recurring frustration at this time because my eyes wouldn't see properly. Occasionally, they would tantalise me by sliding into focus when I was least expecting it .. but as soon as I became aware of it, they would immediately slide out of focus again. Then I would feel my feet curl up in anxiety. It was most odd.

Every so often, I would talk to you about it again, and we would look together for another piece of the jigsaw. One day, lying on your couch, I saw some incredible pictures which related to the whole question of seeing.

"Look in the mirror and see yourself," you said.

There was a woman bent over double, looking at her clitoris, which was long and red and sore. I couldn't see her face. As I looked, I found myself thinking about sex. Sometimes after sex, although I seemed to all intents and purposes to have had an orgasm, I felt that there was something I hadn't done; that things weren't properly complete. And this had something to do with this long, sore clitoris.

"Look at her some more, and try to see her face."

I looked, and I could see her hair all standing on end and frizzing up in fear; her canine teeth looked like fangs, and her nails were long like gnarled claws.

"Do you like her?" you asked.

Well, I did, except for these monstrous features – but I didn't believe that they were really a part of her .. and nor did she. She wanted them to go away.

"What are her eyes like?" you went on.

I could feel my eyes being pulled back by a muscle just under my cheekbone – and I could see my eyeball on a long, thick stalk like a horse's neck, and the top of this neck was all hard and tense and being pulled back. The front of my eyeball was still soft, and I was worried that it would burst under the strain of the pulling back. It was as if it was afraid, like a horse rearing up in fear.

"Let her see now," you said, "and tell me what she looks like."

Her feet stood flat on the ground, and her pelvis relaxed into the right position; her chest relaxed and opened up; her hair lay down and the fangs and nails disappeared; the middle of her forehead came down, and the outer edges of her eyes lifted so that the eyes lay at a different angle in the face. Then I felt the muscles under my arms relax, and the breasts hang properly. That was nice.

"Get familiar with her," you said. "Feel that she's the real you."

You let me digest the feelings of being her for a minute; then you said,

"Fill in the context of this picture."

I looked around, and I could see her lying down, with a baby at her breast and a penis approaching her vagina. It was a very nice picture, but I felt that all its components were parts of me which I'd never integrated properly into myself. Yet as I looked, I felt that I

could distinguish better where I ended and where the outside world
began, and that this was good.

"The outside world was never consistent for you," you said. "So
you projected yourself into it, to make it real; but the price you paid
for that was not knowing where the boundaries between self and
other were."

I could understand that; but now I wanted to incorporate into
myself the bits I'd projected out, and have them as mine. I could feel
the centre of myself becoming full and defined, rather than fuzzy and
indefinite.

"See what she's like."

My eyes and nails and everything were further forward than
they had been; so was my vagina, and I could feel my clitoris small
on top of it. It was as if my vagina and clitoris had changed places.
That seemed rather strange. What was going on? Then I realised that
it was a symbolic picture, showing me that my vagina had assumed
the primary position, and my clitoris the secondary position. I was
very pleased indeed about that.

"Let's find out how all this happened," you said. "Look for the
scene which started it all off."

There I was as a young girl, somewhere between the ages of 1
and 3, in the room where David was born. I had no clothes on and
I was lying on my back. Then I saw mummy with a hole between
her legs with something black coming out of it. As I looked, I found
myself remembering how hysterical I used to get if I got trapped in
anything like my dress over my head, or whatever .. and how I used
to feel as if I was going to die and be eaten up in there. Then I found
myself feeling afraid, like I did when mummy took over some idea
or scheme of mine and chewed it all up and made it hers and so
destroyed it. I could feel myself being sucked into that hole and eaten
up and then pushed out again in her shape. I hated it. My nails turned
into talons again, and my teeth grew big and aggressive. But this
time, I wasn't going to stand for it. I put my hands into that terrible vagina and ripped it apart so forcibly and determinedly that it
cracked right up to her breasts.

It fell into two pieces, and lay there supine; ranks of teeth bristled, serried all up the edges .. but I'd pulled them apart, so they couldn't chew me up or hurt me any more. The relief was palpable; I cried and panted, and just lay there limp and satisfied at last as the feelings swept over me. My jaws, after years of tension, relaxed, and I felt a rushing in my ears. I had so much wanted to do that to her, but I had been afraid that I would kill her. This picture, though, showed me that all I wanted to do was destroy her horrid vagina, so that I didn't have to have it for my own any more.

"Pick it up and throw it away," you said.

But I couldn't; for before I did that, I wanted to chew it all up, so that I was sure that it was really dead and couldn't come to life again. I savoured each morsel of the feeling of it; I experienced such pleasure as I picked off its teeth with mine and chewed each one deliciously into an unrecognisable pulp. Then I felt better; it was done.

But then, as the pleasure faded, anxiety took its place. After all, if that was how I treated mummy's vagina, wouldn't I do the same to a penis? Wouldn't I generalise the pleasure and become a con-firmed sadist?

"No," you said. "Now that the terrible vagina is dead, you'll be able to have a nice vagina – and nice vaginas don't chew up penises."

That made sense, and instilled a huge relief in me. I'd always been terrified to destroy the terrible vagina in case I got stuck in the position of being a destroyer. But now I began to see that there was good destruction and bad destruction – and this took a great weight off my mind.

When I woke up from that session, I felt a bit numb. It took me quite a while to get my mind round anything of emotional significance again. But the sense of guilt that had pervaded my entire life was significantly lessened; I felt that now I'd killed the thing that deserved it, I had discharged a huge quantity of sadistic energy which had needed to be released, and which I had always worried I would let out onto things which didn't deserve it.

The other interesting thing I noticed was that I became far less inclined to defend myself against censure by saying that it wasn't my fault; I was much more able to look at things and see why they had happened. The obverse side of that coin was that when I did do wrong, I was far less likely to look round for someone else whose fault it must be! And all of this made me respect myself a lot more, which was very nice. I couldn't see any better .. but I felt better about seeing, which seemed to me to be a good first step.

ON BEING A BAD SADIST!

Nonetheless, I still kept getting into a state as if the end of the world was coming. And one day, it entered my head that this wasn't either normal or inevitable, but perverse – why should I get in such a tizzy about such trivial things? And why did I always sweat and tremble if I asked for something but didn't get it? I don't know why it hadn't ever crossed my mind before that sensible people didn't get worked up; I suppose I must have thought that everyone did, but that they just didn't talk about it. After all, I didn't talk about it to my friends and relations .. so not talking about it was obviously normal!

I didn't get much joy out of you the day I decided to broach the subject as a 'clinical' issue. You told me that it served me right that I didn't get things, because I didn't know how to ask for them nicely, and therefore I didn't behave well enough to deserve them.

"There's a little savage inside you," you told me. "And she doesn't know how to take no for an answer, and throws tantrums if she doesn't get just exactly what she wants at the moment of asking."

I was a bit shocked that you should talk to me like this – but at the same time, I was relieved, because I knew about the little savage. I thought for a moment and then realised that I really wanted to bash her up when she made my life such a misery.

"She needs to be punished," you said. "We'll have a look at her and administer any punishment she deserves."

I was a bit upset by this, because I felt criticised by you .. yet at the same time, I was deeply grateful to you, because I had spent all my life hiding this savage away, hoping that no one would ever discover her. Most of the time, that was a good scheme, and no one ever suspected that she was there; but it had its downside as well, because it meant that I couldn't trust myself to love anyone or be loved by them in case they encountered the skeleton in my cupboard! I felt that you must love me a lot even to offer look at her, and that went a long way towards making me feel better about her.

Just talking about the savage and how angry she got was a good first step. But I had a very difficult time for the next few days; I kept being assailed by an overwhelming feeling of anger. You were going to hypnotise me, I believed, and bash up my savage; yet, although I hated her running my life, and I knew that she deserved to be put in her place, I didn't want her bashed up, and I was furious with you about it. It never crossed my mind that when we met her, we might actually understand her and be able to make her behave better without bashing her up! But knowing about her certainly made life clearer. I got really angry with people a couple of times during the week, yet I wouldn't let the anger out, because I felt that it wasn't real but, rather, displaced from the anger about the thing in my head that I didn't know about yet.

But at least I didn't have to deny the anger; a couple of times I said to Eddie that I was angry with so-and-so, whereas normally, I would have felt so guilty about being angry that I would have talked round the subject in the hope that he would express his anger as well, and thus make it all right for me to be angry. Fear would have prevented me from really knowing about it. You thought this was all excellent stuff.

"It's the first time you've ever acknowledged that you were angry," you said, "rather than just turning it all inside and just feeling guilty."

But then you went on:

"You're not a very good sadist, you know; that's the trouble."

It took me a moment or two to realise what you meant by this but when I understood, I was filled with a sense of profound relief that you weren't condemning me for what I felt: you were telling me that deep down, I didn't want to be a sadist, and so I wouldn't allow myself the freedom to be one. Unfortunately, however, it didn't feel as simple as that to me; for the fact remained that I kept finding myself up against thoughts and situations which made me think,

"Well, I might not *do* it very well, but nonetheless, all the feelings and desires which make up sadism are there inside me," and it wasn't at all pleasant for me to have to acknowledge my own responsibility for my thoughts and actions. It was only possible because deep down I knew that everything would be all right ...

But you didn't hypnotise me for weeks, and as time went on, I became more and more anxious that you were going to beat up the little savage; I felt that it wasn't fair, since all I'd ever wanted was to be loved, and no one had ever loved me for myself; they'd only loved themselves. And now the little me was going to be beaten up. You tried to explain to me that love wasn't unconditional, and that I had to learn that I had to behave properly in order to get it – but that if I behaved badly, and love wasn't forthcoming, that didn't mean that I was totally bad for ever; it just meant that what I was doing at the moment didn't deserve it. If I started to behave better, then I would deserve to be loved again. Simple.

The trouble was that I didn't feel that things had been like that in my life. Love was conditional – but also cosmic. If it wasn't there, it was because I wasn't nice, not because what I did wasn't nice. Yet as I talked to you about it over the weeks, I slowly began to realise that I was one of the worst perpetrators of the injustice I was complaining about. I didn't want you to beat up the little savage inside me .. because I spent my entire life beating her up myself. Every time she moved, I beat her up; in fact, it had got to the stage where she didn't dare do anything at all. I was the sadist; that was what I didn't want you to find out, because I was ashamed of being like mummy, and behaving so badly and so intolerantly to the little savage. No wonder she didn't know how to ask for things nicely, and had to scream and shout; I didn't let her ask – I just beat her up.

"Actually, you're not like your mother," you said. "She never feels guilty about anything she does; even when she apologises it isn't because she realises she's wrong, it's because she doesn't like being criticised and it's her way of protecting herself."

I was so relieved; gradually, I was coming to believe that she and I were *not* the same. And *that* meant that I could start to like myself properly.

WHY AREN'T I NICE?

I was still having trouble believing that men could like me. Especially when I became excited. One part of me didn't understand this at all, because I thought I was immensely attractive and men were just stupid if they didn't appreciate me .. but I was never very proud of how quickly I fell into this position of despising men for their stupidity; that didn't seem a good way to be sexy and attractive. But where did it all start?

You were in positive mode when I discussed it with you; you wouldn't let me get too obsessed with why I was horrid. On the contrary, you asked me what I thought I had that a man might like. It was curiously difficult for me to make sense of this question; on the one hand I knew that I had a vagina, and that it gave a lot of pleasure both to a man and to me .. but on the other hand, I didn't feel this pleasure as mine to give, because I was afraid that it was only mediated through a man who had a penis. And in any case, I was afraid of taking the penis in case I hurt it.

At this point, you asked me if I'd ever had any problems with eating. I certainly didn't remember ever *not* wanting to eat. But equally, eating had never been straightforward for me; I never knew when to stop eating because I didn't ever really believe I'd had enough. Yet even if the pleasure wasn't straightforward, there *were* immense pleasures to be enjoyed. As a little girl, I used to eat secretly, because the pleasure was only real when I was on my own, without mummy watching me. I used to take biscuits out of the tin in the morning, before anyone else was awake, and eat them in bed. It didn't matter what time of day or night it was, I would be able to eat. I used to go to my friends' birthday parties and, when the food was all laid out on the table to help ourselves, rather than being put on a plate for us, I would eat so much that I would quite literally be unable to move afterwards. My stomach just didn't notice that it was full up until all the food was gone. Then I would be unable to play games with enjoyment because it would hurt so much. Yet I was never sick; once I had the food inside me, it was going to stay there if it killed me!

My mind wandered. I remembered the time when my mother put me on a diet because I was so fat. I was furious about this; on the one hand I didn't like being fat, and certainly didn't like being socially unacceptable because of it, but on the other hand, I treasured my fatness; I knew that I was fat for a good reason. So however miserable it made me to be fat, I didn't want to get thin. I had no idea what made me feel this way, when being so fat was an utter torture to me; the only thing I did know was that if my mother put me on a diet, I wasn't going to cooperate. So I stole money from my mother's purse to buy sweets on my way to school.

They were lovely, those sweets – they were a kind of hard, toffee-flavoured purse-shaped sweet, which took lots of sucking and melted deliciously into my mouth. The buttery, sugary, silky texture and taste made them quite irresistible. I bought 4 oz a day, and ate them under the desk. Such was my determination to defy my mother that I broke with my normal law-abiding habits and flouted the rule that there should be no eating in the classroom. After a while, though, I could no longer make 4 oz last me through the morning; I had to buy 8 oz. But, curiously, that level of defiance wasn't satisfying any more. I'd gone over the top; I didn't want so many sweets .. and the desire to gorge myself soon left me – much to my distress!

I don't remember how much of all this I told you, but you thought that the whole business was very interesting, and suggested that we might look at it further under hypnosis.

"Focus on your lips," you said. "See what they feel like."

I could feel my lips all big and plump .. and as I felt the sensations in my lips, all the aggression slipped away out of my teeth, which had been protecting my lips against feeling anything.

"Let the feeling in your lips flow through your body into your vagina," you told me.

I felt a very pleasant sensation in my vagina .. but it immediately went away again. It seemed to me that the whole feeling ought to be a kind of pulsing sensation which would grow into more and more pleasure .. but which somehow got stopped. Then I felt enormously angry.

"Try to feel it constant and not cut off," you suggested.

That was easier said than done! When I felt that I might suck, I was overwhelmed by a desire to cry because I was sure that it would be taken away. I dared not enjoy the sensation.

Then I saw mummy recoiling from me, and hiding her terror and disgust under a contemptuous laugh at me.

"What's she thinking?" you asked.

I looked, and I saw her hair and nails and eyes bulge out aggressively. She was implying that it was all my fault that she was feeling this. And this implied accusation really made me want to kill her, to chew her up, instead of sucking her nicely. And although I was upset about this, I found myself smirking uncontrollably, just as she would have done at the idea, because I was really so pleased. Then, quite suddenly, I saw her with pictures coming out of her head like I had pictures coming out of my head from lying on your couch. It was like being able to read into her unconscious mind. She thought that she had a penis, and that someone was whipping it with a whip with lots of long leather thongs on it. No wonder her hair was standing on end! But - and this was the wonderful thing as far as I was concerned – it wasn't *me* whipping her .. yet every time I sucked her breasts, she made me participate in this sadistic fantasy. I had confused being drawn into her fantasy with initiating it myself. I was innocent!

Once I'd seen this, and seen that it was not all my fault, I was swept by an immense sense of relief to be rid of that scenario in my brain. It meant that I could have a vagina of my own instead of feeling impelled to kill its sensations because they were always reminding me that I did these terrible things to mummy.

"Look with your inward eyes at your vagina," you said.

I looked .. and it was smiling .. and yet, although its lips were stretched in the smile, that didn't make them thin and nasty and secretive, but caused them actually to become plumper and more succulent.

"That's right," you said. "And the other important thing is that it should be a juicy smile with lots of saliva."

I could feel that .. but the most amazing thing was that I had already known it. For as I felt the saliva coming into my mouth and giving me pleasure, I found myself thinking again about eating biscuits in bed. I had never chewed them, but allowed them to dissolve and become soft and wet in my mouth. That was always the point; I wasn't eating them because I was hungry. But now I had a sucking, salivating vagina which was visible, and appreciated by you .. and I couldn't see what else anyone could want. All was well in my little world.

HOW CAN I BE?

Something that used to happen often was that as soon as anything went remotely wrong in my life, I felt an immediate disinclination to go to work. This was partly because I didn't like my job .. but that wasn't the whole story: the feeling I had felt almost like a phobia. All I wanted to do was stay at home and lie in bed, or sit in an armchair drinking coffee; just protecting myself. I never actually did stay at home when I felt like this, so obviously it wasn't really a phobia – but the resentment I felt towards THEM – the people who were forcing me to go out – was terrible.

I started to become aware that this feeling began as a twitch in my clitoris. There I would be, thinking about doing something interesting or important, and just about to leap up excitedly to do it .. and off it would go; there would be a little twitch of pleasure, followed by a complete withdrawal and shrinking into itself. Then I would feel quite unwilling to push through that feeling, while at the same time feeling desperately miserable that I was held in by it. But there was nothing I could do without risking a total depressive episode – and I'd had enough of them to last me a lifetime. It was as if there was a volcano inside me, which on the one hand was very nice, and whose energy I admired and liked – but which on the other hand I didn't know how to control, and which I was afraid would kill someone. This fear made it difficult for me to accept it as part of myself.

Often, I would be talking to someone, and I'd make some remark about how things seemed to me; this would seem very innocuous and indeed even obvious, but it would meet with utter incomprehension. For example, one day one of my friends was ill. Knowing what I knew by that time about the unexpected effects the unconscious mind could have on the body, I asked her whether she thought she might be unwell because something had happened to her that she wanted not to know about. Needless to say, she looked at me in total unbelief – and I felt a terrible sense of guilt: if she didn't want to know about it, I shouldn't have tried to show it to her; I'd broken her armour and this would kill her.

This kind of thing kept happening to me, and after such an episode, I fell into a frenzy of all-consuming guilt, not knowing what to do with myself at all. It was terrible – yet I didn't want to stop seeing things myself; I liked being clever and far-seeing. But to what extent did I need to keep my enthusiasms under control? How much of my guilt was rationally based and how much was just my mind filling with sadistic fantasies? I didn't know.

You thought that we should ask it a few questions. So I lay down and you asked,

"What is it that you really want to do?"

What I really wanted to do was to have a pee. But as I watched and felt myself peeing, I realised that it wasn't a bit like the way I normally peed; it slid gently out between my legs and made a sort of warm and relaxing bath. I didn't know whether I made this bath, or whether it was actually inside me, or what. But there was a lovely relaxing feeling of wholeness and a kind of whooshing, swimming sensation down my arms and legs.

"Feel your legs relaxed instead of tense," you said.

I never knew how you knew what I was feeling; your acute eye for small details of muscular activity let you see things which most people miss most of the time. Anyway, I let my legs relax, and that was very nice .. but as they relaxed, I found myself afraid that they weren't my legs any more .. it was a curious feeling of alienation.

"What scene comes to mind?" you asked.

I saw myself holding my clitoris. I was a little girl .. and I was holding it in the same way as little boys hold their penises when they're having a pee. I could see it all big and pink and luscious, and I could see myself stroking it and feeling the exquisite pleasure it gave me. But when I came to try and pee out of it, the sensations split apart. I got lost somehow, because I could feel the peeing somewhere else, although I expected it to be coming out of my clitoris. That was very puzzling. But then the penny dropped! For the first time ever, I realised that I didn't have to get lost; it was just that I couldn't pee out of my clitoris – that wasn't how it was built. The clitoral pleasures and the peeing pleasures were actually separate.

Then I felt a great desire to jump up and down; I could see little boys jumping and their penises waving around, and I wanted to share in that pleasure.

"Can you place the scene where you were holding your clitoris?" you asked me.

I was in the lavatory at home when I was about 6 or 7. I was trying to pee into the lavatory standing up .. but I couldn't get the pee to come out in that lovely powerful parabola that boys achieve. It looked like such a wonderful powerful experience, and I wanted to be able to do it and have the pleasure as well. The trouble was that I didn't know how to do it – but after some experimentation, I found that sitting on the lavatory back-to-front gave me enough of the feeling that I was peeing like a boy to be just about all right.

"What happens when you pee like a boy?" you asked.

The only thing I could think was that I got my hands wet! After all, it didn't come out forward. I remembered how stupid and humiliated and ashamed I'd felt, as if I'd been caught out not having what I said I had.

"Stop thinking about peeing like a little boy," you told me, "and pee like a little girl."

There was a moment of the most supreme pleasure in discovery! For a start, all the sensations moved further back, and the area between my legs felt larger and more sensitive. The trouble was that I couldn't sustain the nice feelings; every time I actually tried to do something, to pee, the anxiety at having to do it made all the pee move back up into the reservoir behind my clitoris. Yet I didn't have a hole in my clitoris, so I couldn't pee through that. It was all very confusing.

"Try again," you said.

No luck. Then you asked me,

"Do you have to pee to have an orgasm?"

And suddenly, everything made sense. The way I knew to have an orgasm was precisely *not* to pee; the pleasure was in the retaining of it, and the masturbating with it. Only afterwards did I want to pee. Yet doing it that way was never properly satisfying, so the peeing – and the masturbation – became quite compulsive.

It was difficult, peeing like a girl, because all the pictures involved clenched teeth and blood mixed with the pee; then the passage got completely blocked .. that's why the pee had to get diverted through my clitoris. But I didn't understand why.

"What happened to your penis?" you asked.

I didn't know.

Then, suddenly, without my doing anything to encourage it, there was a picture of mummy's breast. It was blocked, too, and the only way it could achieve orgasm was by holding everything in and having the twitching pleasure. And I couldn't pee properly through my open channels with all the pleasure associated with that, because my only model of orgastic discharge was this tight breast. It got all its pleasure from the holding back, from the struggle to burst or not to burst. There was real orgastic rage in that struggle, and it wasn't that rage or that kind of orgasm that I wanted. No wonder that when I had a real orgasm – not one of those – I found myself puzzled as to where it had come from and what it had to do with me. But now I really believed that we might have laid the foundations for getting rid of the nasty orgasm and replacing it by the good.

"I'd like you again to pee like a girl," you said.

This time, it was all much easier and felt relaxed and better. I felt suddenly that I didn't need to worry about it. But the pleasure was incomplete. What else could I possibly want? Then I realised: I wanted you to come into the picture and watch me. But would you?

"Of course," you said.

And I saw myself peeing for you, and felt that distinctive urethral pleasure which is at the same time the acme of calm, yet the power of the tempest. It was a wonderful, extraordinary, totally enveloping power.

But I worried all night about the question you had asked me about what had happened to my penis. What *had* happened? I just couldn't work it out. Then, just before dawn, I snapped awake in a spirit of discovery. I never had one!

That session was a really revolutionary one for me, because it was the first time that I had acknowledged to myself that what I considered to be normal sexual gratification was actually perverse. The most powerful pleasure I knew was a urethral-retentive pleasure, and it had never occurred to me that this wasn't what people meant by sexual pleasure. Once upon a time, this realisation might have plunged me into a state of the most profound depression – but I was beginning to realise that my unconscious mind could only see under hypnosis things that were there already; therefore, if I could acknowledge that there was another way to sexual fulfilment, it meant that at a deep level, I already understood it. The voyage of discovery through my soul suddenly took on a new dimension; no longer was it merely a search for an escape from chaos – it became also a positive quest for new ways to understand the cosmos.

5
Getting to the Bottom of Things

DOING THINGS AND MAKING THINGS

There was one area which we had never yet discussed, and that was anality. It never crossed my mind to talk about it with you, because it didn't seem to me to be a problem. Admittedly, I did occasionally notice that all wasn't well; after seeing my mother, for example, I would often feel an overwhelming urge to empty my bowels; and on the days when I came to see you, the excitement would often lead to frequent visits to the lavatory. But curiously (or perhaps not!), although the phenomenon – emptying my bowels – was the same in both cases, the feelings that accompanied my despairing evacuation after seeing my mother were quite different from the feelings of anticipatory pleasure of coming to visit you.

But the interesting thing was that I was never aware of any distress or anxiety attached to defaecating in the normal course of events. You used to talk about it sometimes when I came to see you, but always at a general level – never directly associated with me. Yet something inside me often felt that you were really trying to bring something up that I didn't want to look at, and I would become aware of a feeling of unease, as if I was hiding something from you. But when it came to it, I absolutely couldn't conceive of talking to you about it. Peeing was one thing; defaecating was entirely another. In fact, the taboo was so strong that I didn't even know I had a problem.

However, my unconscious knew better. I had developed the most terrible backache, which had almost incapacitated me, and you had been treating it for a number of weeks. It had been gradually getting better, but it wasn't yet quite gone. This worried me; I was

convinced that it wasn't gone because I hadn't yet fully acknowledged the causes of it – and this meant that there was still a risk of
it coming back at any time, without warning. I'd often been aware
of a problem with my back; as a student I used to find it very difficult
to sit at a desk for any length of time without feeling a dull ache in
my back ribs – and when things got really bad, I would feel a chronic
pain in my lower back. But this kind of incapacitating pain – sciatica,
the doctors called it – I'd never had before, and certainly never
wanted again.

Now, if anyone had told me, in the days before I knew you, that
I had backache because there was some unresolved infantile anxiety
about my bottom, I would have laughed at them. What a ridiculous
suggestion! Yet, after knowing you, every time I felt ill in any way,
I would immediately assume that there was a psychosomatic cause,
and set my brain to work to look for it. This time, my brain was
rather slow on the uptake; we spent a number of weeks loosening
things up, and the pictures I saw on your couch were interesting,
though not spectacular. But when the pain in my back – now much
less severe – started to move around, eventually ending up in the tips
of my buttocks, it dawned on me that there was something exceptionally curious going on. You were pleased when the pain moved
there.

"That means that it's nearly coming out," you said, "so we can
now have a look at it."

You let me lie down.

"Focus on the pain and see what is happening," you told me.

I could feel a pain, a tension in my anus and in my bottom, a
holding-back feeling, and a knot as if my anus was a lump of concrete. This all surprised me, because I hadn't even known where my
anus was until that moment. And I certainly couldn't see the connection between this knot and the pain in my back.

"Look and see," you said.

I found that if I relaxed my bottom, the pain went away.

"Look at the woman in the mirror and see what she's doing,"
you suggested.

Her bottom was all pulled back, like a pair of pursed-up lips. I felt an anxiety on seeing this, as I didn't want her to be me; I simply couldn't bear the idea. Then, quite suddenly, I realised that going to the lavatory after seeing mummy was a way of freeing myself from the influence of these terrible lips and restoring myself to myself – and that realisation made me feel a great deal better.

"What does she do next?" you asked.

I watched her squat down and make a big pile of faeces. Then she played with it. My mouth became all wide and relaxed, especially on the upper lip; I felt myself as her, and could smile and express myself and daub it all around and make mud pies. Then she put it in-to her mouth and smeared it around and rubbed it around with her tongue .. and my tongue and jaws felt all liberated, and I became all hot and squiffy with the pleasure. It was a quite different pleasure from sucking – a kind of expansive and creative pleasure; it was wonderful, freeing my fingers and toes and mouth and lips and teeth – fantastic.

Then I found myself remembering how constipated mummy was .. and suddenly I could see her sitting on the lavatory shitting little bits of flint. She was holding it all in for herself, and although she took laxatives, she didn't really want to let it out. My fingers locked in claw-position, and my teeth hurt. THEN .. I saw her with her nails up her anus, tearing and scratching it out – just like she'd torn and scratched to get it in. My mind filled with memories of childhood: mummy had always been terrified of germs. Everything that went into me was somehow dirty; she made me feel dreadful about everything I had inside me – food, sex, anything.

You brought me back to the pictures.

"What's in your bottom?" you asked me. "Let it come out."

I could see a big white worm eating me, and it seemed to me that if I let it out, there would be an orgasm .. but I couldn't see any details.

"What's the blood?" you asked.

I could understand that this was a terribly important question, but I couldn't see the answer. But then it came – and it was at the same time terrible and wonderful. I saw in my bottom all the chewed-up pieces of mummy's breast that I'd attacked and taken in when she wouldn't give her breast to me nicely .. then there were bits of penis as well, and God knows what else!

"The worm is important, too," you said. "It's a kind of destructive revenge-taker and punisher."

Suddenly, I found my mouth able to taste. I discovered, with the joy that accompanies a long-lost memory, that faeces had a wonderful primaeval taste, bringing with it oceans of pleasure and openness and satisfaction. I could roll the taste on my tongue and feel its pungency all through my body. And I realised that mummy held back the taste from her milk; then, deprived of the primaeval taste, which I wanted so much, I chewed her up. But that made the whole business of taking things in a wickedness, and that in turn made eating an ordeal, and food an accusation, to be stuffed down my throat as fast as possible. But now there was the possibility of change. And as I thought about it, I felt that my vagina didn't smell and taste nasty, as I had feared, but shared in the primaeval taste – and that meant that men would like it!

More unexpected pleasures followed: for now that I knew what it tasted like, and had the taste inside me, as it were, I found that I didn't feel aggressive towards the breast any more for denying me the flavour; I didn't need to be destructive, but could be creative. I looked at the pile of faeces that I had made, and I felt that it liked me playing with it. And as I played with it, it changed texture and consistency for me – yes, for me! That gave me the most extraordinary pleasure; I was an active agent, and what I had made liked me. What more could I want?

MAKING WOMEN .. AND MAKING MEN

We also worked on strengthening my image of myself as a woman; I wanted to be a real woman independently of whether there were men around to arouse me and stimulate my femininity. One day, you hypnotised me and told me to see this independent woman. All I could see was a round, open hole – my vagina. At one level, that was rather puzzling; but at another level, just the fact that it was open and not closed was wonderful. Then I felt my shoulders broadening, and my mouth and throat opening to let everything go right down. Then I looked at my legs. There was something not quite right about them, but I didn't know what it was.

"OK, then," you said. "Let them be right."

And I felt my pelvic bones *moving*! They moved further apart, so my legs could come straight down instead of being curved outwards at the top. Then I felt the lumps of fat on the sides of my thighs getting in the way.

"That's just an old habit; tell the fat to melt away."

And as you spoke, I felt it streaming down my legs, out of the way ...

Then I walked on the grass. I felt myself with a big round tummy, and I was pleased and proud of myself. Yet as I walked, I felt uncomfortable. Mummy was going to see me, and sneer and belittle it all. I felt my toes pull back, and my legs and vagina, and my whole body – all pulling back. My face bared its teeth in a painful, clenched-eyed grin.

"It's all right," you said. "Feel your vagina all down your legs."

This seemed a rather strange request, but I felt the power of and from my vagina flowing down my legs. *Then* I saw my vagina itself coming down onto the grass, long and inquisitive like an elephant's trunk sucking and chewing in an open and interested way. It was accepted by the ground, and accepted it. Then I looked at myself, and accepted me; and my toes felt all wide and spread-out, with big pads on them. They could feel; they were pleased.

I walked round for a while, and admired myself. After a decent interval, you asked me what an analogous man looked like. I looked, and he was also relaxed and happy; except for the fact that he had a penis and I didn't, there was no difference in the feelings that we had and inspired in others. Then I watched his penis stretch out – *not* ping up, but stretch out – and that was lovely; it was active and gentle at the same time. I felt his penis start in his abdomen, right deep down .. and then I felt the same feeling in my abdomen .. and then they made love and I felt it all round the pelvic area, into my buttocks and everywhere. And suddenly, I felt that I could just be; I didn't have to do anything, and I didn't have to think .. I could

somehow bypass the thinking while I was making love. It was a
marvellous experience of what it was like to be free.

TAKING IN AND GIVING OUT

You were always talking to me about doing things, and telling me
that psychotherapy wasn't just about the inner world, but also about
relating properly to the outside world. But for a long time, I resisted
talking to you at that level; I wanted to be better before I would dare
to do anything. I was actually afraid to do anything in case it came
out wrong. But there came a day when you decided that this very
fear was a pathology which we could deal with. So you hypnotised
me and told me to search for the memory which caused all the
trouble.

It was very hard to find. Lots of other pictures came into my
mind first. There I was at mummy's hard breast; then there was
daddy trying to make love to mummy, and me in the way; then
there was mummy giving birth to David – a big black hole with
something coming out. And her face was gritted in terror trying to
hold it back, and struggling wildly.

But as I looked, I found that I wasn't really concentrating on
what I was seeing; I was thinking about how I wanted to write, but
how I actually didn't write, or hid what I had written in a drawer;
also how difficult I found it to know what I thought and to express
it coherently in the face of any opposition, real or imaginary. My
voice would stick in my throat, and what I really wanted to say
would have to be forced out. And I was terribly miserable because
I couldn't read. But why not?

"Look at the books as if you were going to read them," you told
me.

It was terrible – far worse than anything I had imagined; they
all stood up on their spines in terror, pulling away from me. And I
was afraid that by reading them – eating them – I'd kill them. I
wouldn't be able to suck in what they said and enjoy it and digest
it; I'd have to race through it, chewing it up and killing it. I was so
upset.

"Watch me," you said. "See my relationship with the books."

As you walked in, I saw all the books lie down on the table, waving their pages with excitement, calling you to come and eat them!

"Now," you said," "read the books in the way that I did, and everything will be all right."

Well, I tried and, much to my surprise, I found that I could do it; but it didn't feel right. I was terribly angry because it was really your way, and you could do it and I couldn't; so by doing it your way, I wasn't achieving any authentic pleasure, but only pretending.

"I know how to do it because I had a nice mother who let me suck at her breast," you told me. "But you had to chew your mother's breast to get anything out, and then you thought you'd killed it. And then the only way you could not kill it was by being dead yourself."

That certainly made sense – and fitted very well with how I felt. But what could I do about it?

"See yourself on the pot," you suggested, "and see how it feels."

My faeces were all wrinkled-up and held in. Mummy didn't like them.

"Never mind," you said. "Take yourself a pencil and a piece of paper and write something."

Well .. I was blowed if I was going to! I was quite defiant and I wasn't going to do anything! But then, as I looked at little me sitting there furious and obstinate, I found that I wasn't angry with her, as I had expected to be; in fact, I found myself thinking how much I liked and admired her spirit. I was sorry she had a problem, but I loved the vigour and determination with which she solved it, and the mischievous glint in her eye. I was amazed to see how much I liked her – and you were delighted that I should have realised it.

"Now then," you said. "Back to the pot. Let it out now."

And I didn't have to push; it just came out, all rich and shiny and coppery. I'd done it – and I liked it, even if no one else did. Yet, even at the height of the creative pleasure, I was sad and angry to think that no one else did like it.

"Smell it," you said.

A wonderful feeling spread through me, making me relax all through my body and down my legs. Then all the tension in two spots at the side of my nose and eyes just melted away. The tense little spots suddenly became little flowers that opened up in the lovely spiritual smell like big blossoms. And I suddenly realised that I had been afraid that I would want to take the faeces back into me again, to protect them from not being liked – but I didn't; after all, now they were smiling at me. And once they were going to stay out-side, so had become real, then I wanted to do things with them, and I started shaping the faeces to give them ears and a nose, and four legs, and a tail .. that was lovely; pleasure wasn't hidden away any more.

But I was still a bit sad, and I could still feel the anxiety in my teeth and nails.

"Look and see why," you said.

I saw myself as a little baby in nappies. And because it was all wrapped up, I couldn't play with it .. so I wriggled in it instead. That was lovely; I could feel it all smearing over me and loving me. Then mummy came in, and I waved my legs at her in excitement. I wanted her to share the pleasure. The trouble was that she didn't like it. Not only that, but she was especially angry that I had managed to get it all over me, and that she couldn't just wrap it up tidily, hide it and throw it away. But I couldn't think why she should be so cross; after all, it was nice. Then I saw – she was terrified! But what of?

"Look at her nose," you said.

It was all pinched round the nostrils, and white with tension, and pulled-in round the bridge. It was long and sharp and she was going to use it to chop up my big fat faeces. THEN I saw; she was terrified to smell it or react to it in case she had to relax (God forbid!) like I had done – for that would break her defences.

Then I realised that what I wanted was for you to come along in your straw hat and look at it properly.

"OK," you said. "Go back on the pot and see me come in and watch."

As soon as I saw you, I went rushing up to you, holding the pot in my hand to show it to you. And you picked me up, dirty bottom and all, and sat me astride your knee .. and we both looked at it and admired it. That was lovely. I was quite surprised at the climax to this incident, since I had thought that what I'd want to do was to look at you .. but in fact, all I wanted was a quick peek to make sure you were looking at my creation .. and then what I really wanted was for it to be accepted fully – by us both looking at it. That was very nice indeed.

WHY CAN'T I LET IT OUT?

You often talked to me about how I was not like my mother. I can't begin to tell you how much I liked hearing this! Yet even as I listened to you and felt myself pleased, I still couldn't really understand what you said. How could I be nice? What did that mean? After all, quite apart from anything else, the rage I felt at my mother was so uncontrolled and so much part of me that there wasn't any room left for the nice me.

You kept suggesting, though, that I should separate myself from her, see myself as different, and then acknowledge what I felt about her. I tried to do what you said; but as I even *thought* about it, I became terribly tense and held-back; I was afraid that in any dispute with her, I would be the one who got hurt .. yet, paradoxically, I also felt that I would be the one who did the hurting. But part of the reason why I got hurt was precisely because I was fighting the bonds holding me back. However it was, it didn't make any difference; the important thing was that I would end up defeated.

You were very interested in all this.

"It seems to me that there is a trauma here," you told me.

I wasn't sure what you meant by that, since everything seemed to be a trauma – but you obviously had something very specific and concrete in mind – and I was, in all honesty, just grateful that you were taking me seriously and wanted to find out what it was that made me feel so helpless in the face of this opposition. So you hypnotised me to see what it was all about.

"Go back in time until you find what it is," you said.

I saw me as a tiny baby; then I saw myself much older. But it was the baby picture that endured. I was lying on my back with my legs open. Mummy was there, with extraordinarily long fingernails .. and she was violating my vagina and clitoris, sticking things, fingers, nails, all sorts of things, up me. And as she did this, I defaecated. I saw it all plop out. But I couldn't understand it; I was sure it had never happened; it didn't have anything to do with me.

"It sounds to me as if your mother is giving you an enema," you said.

I wasn't in any position to agree or otherwise, since I didn't even know what an enema was!

"That doesn't matter; stay with it."

So I looked. And first I felt my bottom tighten up. Then I saw her fingers round a ball filled with water, screwed into a tube. And she put this tube up my bottom. I could feel it all hard and cold and violating. Then she filled me with water and washed it all out. It was terrible, feeling it all coming out without having the pleasure of pushing it, of making it. And I didn't want to believe that this had happened to me; there was a dreadful resistance to believing it. So I died. I detached myself from the feeling of it going out despite me, of me being defeated .. and I felt the pleasure inside instead. I wasn't going to let being defeated deprive me of my pleasure; I was going to assert that it hadn't really happened.

And in a sense, it hadn't – for I had refused to acknowledge it in my soul. And yet I knew it had .. so the pleasure in just letting it go, surrendering, became masochistic .. yet it was for good reasons. But by shouting to you that it hadn't happened, and letting it out, I became able to acknowledge that really, it had. Then I felt my neck loosen and my bottom relax, and the life came back into my eyes and streamed down my legs. I could see the lovely soft stuff in my bowel .. which until then I'd carefully kept empty, just in case it was violated again. Now it could be full and happy and relaxed.

All sorts of thoughts flowed through my mind after seeing this. My first thought was that it must have happened more than once, and that was why my unconscious produced more than one scene when you asked me to find the trauma. Then I found myself thinking that my mother thought that sex was like having an enema; someone pushes something into you and forces you to give things, and hurts you in the process. That's why she thought having a baby hurt, and why she felt such aggression towards my little sex.

"That's right," you said. "She castrates you by refusing to let you do it."

I was grateful to you for this insight, because I was only groping towards it myself. It was sometimes difficult to put all the parts of the hypnotic experiences together to make a whole.

Then you explained to me why it was that she had given me the enema.

"You hung onto your faeces out of revenge because she didn't give you what you wanted," you told me.

When I thought about that, I could even feel quite sorry for mummy, and the feelings of inadequacy it must have engendered in her to have her baby not defaecating for her properly. But at the same time, I *did* find revenge sweet, and I certainly thought that it was just what she deserved. I could see her getting quite hysterical when I wouldn't defaecate for her .. and the pleasure in the power of making her feel like that was quite potent! It was revenge for her humiliation of me. But what was particularly fascinating to see again at first hand was that in fact, the best thing of all was that by not giving her the good thing, I kept the pleasure for myself. And that was very nice.

After this session with you, I felt much better; more 'together', somehow. I had bigger lips and found that I could stand and walk with greater flexibility and ease. But the most remarkable thing of all was that I had more space in my brain. Everyone says that you can't feel your brain, because it hasn't any nerve endings in it, or something like that. But here I was, feeling it!

* * *

That session not only settled a number of anxieties which had been making my life a misery, but was also a real voyage of discovery at an intellectual level. This made it doubly satisfying. I loved getting to the bottom of things.

What was so extraordinary about this particular session, though, was that what I saw had *really* happened. Many of the things I saw on your couch were feelings reified; in fact, mummy didn't peel daddy's penis, or bite it off, and I didn't chew her breast into pulp until it didn't exist any more. What I saw were pictures of the emotions which drove the impulses and made them real. Occasionally, I would talk to my friends about some of the less horrifying things I saw on your couch, and they would say to me knowingly,

"Ah yes, but that never really happened, did it. It's all a figment of your imagination. How do you prove such a thing?"

I tried, often in vain, to persuade them that reality itself was a product of our minds, and therefore it was terribly important what our minds thought was going on, and what they were trying to achieve. But I didn't usually get very far, especially since I was always reluctant to use the argument, "Well, it works, doesn't it?" In fact, though, that was one of the most significant pieces of evidence; but it wasn't in itself a proof.

So it made it all the more interesting to re-experience something that had really happened just as I saw it under hypnosis. I didn't need to create any pictures to make emotions and drives visible and understandable; there were the pictures of a real event, in my memory, and with their own highly developed emotions and feelings. The feelings were real because they were part of a real event. And thereafter, the question of which came first, the event or the emotions, was, for me, one which missed the point; for at an unconscious level, events and emotions are all but indistinguishable. And, as a philosophical insight, I found this quite stupendous!

SEPARATION ANXIETY

I never wanted to go home at the end of a session particularly if we had done work under hypnosis. I used to feel that we'd seen and understood things so profound and exciting together that this made us one, and I wanted only to stay with you forever in the world of peace and understanding. I would find all kinds of ways of delaying you from saying goodbye to me, so that I didn't have to go out into the lonely street on my own, separated from you whom I loved. The little one inside me, whom we had together loved and comforted, couldn't understand how it was that I had to go, and as the end of the session approached, she would prepare herself for the inevitable period of mourning which would follow. Sometimes I would discuss the anxiety I had felt on the previous occasion when I came to see you again, and you would ask me what I thought happened between sessions. But the trouble was precisely that I didn't know, and it was the uncertainty which caused the anxiety.

"What do you think happens to you in my mind when I don't see you for a week?" you asked me.

What should happen? Should you spend your entire life thinking about me as I did thinking about you? How could I expect that? But it was worse than that; I was afraid that you just forgot I existed when I wasn't there, that I was merely a slot in your diary that happened to have my name in it. I wept at the betrayal of our trust, that you should not care about me enough to think of me when I wasn't there.

"But if you aren't here, that doesn't mean you don't exist," you said. "That's what a continuum is."

I dimly realised that you were trying to tell me something I couldn't fully understand. After all, surely I still existed even if you weren't looking at me. But one part of me just couldn't believe it – yet I didn't understand why.

One day I was particularly difficult about leaving at the end of my appointment. I kept you and kept you, until you looked at the clock and jumped with horror. You practically threw me out of your consulting room, hopping around in alarm at how late you were going to be for everyone else that day, and what problems this was going to give you. I walked down the road in a state of near-hysteria. My soul chastised me: I'd killed you; you would never recover from my demands and my desire to stay with you; everyone else for the rest of the day would beat you up because you wouldn't have enough time for them. God, it was terrible.

Then the next phase set in. You would never love me again because I'd put you in this position that you couldn't handle; you certainly would think about me this week while I wasn't there, but it would be with anger and not with pleasure; you'd be saving up your rage for when I next came to see you, and you'd express it either by cancelling my appointment, or by blowing me up when I arrived. What could I do? I was annihilated.

Well, I told myself that I was being ridiculous. Of course you weren't going to banish me to the pit of hell just for making you late. Or were you? It didn't seem to matter how hard I tried, I couldn't convince myself. I settled down for a long, hard week. Should I phone you up? I asked myself. No, that would definitely be a bad idea; if I'd already put you under superhuman strain by staying too long, then God knows what I'd do by ringing up in the middle of someone else's session! I just had no idea what I could do about it all.

After much agonising and self-castigation, it seemed to me that the best thing was just to keep as busy as possible, and hope that time didn't drag too much. I'd had weeks like this before, and I'd survived. I could only think of it all as a life-and-death situation; there was no living core inside me that could cope with it. So the day after seeing you, I decided to go out for the day. That would keep me busy. Anything to avoid coming face to face with the fear.

So out I went, and sat in a cafe with a cup of coffee, on a fine sunny day, watching the world go by. I thought about anything other than you. After a while, I became aware that I had an itchy neck. But it was the time of year when insects are abundant, and I assumed that I'd been bitten. The trouble was, it got worse. And worse. Then I looked down, and found that I was covered with a red, itchy rash. It seemed to start half way down my face and go down my neck into my blouse. A more thorough investigation in a local chemist's shop revealed that the rash ran all over my breasts and down my whole trunk as far as my navel. I bought some soothing cream, smeared it all over myself, and returned to my coffee.

But the rash was having none of that. It got more and more insistent, breaking out in blisters which itched until I felt as if I was in a torture chamber. Eventually, I ended up in a state of clinical shock. My face turned completely green, and I had to lie down on the ground, which I felt was the only place which would support me. Then I lost consciousness completely, watching with an almost detached interest as the world span round, clouded over, and then faded away entirely.

Fortunately, the incident ended reasonably well, as the chemist came back to my rescue with cortisone tablets and a phone call to a local taxi firm to make sure I got home in one piece. But it was a quite extraordinary episode; even as I lay on the ground in a state of total helplessness, I knew that this was an outbreak of hysteria because of what had happened with you – yet that knowledge didn't equip me at all to do anything to stop it!

You were suitably horrified by the extent and ferocity of the rash when I showed it to you. There was no doubt in your mind that it was caused by separation anxiety.

"Interesting," you said. "It just shows how erotic your skin is; skin is prior to the sense organs, and therefore surprisingly important."

I'd never thought of that; I suppose that babies must be a complete mass of almost undifferentiated feeling when they're born. Mouth and skin – no more. But I don't know ..

"You are a bad girl, in a way," you went on. "You did manipulate me into being late and getting into a tizzy. It's a kind of Thanatos; you want me to defeat reality for you."

I hotly denied this. But then I realised that I was denying it because I was ashamed of doing it. THEN I realised that what I was really angry about wasn't that I'd done it, but that I hadn't succeeded! And I had to permit myself a wry smile at this point. I had a grudging admiration for the cheeky little madam inside me!

"What do you want to do?" you asked me.

I didn't know. It was a most peculiar feeling, knowing that the question you were asking me was sensible, and that I knew the answer, but that somehow I didn't know. You kept on at me, and I got more and more upset. I felt that I was having to perform to some preordained schedule, where you knew the answers and I could only guess. It was like being back at school. Eventually, I got stuck in a kind of pit. It was like being all curled up and wanting to start again and come out properly .. but I couldn't; I couldn't do anything

at all. I didn't even know what I wanted .. and I was afraid to ask
for help.

So you let me see the pit under hypnosis.

"See the mirror and look at your unconscious," you told me.

I could see a woman with a huge hole where her genitals should
have been, sucking everything in. She was just a vortex – nothing
else. And she didn't know whether or not she wanted to hide the hole
with her hands. She had a hunched back, and very pale skin, and thin,
weak limbs. I felt that she was malevolent, bringing suffering on
herself.

"Is there anyone else there?" you asked.

There was a man, with an erect penis, jerking back in fright.

"Who is it?"

I didn't know; the only thing that came to my mind was an
overwhelming impression that the scene had something to do with
hayfever/asthma/eczema allergies. As I looked, I had the impression
of a premature ejaculation .. and then appeared a picture of a chicken
having its neck wrung!

"What have you got to do with all this?" you asked.

A good question. I thought I'd pulled his penis off, but I was
puzzled because I couldn't see the picture of myself doing it.

"You haven't, actually. It's just that the man is afraid, so you
think you've done it. Now, what do you really want?"

I wanted to make the man ejaculate. And it seemed to me that
this was nice, and not to be pulled back from.

"I'd like you to look for what started the fear off," you said.

I could see two pictures; one of me tiny at mummy's breast, and
the other of me at about 4 years old in daddy's bedroom. We started
with the second picture. I could see the gap in daddy's pyjamas for
his penis to come out .. but I couldn't see his penis. And then I was
worried.

"How do you know that your father has a penis?" you asked.

Well, I wasn't quite sure. On the one hand, I could feel it when
I sat on his lap .. but on the other hand, I knew it through mummy's
reaction to it. Then I looked again, and the picture changed; the man
jerking back was actually *mummy* having 'her' penis pulled off! I was

so surprised. Then, of course, daddy got worried about his own penis, and then he jerked back .. and so on .. but the primary jerking was hers. He was afraid she might do it to him, too. (And quite right he was to be worried, I felt!)

"Let's have a look at the other picture now," you said, "the one of you as a tiny baby."

I could feel mummy's breast in my mouth. The nipple felt all raw and chapped. And it didn't give out milk – well, not proper milk, but only a thin teeth-paring, yellow liquid; watery, with a bitter, acidic, metallic taste – like the flavour non-stainless steel knives leave on oranges. I was angry; the taste made me livid with rage and distress.

"What do you want to do?" you asked.

I felt blood in my mouth – and it was warm and thick and satisfying. And mummy relaxed because she LIKED being violated; it was what she feared and yet what she wanted.

As for me, I liked finding that the blood was satisfying. Yet I'd only done it because the breast was afraid. It was afraid before I ever got there, so the picture of a full, lovely breast which I had in my head was shattered when she jerked back. She didn't give me a chance to show her what it felt like sucking a nice breast; she broke the picture by pulling back. Yet she loved the exquisite ecstasy of the suffering; she set up the whole scenario so that she should have to suffer. And then I realised that the nasty woman in the mirror, who I thought was me .. was her!

"The pit you found yourself in is a de-toothing," you told me. "When you felt the blood and the attendant horrors, you withdrew from the scene and gave up your teeth to prove your innocence. But then you felt guilty, and you were nothing – just paralysed."

That all made sense; after all, in an important sense, the blood *wasn't* anything to do with me; I had a picture of a nice breast and nice ways to relate in my head, and it was mummy who wouldn't let me live like that. The blood was her fault. I was innocent. Yet, at the same time, I couldn't pretend that it hadn't been my teeth which had drawn it from her. But if she had been nicer, I could have liked my teeth and not had to disown them.

"Let's go back to your father now," you suggested, "and see that, although the penis is slow and shy, it is capable of great pleasure if you treat it nicely. The trouble is that every time you don't have it just at the moment you want it, you are afraid that it's jerking back. And once it jerks back, then you HAVE to have it. Teach her now how to wait, and how, if she waits, it will come."

You spoke so softly and gently, and with such love and encouragement, that I wanted to do what you said; I felt what it was you were trying to help me see. I saw a lovely penis, all soft and relaxed, waiting for me to wait for it. And I believed that it loved me, and I wept.

"That's good, the crying," you said. "It's a play-orgasm, and it's lovely. You'll never have to go back to the pit again."

⋆   ⋆   ⋆

But this wasn't the end of the pleasure: soon after this, you let me see what happened when a penis had a real orgasm. It was one of the most wonderful, moving experiences I have ever had. I saw a naked man's body, and his penis; the penis was so pleased to see me that it was dribbling .. and I found myself overwhelmed by an urge to take it in my mouth and lick off the drips which it was making for me. Then I felt it in my mouth, happy and excited and responsive. I sucked it .. and, I can't explain quite how, it sucked back; it throbbed and pulsated. Yet as it approached orgasm I found myself afraid. Would it pull back at the moment of orgasm and leave me angry?

"Feel its pleasure," you said, " and see what a difference that makes."

Well, that was wonderful. Of course, once I understood that the penis was enjoying itself, naturally I wouldn't expect it to pull back. But until this point, that very thought had been inconceivable to me! Now, though, I could taste its pleasure, all along the shaft .. and then, very gently, it melted into my mouth. I felt all its fluid in my mouth, and down my throat .. and a hole in the back of my head at the base of my skull filled up.

But I was worried now. Was the penis dead?

"Look at it and see," you suggested.

And I looked, and it was soft and little and satisfied .. and then I looked at the face, and it was smiling, and the eyes were gleaming with joy and pleasure – and then I believed it! I was so happy. It was mine, and because the penis liked giving it to me, I felt entitled to the pleasure and the contentment; it was mine by right, and not on sufferance. It was wonderful. I felt my eyes relaxing, and my brain fuller, as if it knew something, and my eyes felt more confident about looking, as if they might really see.

MAKING THE BREAST NICE

I kept hoping that one day I'd see properly – but it soon became clear that this was not by any means going to happen overnight, if ever. But we worked on my eyes quite often, and after each such session, they felt so much better that I wasn't going to complain if they were not quite focusing correctly!

One day, you looked at my eyes and remarked that they could scarcely keep open. I often noticed this; I was very proud of my beautiful eyes and rather upset that they were short-sighted, and sensitive to light, and prone to getting specks of dust in them and twitching just when I didn't want them to .. and I wondered how much of this might be psychosomatic. It seemed rather unlikely on the face of it that getting specks of dust in my eye could be anything but physical .. but I did notice over the months that it very often happened when I was angry. And that surely had to be more than just coincidence!

One day, you hypnotised me and told me to think about my eyes.

"What are they doing?"

I felt them sucking – and then pulling back. But I didn't know why.

"Go back in time until you find the point at which your eyes first became short-sighted," you suggested.

Well, that was very worrying. I found myself terribly anxious just at the IDEA of having to see that. I kept wanting to cover my mouth; I didn't know what to do. But anyway, I suddenly found myself at mummy's breast. It seemed a very interrogatory breast; it was pulling back as if with its eyebrows raised. And I became even more anxious – I had a pain in my clitoris and my teeth were all alerted.

"First see the breast as it really was, and then see it as you imagined it," you told me.

Well, I could see that the nipple was turned up so that I couldn't get at it, and that it was a big, round, full breast. Then I looked again – and in the little holes in the nipple, I saw teeth! And I was afraid. But I didn't know whether I was afraid that the breast was going to attack me or that I was going to attack it. I wanted to put my tongue inside the teeth like one might in kissing a man deeply, and make it all right for her .. but I was afraid.

"What does the upturned nipple signify?"

I didn't really know.

"It shows that it's obstinate," you said, "and isn't going to give of itself. I'd like you just to accept that first."

I felt better just for knowing that. But then I noticed mummy smiling, and I didn't know whether to believe the smile or not. This was always happening; I felt that there was some good in her, and that I didn't want to attack her if she was nice! So I became paralysed; I simultaneously wanted and didn't want to attack her. But then .. I saw her smile growing fangs – and I felt that I couldn't look, because either her fangs would attack my eyes, or my eyes would send out kind of laser beams to shatter her teeth ..

"Accept the anger," you told me.

I felt my eyes becoming warm and full. Yet I was afraid again. My toes all curled up and became rigid.

"What would you like to do?"

I could see a great orgasm of sadistic energy splurging out of my eyes and attacking her. But I didn't want that to happen .. and yet, really, I did desperately want to do it. Then, I believed, I would see. And yet again, I didn't *want* to see on those terms; and so we reached deadlock. I couldn't see how anything could ever change for as long as the breast was armoured in the way it was. So I gave up and armoured my eyes instead.

"What do you want to do?" you asked, again.

You talked for a while about the armoured breast, and as you talked, I felt an uncontrollable urge to bite through the armour.

"OK, then, do just that."

The trouble was that I couldn't distinguish between the armour and the breast, and I didn't want to hurt the breast.

"That's just a problem. Do it anyway."

So I did. And the pleasure! Right down into my clitoris and vagina. And yet it made me most desperately unhappy to do it .. and I found tears running down my face.

"That's why most people get depressed," you said. "Now do it again and feel it flow."

But all I could feel was it pulling back, and my despair.

"Ask the breast why it's obstinate," you told me.

It told me that no one had ever loved it. Then I felt guilty and sorry. It was terrible.

"Stop feeling guilty," you said, "and make it give itself to you nicely."

So I sucked gently on it, and it gave. I was afraid that it would stop giving .. but you assured me that it wouldn't, and that I should go on. I watched myself stroke it underneath and tilt the nipple gently into my mouth .. and then I felt my own nipples connect with my clitoris and my vagina .. and my vagina started to suck just like my mouth – and the sucking on the nipple reminded me of sex of the nicest sort .. and it was wonderful.

It was a bit puzzling, this nice breast. I didn't really know where it came from, and I certainly didn't know what it had to do with mummy; some days when I was at your office, I wasn't able to see anything nice at all which might have to do with her breast .. but other days, it all worked properly. Why was that? I had a picture in my head of a mummy who tried, who wanted, to be nice, but who just couldn't manage it. And I felt a certain compassion towards her .. but at the same time I didn't want to believe in her niceness because I was afraid that if I trusted it, it would let me down.

You let me look at all this.

"Go back to the time when you were a little baby," you told me.

"Now see your mother and see the nice breast."

I could see the nice breast, but it didn't seem to have anything to do with her; by the time my lips got to her, the nipple had become hard and cold, like a ball bearing. I was so confused that I felt my head swimming, and a total detachment of myself from the outside world – as if a veil of gauze had been put between me and it.

"OK," you said. "Where does the picture of the nice breast come from if it isn't a 'real' picture?"

I didn't know.

"Feel your lips and see what they feel like."

They were big and warm and tumescent. I could feel them inviting mummy to come and share pleasures. It was I who was the protagonist, not her! That was such a pleasurable reversal from how I'd understood things before, with her in control of everything. The picture of the nice breast was created by my brain in response to my lips; MY LIPS made me the picture. That was amazing. Yet she denied me by not responding to my invitation; it was at that point that I became nothing, could do nothing. And that was terrible.

"You must just accept that that's how things are, and stop thinking of it as your own fault," you said. "Let's ask your mother why she's unyielding."

That seemed a good idea. I wanted to know. So I asked her – and she started to cry. That was just the kind of thing that happened in real life, and I wouldn't have been able to get any further at that point, because I was overwhelmed by compassion for her suffering .. but you said I was to ask her again, and not to let her get away with it by making me feel sorry for her. So I asked her again – and she said that she felt a failure. She felt that her failure was cosmic and inevitable, and that made it intolerable, because there was nothing she could do about it. Then I saw her father with a long, sharp sword, cutting off her penis! At least, that's what she said he was doing; in fact, I could see that she didn't, in fact, have a penis to be cut off. Anyway, he was certainly punishing her.

Then I saw *her* mother's fangs smiling with sadistic pleasure at the castration by her father. And the small mummy turned into a little animal; she started to have a kind of epileptic fit, and she turned green and scaly, like a dragon; her fingers became long, with gnarled nails, and webbed .. and she attacked and scratched her clitoris until it bled. Then she rolled in her own excrement, and daubed it on herself and round the walls .. and her parents watched with a mixture of sadistic satisfaction and sadistic disapproval.

"Your mother must have been an assertive little thing, even as a girl," you remarked. "Her parents didn't accept her mouth, or her hands, or her bottom. So they will have entered a vicious circle of anger and punishment."

No wonder my eyes recoiled from seeing all this; for the whole picture was contained in her breast.

Part of me felt very sorry for mummy; it wasn't, after all, her fault that she had these horrible parents. But what I couldn't forgive her for was making *me* play the same sadistic games because she was jealous of my nice pleasure. She couldn't quite bring herself to attack me openly, because she remembered what it was like; instead, she encouraged me to attack her by drawing her breast away from me like a knife she was unwilling to use – hard and sharp. Then she wailed because I too had hurt her, just like everyone always had .. and then the guilt was mine and she was the innocent victim.

Now, though, I understood that the baby invites the mother, that my invitation was nice, and that she'd rejected the offer to participate in a happy world, and this realisation made me feel much more confident about myself, and more able to be compassionate towards mummy without having to take the responsibility for her suffering on myself. For it was that which really hurt.

THE TOTALITARIAN SUPEREGO

You didn't do all your work through hypnosis. I liked the hypnotic bits the best, because they were so vivid and exciting, and so new and interesting, and because they brought out ideas and feelings that I'd never known about before. The other thing about hypnosis was that there were no distractions; I was fully focused on whatever was important at the time, and nothing else counted. That made the experiences very direct and very intense – two qualities I've always loved.

But I remember a particular time when I had been having a row with Eddie, and I hoped you might help me understand what had gone on by hypnotising me. The only trouble was that you wouldn't; you made me come to terms with it at a conscious level first. The problem was that I'd been talking with Eddie quite normally – or so I thought – and suddenly he had snapped contemptuously at me for talking too much. I was totally devastated; I felt that he'd gone away and was never coming back. Yet at the same time, even though he said it was all my fault, I didn't believe him and I was outraged. But I wanted him back on any terms – any at all. So I started off by apologising. Then I tried telling him how lovely he was. But I didn't mean it; I was angry with him .. it was just a kind of encouragement to him to come back – a showing him that it was all right because I would love him. Yet it was I who needed him! I hated grovelling to him, yet I had to appease him; I wanted him to apologise to me, but I couldn't wait for him to be ready; I didn't even know that I believed he would ever be ready! If he was turning away from me, then I believed the picture of myself that he was showing me, and I couldn't live with it. I had to be forgiven. Yet, at the same time, I was sure that I hadn't done anything wrong!

This kind of thing happened to me often. My first inclination whenever there was a difference of opinion was always to climb down – and not just with Eddie. It happened at work, too, with my extremist colleagues; I had to keep such a hold on myself not to give in to them. One part of me wouldn't let me, but the other part wanted to be loved at any cost. What I didn't realise was that neither party ended up with any dignity if I went in for full-scale appeasement.

I remember you being very interested in the row with Eddie. You said that I thought Eddie had gone away because I was afraid that my aggression had killed him. Still without letting me lie down, you asked,

"What would you like to do to him when he stops you talking?"

I could see myself beating him up .. but that didn't satisfy me, and in any case, it exacerbated the guilt.

"OK then, find some other way of dealing with the situation."

I saw myself acknowledging that I didn't like what he was doing, but then shrugging my shoulders and turning away to do something else. I felt that that was what I ought to do .. but I didn't trust him to understand my point of view and to come and apologise for his part in things unless I impressed it upon him. And I couldn't bear the fact that he didn't understand.

"That's very important," you said.

Then you went on to tell me that I had rather a tendency to see things as all good or all bad, with no grey areas.

"That's exactly right," I realised. "That's just how I do see things, and I think it's fundamentally the right way to see them."

"Well, I don't; it's totalitarian."

I was really upset by this – yet I wasn't able to tell you I disagreed with you, either. In any case, something inside me rather feared that you might be right. But if I was a totalitarian, then I hated myself. How, then, was it possible for you not to hate me?

"Because it's your superego, not your ego, which thinks like that," you replied.

That didn't really make any difference to how I felt; if I also thought like that, then I was identified with my superego .. and that in turn meant that I was like mummy. God forbid! I didn't know which was worse, being a totalitarian or being like her. But you explained that my ego (and my id) was not my superego, and the fact that I didn't like what I found myself thinking proved it!

Then you went on to tell me that I had a tendency to treat Eddie as a superego figure, and to want him to protect me from the bad superego .. and that every time he failed to do that, or became aggressive in his own right, my ego got swamped by the bad superego and everything became terrible.

"But," you said, "there's a difference between your ego being swamped against its will by the bad superego, and its taking on willingly the characteristics of that superego."

You suggested that if I could regard Eddie more as an equal, and accept myself, rather that needing to be accepted by him first, then life would become much easier for me.

I was very shaken up by this episode. One of my most cherished moral beliefs had been assailed and attacked by you and shown to be totalitarian. When I thought about it afterwards, and wondered why I had such a strong attachment to it, I realised that it must have been the only way I could protect myself against the crazy aggressiveness of mummy, just to declare her all bad; for as soon as I engaged in dialogue, she would pull me into her territory and swamp me .. but I was very ashamed to think that I'd generalised that way of thinking. I had often wondered about morals and free will, and whether we were free to be good or bad .. and this whole session stirred me to further thought. Which bits of me are free?

CREATING A GOOD REALITY

It was a very long time before I could stop worrying that I was really like my mother. Sometimes I'd be angry with Eddie about something, and I'd explode into fury. But one day I realised that what I was upset about wasn't what he was doing – or not doing, as the case might be – but that I could feel mummy behind me saying, "you see, he's not good enough; I told you so." I had a real problem: I didn't want to behave like her, but unless my man was perfect, I didn't seem to be able to help doing so.

"You should let your ego become stronger," you told me, "and stop capitulating to her all the time."

I could see that you were right; the trouble was that I couldn't see how I could actually *do* it, and I felt that you were sending me to the lions. It was as if the Good was only a fantasy, and only the Bad really existed. I didn't really believe that, but I found it terribly difficult to hold on to the affirmative image in the face of the other. When you told me to be strong and go out and be myself, I didn't feel proud of myself that you thought I could do this; all I felt was that you were totally abandoning me to deal with her all on my own, when this was a complete impossibility for me.

"I'll show you how different you are from her," you said. "Lie down and we'll see."

I went to lie down, but as I reached the couch, I rolled up into a little ball and cried and cried like a baby; I was so wretched. You just let me cry it out. You didn't judge, or offer sympathy; you just respected that this was what I had to do. But when I'd recovered, you hypnotised me and told me to see myself in the mirror. I looked – but there was only a shadow there. Mummy was leaning over my shoulder .. but I didn't exist.

"Have a look and see why," you told me.

I was completely terrified by this idea. I screamed and cried, and shouted,

"I don't want to go!"

I could feel my vagina stretching, and my nostrils flaring like a frightened horse .. and then my mouth stretched and flared as well, and my teeth became horribly sensitive. Then I saw a raw, red penis lying stretched out on a chopping-board, being cut off! It was awful.

"It's all right," you said. "I'll count to five and then you'll go back in time until you find what's triggering all this."

As you finished counting, I felt myself all rolled up like a little baby. What was the matter? I looked around .. and I was curled up in grief because daddy was dead, and it was terrible.

"Where is the dead daddy?" you asked.

I could see him lying, post-ejaculation, limp, on mummy. And her mouth and teeth were covered in blood, like a lioness', because she'd had his penis. She was delighted to have had it, because she *had* to bite men's penises off, and once she'd done it, she didn't have to do it again .. and she was relieved that it was over.

I had felt that daddy was dead by my fault – or at least, that she had said it was my fault. And certainly, I felt myself somehow involved in her pleasure .. and thus incriminated by her guilt. I kept saying, "It's wrong." And she kept saying, "No, it's right .. and anyway it's good and you like it." And it was particularly dreadful because I couldn't help feeling the pleasure .. but I thought it was wrong, and so I was bad; and morality all got turned on its head. It was terribly confusing.

"It's especially confusing for you," you said, "because you would have attacked her cold breast, and that made you worry that you were naturally sadistic and thus inclined to bite penises off."

"Now then," you went on, "let's give your father ten minutes and then look at him again."

So I looked at him as he was ten minutes later .. and not only was he alive, but his penis was erect again.

"I'd like you to notice that he isn't dead," you remarked.

Indeed he wasn't; as I looked, he started to use his penis to beat mummy up, thrusting it into her .. and so the sadistic pleasures started again. I wanted to die rather than be involved .. but once again, I found that I couldn't help feeling it all. It was at least pleasure, and there wasn't much of it around – still less was there much decent pleasure. So I felt caught between the devil and the deep sea: bad pleasure or no pleasure. What was a little girl to do?

"Perhaps you could show them how it's done," you suggested.

So I invited daddy into me. He came, bringing his penis, and put it into my vagina. When he had put his penis into *her* vagina, there had been a gap between them; his penis wasn't gripped nicely and firmly by her, because her vagina held back from it a bit. But I sucked his penis in close so that there was no gap, just a snug fit.

"That's terribly important," you said. "The gap was to make room for her teeth. Now, is your father enjoying himself?"

I watched him pull back slightly in fear of the pleasure .. but when he found that it was nice pleasure and not sadistic pleasure, he relaxed and the sensations all built up inside him – or was it inside us? No matter, it was all the same anyway. Then, instead of spitting his ejaculation out into me like he did into her, he melted into me. That was wonderful.

"What do you feel?" you asked me.

What I felt most of all was that I should hold back in case my vagina also sprouted teeth and hurt daddy.

"Your vagina doesn't have teeth," you said. "Just relax."

It took a while to overcome the fear, but gradually I felt my vagina becoming full, and my eyes relaxing and the back of my neck filling out. That was wonderful. Mummy and I were *not* the same.

When I woke up, I felt much better; I didn't want to kill myself any more. And I wasn't angry with Eddie any more, either. You told me that the gap discovery was momentous; that sadistic people drew their lips back – not initially out of aggression, but to withdraw. Then they could only feel with their teeth, and then they had to bite to relate. But the no-gap sucking feeling allowed me to touch and taste and feel. I loved hearing you say all this .. and as you spoke, I looked at you and felt that you were actually *in* my eyes, you were so close and I could relate so well. Imagine not being like mummy! What freedom to do nice things ..

MAKING THINGS WORK PROPERLY

It was remarkable how the capacity I had for pleasure and niceness increased after this; and I became a great deal more civil and agreeable to Eddie. But the depth of anxiety in my soul was so great that it couldn't all be disposed of in one go. A pity, but that's the way it was! I didn't immediately give up my fears that other people would be horrid to me, either. And, extraordinary though it seemed to me, I spent vast amounts of time and energy worrying that when I arrived at your consulting room for my session, you'd torture me, and that would be dreadful. I didn't know where this anxiety came from, since in fact you never did anything remotely like torturing me .. but nonetheless, it was there. It wasn't *only* you I felt it with; the worry came out in all areas of my life .. but it was particularly heightened with you, as you were the person with the key to my inner soul.

When I told you about this, you weren't offended and you didn't throw me out! It didn't occur to me at the time that it might be offensive to you if I suggested that what you were intending to do was to torture me; it was so much a part of the way I thought about things that it seemed only natural to say it. Fortunately for me, you understood.

"You have adopted me as your good superego," you said. "What more natural than that you should believe I'll beat up the bad one?"

Then you let me lie down to see what was going on.

I felt that I was lying in a bath of cream cheese, and that this was a very sensuous and reassuring thing to be happening to me. But the sensuality was broken by a tension in my bottom .. and soon I started to see baby pictures. I could see myself lying on a dirty nappy, and wriggling my bottom in it like in the cream cheese .. it was lovely. But at the same time, I could see mummy's breast withdrawing in pain. I was angry. If she wouldn't have pleasure in feeding me, and I didn't have pleasure in defaecating for her, then nothing connected up any more. Then I saw myself, rather older now, sitting on the pot, feeling angry that there was no time and no space to experience and control the pleasure, and that my defaecating had become alienated from me. I was expected to shit in the pot just because it was convenient, not because it was nice. And that was all wrong.

"Do it how you want to," you told me.

My first awareness wasn't of how I *did* want it, but how I *didn't* want it. I could see it coming out hard and greeny-brown, in a long sausage. And because it had to go into the pot, it couldn't fall out naturally behind me, but had to be directed forward to that it could fall in the right place. It was ugly, and it smelt bad, and I didn't like it. It reminded me of a frightened penis.

"Look at the nipple," you said.

It was hard and green and somehow gritty in just the same way.

"You make your faeces in the image of the breast," you told me. "Now, what's your mother doing?"

I could see her, but somehow she wasn't there. She was so busy dissociating herself from it all that she took no part in it. Then I saw her with baby me and the dirty nappy – and she was terrified at having to yield and be soft and sensuous like the faeces.

"Do it again how you want it," you said.

I felt the crack from my front to my back all open up and become wide and relaxed .. and the vaginal and anal and urethral sensations all connected up together. That was revolutionary – a most wonderful feeling of oneness. Then everything inside me fell; I didn't fall out of myself, as I had worried I would when I held myself together .. but I discovered that there was a proper, relaxed position for everything, lower than the tense position. Then I saw myself – and this is the truly extraordinary thing – doing little pats of soft, yellow faeces which fell gently to the ground and took up the shape of succulent, giving breasts with eager, lively nipples. And they were golden, and they shone and sparkled and told me they liked me. I was so happy that they liked me; I felt truly accepted and relaxed in the middle. Their eyes looked at me and loved me .. it was such a pleasure.

Then I found that I had a great desire to take things into my mouth and into my vagina. And I looked at the gleaming, happy. breast-shaped faeces and felt the pleasure of making them, and of controlling the pleasure and not being controlled. I wanted to play with them, and not any longer to re-introject them. I was now free to take other things in. Then I felt a great sensitivity in my lower lip, and I saw a breast and realised that if I coaxed it just underneath the nipple, it would just let milk flow into my mouth without my having to squeeze it and force it. That was lovely; as I felt the milk coming into me nicely, my back became straighter, and my pelvic bones moved again to bring my bottom forward and let me be proud of showing what I had. It was all lovely ...

6
The Real World

Once I knew more about the relationship between the conscious and the unconscious worlds, I became fascinated by the moral issues which arose out of their interaction. Each world had its own morality, but I often found that the demands or judgements of the two were somehow in conflict – a state of affairs which left me very confused.

This confusion came out in all kinds of strange ways. I kept returning to my sneaking sympathy for feminists, for example. It wasn't just that I believed that what they said was rooted in truth – which, indeed, some of it was – it was that I was horribly attracted, quite against my will, to some of the more destructive aspects of their philosophy. And as I felt this attraction, I feared that I, too, was basically a man-hater. For that was what I considered the feminists to be. The fact that there was a certain justice and logic in some of the things they said didn't alter the fact that their major aim was to castrate men and take the power for themselves. But why should I, who loved men, want to do that too? Perhaps I didn't really love men? Oh dear. I was always cautious about falling in love; I was afraid that it would hurt the men I loved .. and suddenly I found myself wondering whether all these things were connected.

Another thing I noticed was how often I would read something, or hear someone else talking, and realise that I had had the same idea, and that it was a good one. Then, instead of being pleased with myself and agreeing, I would be consumed by outrage:

"I thought that! It's not fair. Why did no one listen?"

When I told you about all these thoughts, you were delighted.

"The underlying feeling of all this is, 'I've got that!'" you said.

"Shall we look at where it comes from?"

Sure thing! I lay down and you told me to feel my teeth. They felt enormously big, and as if they were connected with my eyes and with my pubic region.

"Your eyes and teeth are both stretching out for something," you told me. "Now, tell your eyes to see."

I saw a penis – but I immediately became anxious and blotted out the picture, as if I ought not to have seen it.

"Look again," you told me.

I saw teeth round the penis; I was afraid that they would bite it off. But I didn't know whose teeth they were (although I was afraid that they might be mine ..). I felt that I could only look at the terrible things they were going to do if they were not mine. Yet I knew they were ...

"Look," you said.

And I watched the teeth feeling the penis, getting to grips with it. It was wonderful; my teeth could feel every bump and every nobble on the penis. And I *wasn't* doing anything terrible! But I was afraid; I was worried that it would become erect and that that would mean it was hostile towards me. Then I'd have to draw in my teeth and let it have all the power and all the pleasure, and the only pleasure left to me would be that of passivity.

"Feel it some more," you told me.

I did .. and it was a most exquisite kind of sensation – a sharing. But then I began to see childhood pictures: I saw daddy and David with their hands over their penises, hiding them from me and not letting me even see them, much less play with them. And I became furious; if they weren't going to let me share their penises, then I wanted them – or do I mean it? – for myself. I ripped their penises off so that I had them .. and David and daddy cried .. and I was pleased. I was so outraged by them that I felt (even now that I had stolen their penises) that they deserved to have them torn off, and that I was glad I'd done it; it was what was right.

Then, much to my shame, I felt that I understood deep down the motives of feminists in castrating men. But, I protested, I didn't really hate men, and I didn't want to castrate them. It just happened that those particular men – David and daddy deserved it. That didn't mean that all men deserved it! Yet now I felt like a man-castrator, and that was truly terrible. I wanted to kill myself, castrate myself to punish myself. No wonder I'd always warned my boyfriends away! I felt dreadful.

"We're going to change this story," you said. "See a boy who *does* like having his penis played with."

There he was .. and his penis became erect – but it was because he wanted to give me *more* of it, not *less* of it! He shared it with me. And I sucked it, in my mouth and in my vagina, and I felt the pleasure in it and in me. There was a little pool just behind my pubic hair that I had been afraid was full of poison.

"That's not poison," you said. "It's an orgasm. The boy doesn't lose his penis; he loses his orgasm; that is, he gives it to you, he lets it go."

I looked, and the boy wasn't afraid .. and I watched him have an orgasm .. AND HIS PENIS REMAINED INTACT! Smaller – but still there. And how did I know he hadn't lost it? Because he was smiling; he looked totally happy. Me too.

A most unexpected side-effect of this session was that my feet became straighter. They lay much better on the ground and my ankles were less tense. It was rather bizarre until I got used to it, though, because I didn't know where my feet were, and kept tripping over things! But my body very quickly became used to postures closer to the essential me; it must always have known what was right, and just waited for me to find it.

THOUGHT VISIBLE

At this time, it still seemed to me that to have an orgasm was to make an unconditional declaration of existence. I felt that, as yet, I was still dependent on the man to make declarations of love and surrender first. Yet I wanted to be able to make such declarations myself, and I was rather ashamed because I couldn't. But why not? When I talked to you about this, you said that I was afraid of being hurt by an aggressive phallus which thought only about itself and not about me at all. And one day, this anxiety revealed itself in the most extraordinary way.

I attended a performance of a play in which the lead female part was played by a gay man. He was dressed up to kill, in falsies, slinky stockings and the tiniest of tight mini-skirts. In one scene, his part was to try to seduce an older man, and it soon became apparent from the bulge which appeared through the mini-skirt that he was finding this more real than pretend! Since I considered myself to be more than normally "liberated", I was rather surprised to find that I was immensely and almost paralytically shocked by this. I felt that he ought to hide his erection from us, because it was something which was private to him and which he ought not to thrust upon his audience against their will. The actor didn't have any such inhibitions, however, and I became rather confused as to whether or not my reaction was reasonable. I turned to one of my friends who was sitting next to me, to ask her what she thought .. and then I found that I couldn't speak. After all, I reasoned, she might not have noticed – as if anyone could not have noticed! – and then I would be aiding and abetting the exhibitionism that was so embarrassing me. So I didn't speak.

I got home in the evening, and thought I'd tell Eddie about it. But, once again, I found myself unable to find words to do so. I mentally shrugged my shoulders, and busied myself with something else. But the evening didn't go quite as I had anticipated. As I was peeling the potatoes for dinner, I found that the index finger on my left hand was rather painful. I didn't think much more of it, but rearranged the potato in my hand so that it didn't put too much pressure on the finger. But the pain got worse and worse, and gradually, the finger started to become rigid and to swell up. Overnight, it went yellow with tension, and became very painful indeed. I couldn't bend it at all, and every pressure on it was an agony. But I couldn't think why it had happened. Had I bumped it? Had I shut it in a drawer? I couldn't remember anything which might have caused it. But as I felt it lock into such a position that I couldn't even bend it at the knuckle, far less at the joints, I began to be rather worried about it. Unfortunately, it was by now Saturday afternoon, and the doctor's surgery was closed until Monday morning. What could I do?

Eventually, I thought of the local chemist, who was a good friend of mine. I went round to visit him in his shop, and showed him the finger and asked him what I should do.

"Hmm, interesting," he said. "It looks to me as if it should respond to massage, to take the pressure down. Soak it in cold water, and then rub it gently like this .."

He took his right hand, and cupped it gently round his left index finger, in such a way that the right-hand fingers gripped the finger that was causing me the problem .. then rubbed them up and down along the shaft of the injured finger.

"If that doesn't work, then I think you ought to take the finger to hospital, because it's so swollen that it's probably liable to suffer internal damage if it goes on for too long."

But I didn't need to – he had solved the problem for me!

There was something about the way his fingers gripped the offending finger and then massaged it – up and down, up and down – that reminded me of a penis in a vagina; in and out, in and out .. and I suddenly became aware that it was my inability to come to terms with the episode of the day before which was causing this physical symptom. I went home and sat Eddie down, and said,

"There's something I have to tell you."

I told him the story of the erection, and my reaction to it .. and as I got to the end of the story, I felt the locking in my finger release itself. It was no longer panic-stricken, and could relate again to the outside world. The swelling took about as long to go down as it had to go up .. but the moment of discharge was immediately palpable as I finished telling Eddie all about it.

It was one of the most bizarre things that has happened to me in my entire life, and a simple, yet extraordinary, proof of the power of the unconscious mind. I felt the actor's phallus to be aggressive, I was afraid that my fingers, teeth and clitoris were also aggressive; I couldn't face that, and couldn't face the idea that maybe sex meant being attacked by an aggressive penis .. so I created a symptom instead. God knows what other, more serious symptoms can be caused by infantile traumas, where the conscious mind isn't big enough yet to deal with them. I was relieved to have suffered only such a minor inconvenience!

SHOWING MYSELF

Then I found myself remembering episodes of showing myself when I was a little girl. I had wanted desperately to join the street 'gang', which was entirely composed of little boys. For, by coincidence, I was the only little girl in our street who was of a suitable age to be in a gang. The boys were very happy to have me in their gang, and I was duly proud. There was just one thing they wanted me to do; they wanted me to take my knickers down and show myself to them. This was to be my *rite de passage*.

I couldn't see why I shouldn't do this. After all, my mother had always said that there was nothing wrong with being naked. To be fair, I should have suspected a rat, because she also went on to tell me that other people thought that nakedness wasn't nice. But, she reassured me, we were right and they were wrong; the only thing was that we had to be careful who we told that this was what we thought. I suppose that even as a child I must have detected the duplicity in this – after all, either it IS all right or it isn't; but to say that it is all right but no one is allowed to know about it is crazy, unless, of course, you live in a totalitarian dictatorship, where no one is allowed to say openly what they think. I didn't realise that my mother's superego was indeed totalitarian, and that that was why she was always trying to avoid upsetting it; I just took it for granted that she meant what she said.

So one wet day, I went with my friends the little boys into a red and white telephone-engineer's hut which happened, fortuitously, to have been left outside our houses for the weekend, and we had a grand ceremony. Down came my knickers, and they all crowded round me. They all had a look; but of course, they already knew that little girls didn't have penises – that was why they wanted to look at a little girl naked. Yet they weren't really interested in what I *didn't* have; what they wanted to know was what I had instead. They asked me to spread the lips surrounding my vagina so that they could see what was there. I was so delighted; they knew that there was something there, and they looked with reverence and interest. Then they pulled their trousers down and let me see their penises; that was very interesting for me, because I'd never seen a penis that wasn't circumcised before .. and then we all got dressed again and I was a member of the gang.

Foolishly, I suppose, I told my mother about what I'd done. I rather naively expected that she would be pleased with me for spreading pleasure and enlightenment! Nothing could have been further from the truth. I thought the skies were going to fall in. Off she went into an hysterical tirade: the boys would despise me now; they'd never be my friends again; she wouldn't let me go out with them again; how could I do such a thing when she'd told me that not everyone understood .. and so we went on. I tried in vain to tell her that everyone in the telephone tent had had a pleasurable, enlightening and dignified time .. but there was no persuading her. I was a bad, dirty girl and the neighbours would never speak to her again if they knew what her daughter had done .. the sins of the world were visited upon my shoulders. It was quite terrible.

I told you about this episode. And, for the first time in twenty-odd years, sanity returned.

"Of course it was a nice thing for you to have done," you said.

I was so relieved. I hadn't realised to quite what an extent I had accepted her judgement that I'd been a bad girl until I heard you so uncompromisingly on my side.

"Your mother was afraid that they'd hurt you with their penises," you went on. "She was afraid of rape."

It certainly fitted with our earlier conversation, and you deemed it sufficiently serious to deserve hypnotic consideration.

"Look at the blank," you said, "and tell me what you see there."

There was a picture of me as a tiny baby; mummy was looking at my little vulva and having to hold herself back not to poke her finger aggressively into it. She could see blood, and she was afraid that I was castrated. Then she was angry with me because she felt guilty because she thought she'd done it. I didn't know whether I was supposed to have a penis or not, and so whether it was true or not that I was castrated; I felt that I didn't know what sex I was. As I looked at this picture, all the life drained out of my vagina and my genital area.

"How do you feel if a nice penis comes?" you asked.

Well, I felt wonderful; the life rushed back .. but then I didn't believe it, and everything seized up again. I was afraid that the nice penis wouldn't come because I was nasty and going to bite it off.

"Feel your vagina unfreeze and see what it feels like," you suggested.

I could see a kind of tube with a kink in it, like a bent straw, so that nothing could get through. I began to feel it straighten up .. but suddenly there was mummy's breast with a kink in it .. and then I couldn't see anything else.

"Show the good vulva to me," you told me. "Let me see it, and watch my eyes watching it."

I cried and cried; I didn't believe I had anything to show you; only men, who had penises, could see and feel things; if I showed what I had to a man, he'd have to force his way into nothing by making a hole and hurting me .. and so it went on.

"But you do have something," you insisted. "I'll look at it, and I'll like it."

I felt a warmth unravelling inside me .. and I watched my vagina shining. Then I saw it open up like a flower, with a warm and soft sucking centre, and its focus of feeling in the middle and not at the edges. I wasn't sadistically scratching at things to draw them into me; I was sucking them in, and I was sucking them *with* something. I had something, too – and that was wonderful; something for men to respond to. But the most remarkable thing about this was that I felt that it was the first time that I'd ever had such thoughts; the conviction that I had nothing ran very deep indeed, and was not ever overcome by the evidence of my conscious senses, which could see and feel clearly that of course I had something. That was very interesting indeed .. Not only had I gained a sex organ; I had also gained an insight into the relationship between my conscious and unconscious minds.

All this started to pave the way for me to come to understand that my fingers and teeth and nails weren't nasty because they were aggressive. I had always been worried to do or think anything in case this destroyed people. But once there was a nice warm centre inside me, there was less need to attack other people to get things .. and then I became able to be aware that, in fact, I'd never wanted to attack them anyway; I'd just wanted them to let me explore, investigate, uncover .. and that was nice. What a revelation this was to me! Yet I hadn't even been able to begin to think it for myself before it was safe to do so. You had often told me that I wasn't aggressive, but I had been quite unable to hear what you said – even though, of course, I heard what you said. This was very strange.

Another interesting aspect of this was that I often felt myself under an enormous obligation towards you. I believed that you were somehow putting yourself at risk, or doing something quite unpleasant, by treating me and looking at my unconscious – uncovering me, letting me show myself – and I spent quite a lot of time worrying that I ought to stop you doing it, or else find some way of paying you back for your favour to me. It wasn't a straightforward desire to do something nice for you because you had done something nice for me – although that certainly came into it – it was more a feeling that I owed you a debt that I had to pay. I resented this very much, because I wanted you to like looking at me and I wanted our mutual obligations to be free ones, entered into through desire and pleasure .. but I couldn't make myself believe that you liked me and treated me because we had a relationship which we both found rewarding and valuable. As I came to realise this at a conscious level, I found that my brain was able to generalise what I felt so that I had a far deeper insight into obsessive morality; and that was fascinating.

BREAKING MUMMY'S POWER

Once I felt so much stronger inside myself, I found myself able to acknowledge many more things about myself – in particular, the extraordinary power that my mother wielded over me, and the shame that I felt at being so helplessly in her thrall. You were very helpful to me at this time; you talked to me often about the relationship between my ego and my superego, and how my superego didn't like the drives of my id. You were most insistent that in the course of time, I would learn how to accept and love the desires of my id, and that my ego would learn how to deal with them in a way which didn't involve copying my superego and bashing the drives firmly on the head. I was always rather embarrassed when we had these conversations, since I was aware of how very much I still was under the control of my repressive superego – but it certainly was reassuring to know that this would not be the case for ever. And it certainly, also, spurred me to braver thoughts of rebellion than I had ever allowed myself in the past. The past, in fact, provided me with much of my conscious speculation at this time.

For example, I had always felt an anxiety about the relationships I had with men – or even boys. As a girl, I didn't really have many boyfriends, because I didn't know what to do with them or say to them. Socialising was never my strong point although I thought of myself as popular and gregarious, and I think I was considered that way by people who knew me. I suppose that underneath, I must have been so afraid of hurting the men I went out with that I walked around with a kind of 'beware of the monster' sign inscribed on my brow. Certainly, I did my best to let my boyfriends know good and early what they were tangling with; after all, if they wanted to persevere, then the responsibility would be theirs if they got hurt. Not mine, God forbid!

For many years, things went along without my realising quite what was going on; as a child, I didn't feel a burning need for a boyfriend anyway, and my mother always consoled me (!) that the reason I wasn't terribly popular with boys was that I was too clever for them. In retrospect, I considered this to be one of the wickedest things she ever did. For a start, although I wasn't in the greatest demand as a girlfriend, boys did like me, and my mother ought to have helped me understand that adolescent relationships are, by their very nature, short, because it is a period of experimentation and finding an adult self with which one is happy. And secondly, her insistence that I could be attractive *or* an intellectual, but not both, set up all kinds of conflicts which just waited for an opportunity to emerge fully-fledged. My mother taught me that I could be satisfied, or the men could be satisfied by me, and that the two states were incompatible. This didn't contribute to my ease in sexual relationships generally!

She also had the most insidious way of getting rid of my boyfriends. Occasionally I would bring home a boy whom I really liked; but as soon as she smelt this, out came all the big guns. I remember one example in particular. I had been at university for a couple of years, and while I had had the odd minor flirtation, I had never had a serious relationship. I was still a virgin, and knew little or nothing about sex. Before I had gone to university, my mother had taken me aside and told me that I was to sleep with as many boys as I could while I was a student. This sounds like the advice of a kind and liberal mother .. but, as usual, there was a sting in the tail, of the kind that at the time drove me to insanity like a gadfly:

"If only I'd slept with your father before marrying him, I'd have recognised that he was a bastard, and I'd never have married him. You must protect yourself against my mistakes by checking the men out first."

In the event, I had not taken her advice .. but, foolishly, I had believed that she was sincere in offering it, and, even more naively, I considered myself fortunate not to have to hide any possible sexual exploits from her, as some of my friends had to from their prudish parents.

So, there came the day that a boy truly fell in love with me. I was quite unaware of his feelings until one evening I met him on the stairs, and he invited me to come and visit him later that day, after he expected to have finished his work. I thought nothing of it, because I didn't really know him very well, and wasn't harbouring any unrequited passion for him. It seemed the most natural thing in the world that near-neighbours should visit each other for coffee – why not? Anyway, to cut a long story short, I went along to his room at about one in the morning, after I'd finished my work for the

day. A muffled "come in" could be heard through the door, so I
turned the handle and went in.

There was such an atmosphere of peace in his room. I knew him
sufficiently little that we'd done no more than nod on the stairs, and
I'd certainly never been in his room before – and never in anyone's
room at this time of night. But he hadn't finished his work yet. He
sat at his desk, illuminated by a single bright light in an ocean of
darkness; yet it was darkness which lapped around his body, sucking
gently, beckoning him into the realms of peace and contentment.
Only the one spot of brilliance disturbed it .. yet even that was quiet
and accepting, admitting no rush or urgency, but just a gentle movement forward. He patted the surface of his desk next to his books,
and motioned to me to sit down. Why not? I sat, quite quietly,
waiting for him to finish. There was no hurry. I cannot begin to
express what an extraordinary thing this was for me; normally
everything was in a hurry, and in the absence of frenetic activity, I
became anxious and agitated, lost in the void which failed to define
me.

I sat, and felt embraced and caressed by the quiet, deep silence
which this young man had the ability to create around him, and into
which he had done me the honour of inviting me. I didn't need him
to be looking at me, or talking to me, or otherwise engaging me; just
his presence was enough. I could make out a cello in the corner. So,
he was a musician as well. I had had no idea. How wonderful. The
smell of his room was sweet and rich, with no hint of bitterness or
acridity .. and the atmosphere throbbed with life and pleasure.

Eventually, he finished what he was doing, and rose to turn on
the central light. The room lost its almost supernatural feeling, and
became any other student's room, normal and without magic.
Almost; the smell remained .. and now there were his eyes and his
gentle, relaxed gestures as well, better defined by the greater intensity
of the light. We made coffee, and sat by the fire in the thick silence
of the middle of the night .. and talked. I no longer remember what
we discussed; it was, in any case, of no importance. What was important was what we were communicating without words. And,
without words, we found ourselves lying on his bed; still fully

clothed – but naked in our souls. He leaned gently over, raised my
jumper, unhooked my bra, and began, with an air of total acceptance,
to suck my breasts. No one had ever done anything like that to me
– ever. I was overwhelmed by a warmth that I'd never felt before
and didn't expect ever to feel outside my dreams.

"It makes you feel nice down here, doesn't it?" he asked,
stroking me between my legs.

Such an idea had never entered my head. What had the two got
to do with one another? But, my God, he was right. I felt enveloped
in a feeling as warm and comforting as a quilt of down, wrapped
round me, embracing me with its kind, soft acceptance.

He was touched by my innocence.

"A virgin, are you?" he asked, with not even a hint of the contempt such a question often carried in student circles in the seventies.
And – so much more wonderful for me – not even a hint that this
was going to make any difference to how he would treat me as a
woman. He knew about pleasures I didn't know about, and we were
going to share them. He put my hand on his penis and showed me
how to stroke it so that it felt nice. I didn't know that penises liked
being stroked; I had no conscious pictures at all of what sex could
possibly be like. What I wasn't at all prepared for was the impact of
the wave after wave of pleasure which just cuddling caused in me.
How could this be? For the first time in my life, I wanted to make
love with someone. I didn't have to ask why, or whether it was right;
I just wanted to do it.

But we were prudent – unfortunately. First lovemaking should,
we thought, not be approached with precipitate haste. In any case,
the unexpected nature of the encounter had left him – for it would
never have occurred to me – without contraceptives .. and we
weren't that lacking in forethought. Would that we had been!

"They all say you're frigid," he said.

I laughed. What an outrageous idea .. and yet, my 'keep off'
signs had worked.

"I knew you weren't, though," he went on. "That's why I chose
you – and I was right; you're as warm as toast."

My soul swelled in gratitude. He had understood. I didn't even bother to try and put him off me. He understood; it wasn't necessary.

My body responded very quickly to all the stimulation it was suddenly receiving. A few days is a long time in the life of a student. My eyes shone, my lips became blooming and responsive, my hips swayed proudly .. and I licked my lips at intervals all through the day in memory of the kisses which had been lavished so gently, yet with such passion, on them the night before. It was like being a different person. And it was all a preparation, a building-up to the inevitable consummation of our relationship. There was no hurry; we loved each other so much that a week or so's delay would make no difference .. why not savour the pleasures of each stage in their proper place? The outcome was not in doubt; so we could even enjoy the uncertainty about its time and place. It was a most extraordinary experience for me, and one whose like I had never imagined possible.

It was not fated to end well, however. The vacation intervened before we had come to the end of our courtship. But it didn't matter – or so we thought. He would come and stay with me. If only I'd gone to stay with him instead .. but it was easier, for a number of reasons, for him to come to us. We planned that we would spend a few days alone with our respective families, and then arrange a visit. My mother came to pick me up with my luggage at the end of term. We piled into the car and headed home. But we hadn't gone more than half a mile when she said,

"New boyfriend, eh?"

I can't remember any longer what I had or hadn't told her about him. I only know that I didn't need to tell her in words how I felt about him, because it was obvious from every pore of my body.

"You haven't slept with him, have you?"

I knew she'd be pleased if I had, because she'd told me to get as much experience as I could in bed with young men. So it never crossed my mind to dissemble. I must have been mad!

"No, but I'm going to."

Her reaction was the last thing I'd ever conceived would happen. She wasn't pleased! I couldn't believe it. But she didn't scream and shout .. she went completely silent .. and her shoulders started to shake with silent sobs. The tears ran down her face until her hands were wet as they gripped the steering wheel. But she said nothing. A friend of hers who had come with her to collect me observed that it was not right of me to put my mother to such grief. I couldn't believe what I was hearing. It didn't cross my mind that she might be jealous for all the pleasures that she hadn't had, and that it was outrageous that she should try to deprive me of them merely out of jealousy; I truly believed that I must be doing something terrible if it was having this effect on her. What could I do?

I heard her incoherently babbling on:

"You've built up such respect for yourself; no one will ever think of you so highly again; what will happen if you need a reference; oh, how could you, how could you?"

I couldn't see what any of this had to do with what I was thinking of doing.

"No one respects a girl who isn't a virgin; you'll cheapen yourself not only in the eyes of your tutors, but in his eyes too. And I always hoped you'd marry one of your tutors, someone intellectually worthy of you. No little boy could be worthy of you; don't throw yourself away."

It really was like something out of a cheap novel. But it happened in real life. And despite myself, as I've now seen it happen so often in hypnotic sessions at your consulting room, I found myself drawn into it. My breasts and my clitoris and vagina, which had been so proud and happy to be loved, felt devastated and unworthy and as if they had to hide away; my entire body just became a living pain, and I screamed inside myself – just shut up, shut up; I'll do anything you like if you only leave me alone!

As I sat in the car and listened to my mother, and felt my reactions to what she was saying and doing, I felt that I had betrayed that nice, gentle young man to her clutches. I feared desperately that I had not stood up for him sufficiently – not even to myself; far less to her. In reality, I made a valiant attempt to keep my end up .. but arguing with her is just not possible, and the more you argue, the more you end up on her terms. I should just have left home there and then .. but I was afraid of killing her. I was too dependent on her; that was the trouble; that was why it was so difficult for me to understand that she and I were not alike.

Anyway, suffice it to say that he came to stay with us. But it was never the same again. The feeling of uncomplicated abandon that I'd felt in his arms became lacerated by guilt, and I wanted all the time to ask him:

"It's not dirty to walk round the streets holding hands, is it?"

I hated myself for needing to ask such questions .. so I didn't ask them; but their unanswered ghosts hung in the air and polluted our relationship. Mercifully, I don't think he noticed .. but I didn't love him any more. I was too ashamed. But I wouldn't let my mother know how I felt; to her I showed the face of a girl in love. The sadness of it; I was lying to her so that she wouldn't know that she'd won.

But she won anyway, in the end. I took him round to the station on his last afternoon with us, and saw him onto the train home. I walked slowly home, thinking that at least there would be some peace and quiet now .. But no such luck. As I walked in the door, there was my mother, her face swollen and distended by weeping. She had apparently started crying the moment I left the house, and hadn't stopped since. As I entered, she made a show of trying to pull herself together .. but she didn't really want to pull herself together; what she wanted was to tell me what she thought. And that she did – with a vengeance.

"It's worse than I'd ever thought. Not only isn't he clever and worthy of you .. he's .. common!" she spluttered.

This was her ultimate term of contempt. I couldn't have cared less whether my boyfriends were lords or plebeians, provided that they were nice .. but she'd already won her battle, had she only known it, and was therefore wasting her time keeping it going.

"What will your tutors think of you? How could you walk along the street holding his hand; everyone will see you and know that you are a person of no taste; how could you let yourself down like this?"

Images of myself as a total pariah, held in absolute contempt by everyone I'd ever known, filled my head. I quite literally could not bear it. And yet I couldn't see how to maintain my pictures – the lovely ones – in the face of such determined sadistic destruction.

Not surprisingly, the relationship didn't stand the strain; he was willing, but I felt like a block of ice in his arms; my back became totally rigid and I couldn't feel any of those wonderful whooshing sensations that had characterised our togetherness. Who says sex is just a physical thing? But my soul went into mourning, from which I don't think I recovered until I met you and started to rebuild my life. That destruction was a real trauma for me; the first meaningful act of my adult life was trampled on by my mother, reawakening all the childhood memories that I might never have needed to relive if my adulthood had been properly affirmed by her. I literally didn't think I'd ever believe in myself or in my powers to affect the world for the good ever again. It was a nail in my coffin .. and I was only twenty!

But did I really have to kill myself – or my libido – in order not to kill her? That was the real issue. I talked to you about all these painful memories, which I had thought buried; I hadn't even realised how important they were. And, much to my relief, you let me lie down and start to find out what was going on.

"Feel your body and see what it's saying," you told me.

I felt a trembling of expectation .. but I wasn't sure whether what I was expecting was nice or not. I thought it was – but then I felt my clitoris pull back in pain.

"What's happening to it?" you asked.

I found it difficult to look; it was somehow hiding and I felt terribly guilty.

"Look and see what it wants."

But all I could see was it being bitten off.

"Let's have a look at it in slow motion," you said, "and we'll be able to see what's really going on."

I could see a mouth sucking my clitoris .. and that was nice .. but then – there was the pain again. And no more pictures.

"Let the energy come into your clitoris and into your eyes," you told me.

I felt my clitoris getting big .. and then I saw me and David, playing games with our tongues, licking each other's tongues and seeing what it felt like.

"That's a sharing; it's nice," you observed.

I'd never thought of it like that. My clitoris and David's penis.

"That's how women know how to take penises, because they know what penises like because of the model of their own clitoris."

That was interesting; I'd never thought of that, either! Meanwhile, I could see the clitoris big and red and swollen and hard. Then I felt teeth bite it and let the energy flow out. One part of me was pleased at this, because it was a lovely feeling having the energy flowing out; it was like the feeling of orgasm .. but part of me was shocked by the sadism involved and grieved by the pain.

"What does the big red clitoris remind you of?" you asked.

First of all, I thought of a penis .. but then I found myself thinking about mummy's nipple. And I'd started by sucking it nicely .. but it hadn't worked, so I'd had to bite in order to get anything out. And now I was afraid that my clitoris, too, would have to be bitten.

"Make yourself a nice breast," you told me.

That was easier said than done; I found it enormously difficult to do. For a start, I was afraid in case it was too nice, which I didn't quite understand, but recognised as a feeling which I often had in the 'real' world as well. Secondly, I was afraid to put aside the armour which I had against it, since it had always been horrid to me. Then I was afraid that I'd bite it .. and that would be terrible. I think that you started to feel that I was just making excuses, because you said,

"No you won't; now just get on with it!"

I saw a breast with huge trumpet-shaped milk ducts .. but when I looked, that was just mummy in disguise, giving me too much and drowning me to prove that she could give. I kept seeing a jaunty, high-nippled breast, but I couldn't get my lips around it .. and that was all very puzzling.

Fortunately, you realised what was going on.

"You're too loyal to your mother," you said, "and keep preserving the image of her breast, because you're afraid that you're betraying her and killing her."

You were absolutely right; immediately, I felt better, and I could see the nice breasts hanging low and full, with dark, long nipples. The nipples were somewhat erect .. but because the relaxed breasts were now hanging downwards instead of pointing upwards, the slight erection meant that the nipple pointed straight and easily into my mouth. And I sucked and felt contented, and felt the nice mummy just yield peacefully to me; her vagina was connected to her breasts, and it sucked too, and cradled me nicely in the middle. The feeling of 'too nice' went away; it had been just mummy's fear that her armour would break, short-circuiting the desire and pleasure into quasi-electric shocks. But now there was just peace.

Then – and this was wonderful – I felt the breast respond and come alive and communicate with me; it had desires which fitted mine and fulfilled mine. Then my clitoris relaxed and fell back into my body, as my body did into where I was lying; I was supported. Everything felt wider; my pelvis broadened at the top of the legs, I felt my bottom fall from higher up my back, and my clitoris, although big, wasn't aggressive or red or hard. It just spread around further ...

Once all this happened, I felt my fear of being a nuisance diminish perceptibly; I wouldn't, after all, do bad things which would make me a nuisance. Suddenly I was nice, and more visible. No more biting; no more being like mummy. I was accepted – at last!

7
On Getting my Teeth into Things

BEING AN INTELLECTUAL

I had always had an ambition to be a real, high-powered academic
– but somehow it had never quite worked. When I was at school,
I assumed that it was because I was too young; it seemed that we
never got to grips with important issues, but only skated across the
surface. I remember studying Sartre and Camus, and thinking that it
was all very well, talking about commitment and absurdity, and how
the one was supposed to solve the problem of the other .. but that
the real question was what it was all *really* saying. If the world is absurd, what does that mean to us, and why is it important? What
would a non-absurd world-picture look like? Wouldn't it be a
challenge to find that out? Isn't accepting the absurdity a defeat to the
intellect? And so on. The trouble was that there was always the
tyrannical pressure of external examinations, and the important thing
was to learn the books and be prepared for whatever essays there
might be to write. Never mind, I thought. There's always university.
That will be the place where real questions are asked and answered.

I couldn't have been more wrong. I had chosen to study
philosophy, amongst other things, and was very excited: I was going
to discover all the truths about the universe that I'd always wanted
to know. But it was all so boring! What did I care about truth tables
for? I wanted to know what truth WAS! Unfortunately for me,
linguistic philosophy was fashionable while I was a student, and we
spent hours chasing our tails through articles and books, trying to see
whether you had uttered a true statement about someone if you
referred to them with a nod (so that they were securely identified) but
then got their name wrong. Gosh; what earth-shattering stuff!

Then there was moral philosophy. Things were no better on this front. For a start, no one seemed quite sure what a person was, and it was difficult to talk about morality when there wasn't any sense of Self. How was it possible for me to identify myself as a moral agent when I'd been broken down into my component parts and it had been proved that, since none of my cells were the same as the ones I was born with, I couldn't possibly be the same person? All this meant that there was no sense of continuity through time .. and therefore morality didn't even make sense as a concept. I suppose there was always utilitarianism .. but I could never see what that had to do with morals. It, too, didn't start from the person, but from an abstract concept – happiness – which, presumably, we were supposed to measure in order to weigh up the relative merits of different courses of action. Morals became a matter of statistics.

Then there was the professor who wrote a book in which morality was so much a matter of what seemed right to you when you were being sincere (or something) that there was no way left to condemn even Hitler for immorality. But no one said: we find this unacceptable, and therefore, by the good logical argument of *reductio ad absurdum*, we'll throw the whole lot out and start again. It was terrible! Nothing connected. Any residual desires I had to be an intellectual faded away.

Yet, at the same time, it was what I really wanted most of all. The trouble was that, in truth, I was outraged not just by the academic establishment, but also by my own inability to put my finger on what it was that was the matter with it, and to express what I felt coherently, so that I could believe it. If I was out of step, then, I felt, I must be wrong. Yet I knew I was right. The result of all this was the normal manic depressive cycle: I got on top of it, and everything was wonderful; then it got on top of me and everything was dire. And eventually, I lost faith in my ability ever to understand the rules of their game, and equally in my ability to explain the game I wanted to play .. and the whole business of being an intellectual faded into never-never land. That was what was so wonderful about meeting you. Suddenly, things connected, and the universe made sense.

The trouble was that you were always encouraging me to fulfil my intellectual potential: write a book, or a play, or whatever – anything to express my power and stop feeling so helpless. I thought of it as a 'trouble' because, although I loved the fact that you recognised the power of my mind, it depressed me enormously that I was quite unable to do any of the things you were encouraging me to do. I was sure that the habits of feeling that it was all too much while I was at university were rediscoveries of old habits set up when I was too young to remember, and that if I could get to the bottom of them, I'd be ready to start thinking again .. but it was difficult.

Then, one day, I found myself thinking about why daddy didn't give me his penis. And I didn't know what to do. Interestingly, though, it felt like the same not-knowing-what-to-do as I used to feel when you asked me about my non-existent intellectual life. At this point, we entered into a new phase of exploration which had quite a profound effect on my attitude towards my work.

I felt that somehow if I made it all right for daddy, he wouldn't be afraid any more.

"You've spent your whole life trying to make it all right for your father," you observed. "Or even trying to do it for him."

You were right. I had expended an enormous amount of energy making everything all right.

"Nothing's too much trouble for you," you went on. "It has led to an enormous generosity .. but you don't feel satisfied by it."

The trouble was, I thought, that I didn't know how NOT to do anything, either. I got into a state of trembling anxiety at the idea of just letting things happen. Yet at one level, I knew how it was that it ought to happen.

You let me lie down and see what was going on. Immediately, before you'd even finished counting, I saw that actually, it wasn't me that wanted daddy's penis and made all the advances, but he who wanted to give it to me. He was standing there, holding out his nicely erect penis to me, inviting me to make love with him. He was telling me that I was nicer than his wife, and that he loved me. (And they say that the Oedipus complex is nonsense!) That was very nice .. and yet I felt somehow that something was all my fault. I felt angry and contemptuous of the penis because it had to come to me and couldn't give itself to mummy. And it was I who didn't know what to do – not him. I kept on thinking that I didn't want his penis as a cast-off and as second choice; I wanted to have it because he wanted to give it to ME because that would be nice for both of us. And I couldn't feel any libido at all; I felt that he ought to leave mummy first ..

"You've got yourself into a confusion about who you should be loyal to – your mother or your father," you said.

It was certainly true that I felt highly responsible for their relationship. I didn't want daddy to love me instead of her; if he loved her, I'd be jealous, but that would be tolerable – or at least normal!

"Why don't you forget about your mother and concentrate on what *you* want to do?" you asked.

Good idea. I was so relieved. I suddenly realised that all those destructive thoughts about daddy were *hers*, as she did her best to mess things up. I was so delighted just to be able to tell her to go away.

"She always tries to mess things up," you observed. "You'll get on better without her."

"Now," you went on, "what's happening?"

Well, I didn't *do* anything. Daddy came to me! And he picked me up and took me into the bath with him. The water was all slippery, and my vagina was full of lovely feelings, wanting daddy. But it was too little for his penis. Yet the slippery water let it slide in, and he rocked me up and down on his penis, and I felt my vagina full. After a while, I slid off and felt the penis still erect next to me. But it wasn't because the penis couldn't ejaculate and was holding back; it was a symbol of its always loving me and being there for me – so I didn't have to have it inside me to believe it was there; it was there anyway. I felt a wonderful sense of continuum.

That was enough. I didn't often ask you to wake me up because I'd had enough; but this time I felt that I'd seen what I wanted, and wanted the chance just to digest and enjoy that. I went home with a very unusual feeling inside me. What was it? Then in the middle of the night I woke up with a sudden sense of realisation; I was happy!

BUT WILL THE TEETH GET IN THE WAY?

My eyes began to interest me again at this point. I became aware of a feeling that they were hard on the outside but soft in the middle; and even though I loved reading, I found my eyes very reluctant to take in what I read. There was a very deep level at the back of my brain – almost like an x-ray – that understood what I read, and savoured it, but I felt that the centre of my eye was starved of goodness to suck and chew on by the outermost part, which wouldn't let the everyday bits in for me to enjoy; it was, indeed, almost as if it reflected it all away again. This gave me a most ambivalent attitude towards books. The best book was one that I'd already read; one which couldn't threaten me any more with things I wasn't going to be able to take in properly.

You let me lie down that week, too, and told me to focus on the middle bit of my eye. I could see it sucking and chewing with gusto .. but I was afraid of what it might do. I felt that I ought just to lie there and wait for things to come, but I wanted to go out and find things, too, and draw them in. Yet I was afraid that that meant biting and clawing at them and destroying them. And in that case, it was better to have nothing; not to see. Yet while I wanted to be passive/receptive, I also really wanted to make things mine by going out and exploring.

"You learnt as a baby that things didn't come if you just lay there," you said. "But in any case, it is part of your personality to like exploring, and you mustn't be afraid of doing so. Let your top lip come forward, looking for something to take in."

I was afraid that my teeth would go forward too, and would destroy things. I wanted to go forward and stay with the sensation, as you suggested .. but, while I could feel the most enormous anticipation of pleasure, I wasn't convinced that if I let it happen, it wouldn't actually be pain.

"Get it into your brain that your teeth are nice, will you?" you said. "They only want to caress things and feel them. Now go back to them and feel their pleasure."

And I could! It was just a relaxed feeling – no pain. Then I could

see my lips and my teeth and their counterparts in my eyes feeding
the bit at the back – the nice bit – like birds feed their young. That
was lovely. Then I realised quite suddenly that mummy didn't know
that if you sucked things, they flowed, and that if she would flow to
me, my libido of sucking would flow to her. She was afraid that if
she gave to me, she would become empty; she didn't understand the
reciprocity of giving and taking.

And as I watched, the hard bit at the front of my eyes shrivelled
up like an old scab. It lost its tyrannical grip on the middle bit, so that
the middle and the back took charge.

"Can the scab fall off now?" I asked you.

"Yes, of course. Now look at what the middle bit does."

I looked, and saw it all silky wet, flowing forward and going out
into the world.

"Now look at me and see what your eyes want to do," you said.

I could see all the fluid caressing you and enveloping you and incorporating you; drawing you in.

"Do you mind?" I asked. "Are you afraid of being smothered,
or held in, or contained?"

You said that of course you weren't – that for a woman, taking
in is giving .. and that's lovely. I was so pleased.

Then I felt that I could at last understand how to read books. I
had always been afraid to 'contain' material within a theory, so I had
had to hide what I thought from myself, almost. And while I had
been proud of having such a profound brain, I had found it difficult
to use or enjoy what was inside it, and had let everything in it lie in
the back, in a kind of chaos, just in case I hurt or imprisoned it.

"Start now to use it," you suggested.

Then I was swept away on a tide of blissful and passionate feelings that I almost didn't know existed. I didn't ever want to have to
wake up; life was so breathtakingly fulfilling here in my unconscious.
Unfortunately, though, all good things have to come to an end .. yet
when you did wake me up, I didn't lose the feelings; I still had them.
That was wonderful. My face was wider, my eyes more relaxed ..
but, best of all, my brain was bigger!

AND IF PEOPLE LOOK?

Shortly after this session, I went off to a conference. I had not planned to speak at it, but circumstances conspired to encourage me to speak out about something particularly outrageous in 'loony left' ideology .. and before I knew where I was, there were my remarks splashed across the pages of quite a number of national newspapers. I had expected to be really nervous and neurotic about this, in case I was carpeted at work for spilling the beans .. but actually, when I saw the reports, I was conscious of nothing except a sense of profound relief at having spoken, and having freed myself from a kind of tyranny of silence. I was quite sure that I could not have done this at all before knowing you – and certain that even a few weeks earlier, I would have been able to do it only at the cost of sleepless nights and hot sweats. All this made me very pleased and proud of myself.

On my return, the night before I was next due to see you, I had a most curious dream, in which a colleague of mine was talking to my mother, who had three festering cuts on each side of her neck, under her ears. My friend said to her:

"I know what's wrong with you; you've got gonorrhoea."

I woke up with the shock, and wondered what this meant. And the thought suddenly flashed throuh my mind:

"That means mummy has a dirty vagina."

And I went back to sleep. But when I woke up again, I found myself wondering about my vagina. Was it dirty? Then I remembered how in bed, during lovemaking, I would often reach the point of orgasm and think not "Shall I let go?" but "Shall I let it out?" Why I should ask either question was in itself a puzzle; but the particular way I chose to phrase it to myself was interesting. What was it, I wondered, that I was afraid to let out.

I talked to you about it all, and you were very pleased. You said that the cuts on my mother in my dream were in the 'stubborn' muscles .. and that it would be a good idea to look at it all under hypnosis. So I lay down. There followed one of the most extraordinary sequence of pictures that I've ever seen at your office.

"Look at what it is in your vagina that you are afraid of letting out," you told me.

I was afraid; I was going to see a dragon. But in fact, all I could see was a big, powerful mouth and tongue, sucking. It was very nice, but I felt rather apprehensive about it. Then I felt a pain at the sides of my eyes, going down towards my ears.

"That's good," you said.

Then I wanted to take my contact lenses out. And as I did, I found myself remembering how I always thought that my eyes were too short (!), and were always having to stretch to get things.

"That's right; they are too short," you confirmed. "A very good observation."

"Go on feeling the sucking in your vagina," you went on.

I kept finding as I did it that although it was very nice, I was afraid that it wasn't real. Then I felt my fingers and my teeth and toes and the very outermost extremities of my vagina all tingling. The sensation felt as if it ought to be pleasure, but it was so tied up with nervousness that it was nearer pain. Then I felt a blockage in my vagina just under the pubic bone .. but I didn't know what it was.

"Have a look, then," you suggested.

I saw a set of clenched teeth! I looked at them and wondered whether they were angry; I rather thought they might be. Yet anger wasn't quite the word I would have chosen; there was something else.

"Would 'control' be a better term?" you suggested.

That seemed right. A tussle was going on in my soul; I felt that someone was angry with me, and that I was angry with them for having the cheek to be angry with nice me. Yet, because another part of me was afraid that they were right, I held on to my anger.

"What is this all about?" you asked.

I could see a picture of me as a little baby, lying on a dirty unwrapped nappy, with mummy there, angry, and daddy behind her not angry, but participating in the outrage by allowing mummy to do it to me. Then I looked some more. I kept feeling that it wasn't my bottom that was dirty, but my vagina. But little babies don't have things coming out of their vaginas .. or do they? I was puzzled.

"Why is there a connection between your vagina and your bottom?" you asked.

I thought .. and then I felt that they both saw (*sic*), so they were both connectors and communicators between me and the outside world. Then I realised that I'd been afraid that both were dirty. But why should I think that? I wondered if it might be through having faeces in my nappy splurging around; that was why I could see mummy wiping my vagina clean. BUT .. as I looked, I saw that it wasn't like that at all! In fact, she was digging her finger into my anus, and wiping dirt *into* my vagina, not away from it. But why should she want to do that?

"Ask her," you suggested.

She said that she was doing this so that I shouldn't ever suffer the humiliations of being a woman. She was doing me a favour! She wanted to hide my vagina behind shame, so that I wouldn't ever want to show it, and then I'd never have men looking at it and doing terrible things to it. That was bad enough – what a favour! – but the thing that outraged me most of all was that she made this a secret that I wasn't ever to tell anyone; for this meant that I was in her power for ever. It was just like when she used to tell me that if I was clever, it meant I couldn't be sexy .. but that it was lucky I was clever. A kind of double bind. I felt abused .. but no one could see.

"What would men see if they looked?" you asked.

I saw mummy naked, with blood between her legs.

"What is the blood?" you wanted to know.

And as I looked, there was the dragon. A dragon with big teeth and huge bulging eyes reared up. And I wanted to attack it. She had never let me see it .. but she *loved* it. She was riding it, and smacking her lips together in a smug, self-satisfied sort of way. I hated it .. and yet I was relieved to see it after all her lying protestations of impotence and humiliation. I had always known that she wasn't really either impotent or humiliated, but only guilty. And she wanted to be the boss.

"The dragon is something significant," you said. "What is it?"

It was a penis-substitute!

"That's right," you commented. "But it's also the castrator of men's penises."

Then I became worried. I could feel a little dragon stirring inside me too. And I looked .. and it peeped out. But it wasn't a horrid dragon; it was nice. It sucked and slurped and smiled, and looked at things. I loved it. But I didn't want it to be like mummy's.

"It's not like your mother's," you reassured me. "It really is a lovely little dragon. And now I'd like you to get your mother to have a look at it."

I had expected that something terrible would happen to my lovely dragon if I let mummy look at it .. but in fact she was so terrified – and so was her dragon – that they fell over themselves and over each other in their desire to run away as fast as possible! I laughed and laughed. I was so relieved; I'd thought her dragon would eat mine. But it hadn't. Then I realised that there was another thought there; I'd been worried that if her dragon ran away from me in fear, then so would everyone else. Then I *really* felt I'd better hide it. And so everything reinforced the same action: the hiding of the dragon.

But it was lovely with it out, and stroking it and playing with it and feeling it – and my fingers – all alive and good. I felt as if everything had rushed to come to it in the place where it had hidden from mummy; it was popular and loved. So she had had to scratch it to bring it to her.

"The little dragon is your clitoris," you told me. "And as it grows active and longer, so will your eyes. Now, how does your vagina feel?"

I felt my vagina .. and it sucked in my clitoris to make them a single thing. That was lovely.

Then I looked, and mummy was gone. So she was no longer standing in front of daddy – and that meant that I could see his penis. And once I could see his penis, I could begin to understand what being a woman was. For how can female understand itself without male? Then .. I watched my dragon lean out and take daddy's penis in its mouth. And daddy liked it! It wasn't sex, but a preparation for sex. I found myself thinking that daddy had always been nervous in case he ejaculated prematurely at this stage – and so had drawn back. But my dragon could reassure him that it was just pleasurable foreplay .. and he began to lose his fear and enjoy himself. And that gave me such pleasure; it was wonderful.

An interesting side effect of this session was that when I ate, I didn't swallow the food immediately, almost without chewing it; I could keep it in my mouth and caress it and let it get wet and soft before letting it go into my stomach.But the really important thing about the session was that I was left with much greater confidence to relate as an equal with men. I had a dragon; they had a dragon – and both were nice! So we could be friends, and we could play together. What more obvious? But the thought was new to me, and had a profound effect on my expectations. I didn't need to be afraid of men, because I wasn't jealous of them any more. It felt like a real breakthrough.

★   ★   ★

It took me a long time to acknowledge how much I hated my parents – especially my mother. I suppose that I loved them too, and that was why I was so reluctant to admit to the hatred. I invented a story when I was a little girl – no doubt it's the kind of story that all children invent, but I was particularly concerned with my own version – in which I wasn't the real child of my parents, but an adopted princess. I used to tell my friends this story, and hope that they would love me for it. I suppose I thought I wasn't lovable if I had anything of my parents in me .. but, oh, the guilt I felt in case anyone found out what I'd done. My parents would kill me, I felt. Yet it was worth the fear to assert my difference from them. And here I was, all these years later, doing it again with you .. but this time doing it properly!

VAGINAS

The question still was, though, what to do with a vagina. I knew that men did things, because they had penises. But it was no good trying

to do things in the way men did them, because I didn't have a penis.
I fell out violently with a number of my feminist friends over this.
They were angry with me for saying that there was a difference be-
tween the things men could do and the things women could do.

"Why should women stay at home with babies while men go out
and do interesting work with computers and business?" they would
ask me. "You're consigning women to servitude and dependence,"
they shouted. "And you call yourself liberated!"

God, they were furious with me. This was the beginning of the
end of my uneasy relationship with my feminist friends; we had
become too different, and I was no longer prepared to compromise
my instincts for the sake of a friendship which denied their validity.

For I felt that I knew more about the needs of my soul after
looking directly into its depths than they did from trying to interpret
the messages which had come through the layers of their mind and
been distorted in the process. I knew from my own experience how
easy it was to be furious with a man for not being as I wanted him
.. and then to find that if only I had a better idea how to relate to
things, the problem went entirely away. It seemed to me that by
pinning all the blame for the ills of society on the men, these women
actually admitted their total dependence on them. For they couldn't
see any other way things could be organised.

I did try talking to them; I explained that the fact that I didn't
go along with their solution to the problem – and, indeed, the fact
that I didn't even accept their interpretation of reality – didn't mean
that I thought everything was hunky-dory and that there was
nothing wrong. It was terribly difficult, arguing with them, though.
It was as if there was a 'sound' ideology which one had to accept in
a totality – as a package. And if you wanted to disagree with any of
its parts, then you were a traitor. Their minds were so closed – in
the literal sense of not being able to admit any information which
couldn't be accommodated by the current theory – that it actually
wasn't possible to introduce new ideas. In one way, I could see their
point; if you accept a package of interdependent ideas, then it
genuinely isn't possible to change one of them without having a
knock-on effect on the whole system. And without a system of inter-

dependent ideas, we wouldn't be able to think anyway. But to elevate the conclusion of a system of thought to such a status of dogma that you can't admit any thoughts whose knock-on effect might endanger the conclusion seemed to me to be totalitarian. The end justifies the means. And the end is accepting the dogma; so the means is paralysing your brain. It didn't seem right.

I agreed that it wasn't right that only men could do things; I even shared the societal hang-up – the fear that this was actually true. But I didn't accept that this meant that all men were bastards if you only dug deeply enough; nor did I accept that the way to solve the problem was for women to have access to high-powered jobs in management and computing. For management and computing, it seemed to me, were the epitome of success in a society which had been made and moulded by the will of men .. and thus the women who went down that path were taking the route of 'Animal Farm'. Good luck to them, I thought. Why shouldn't women be managers or engage in traditionally male activities like engineering or computing, if that's what they want and they have a natural talent for it? Quite right. What I couldn't tolerate, though, was the myth that by taking up powerful positions in a man's world, women were somehow liberating themselves and each other from the subservient position men had put them in. By accepting men's standards, the women showed that they had no original thoughts of their own to put in their place. And that seemed to me to be an enormous pity, and at the same time, a terrible deception.

I suppose that I shouldn't have been surprised. After all, I had been through exactly the same process in my relationship with my soul. For when I first started coming to see you for analysis, the thing that struck me most forcefully was the intense power of my righteous indignation. The single emotion I felt most strongly was rage – and I felt totally justified in feeling it, and would have relished the opportunity to let it out and destroy things. I had been oppressed and crushed all these years, and had held the fury in and not been able to discharge it in a proper way. And the fury was real, and the injustices which I complained of were real. The trouble was threefold: firstly, most of the injustices of which I complained had actually occurred a quarter of a century earlier, when I was a child; secondly there was so much anger stored up that I didn't know how to let it out safely; and thirdly, my soul had actually been warped by the repression into an unnatural shape, so that I had no confidence in my own judgements about what was right and wrong any more. We needed to reestablish my positive self before I would feel able to act with conviction. Otherwise the only thing I would be able to do was to take revenge. And there's nothing constructive about that in the long term; it just perpetuates a cycle. If the oppressor becomes the oppressed, that makes the new oppressor happy – but it's only a superficial change; it doesn't change the underlying structure of society.

I tried to explain all this to my feminist friends, and to tell them that being angry and wanting to destroy the men's world – either overtly, by behaving defiantly, or covertly, by taking over men's roles so that the men have to share power – didn't solve any ultimate problems. For as long as they were either still angry or subject to the norms of patriarchal society, nothing fundamental would have changed. But they were too angry to listen to me.

There was a real problem to be addressed, though. What should women do with their vaginas? And how could they have what they wanted without grabbing it, and without hurting it? These were big questions for me. Yet I felt that it wasn't just I who was affected by them; the answers could hold the key to a new era in human harmony. Psychoanalytic understanding had something to say about society at large, as well.

WHAT IS AGGRESSION ANYWAY?

Suffice it to say that at this time I was extremely preoccupied in the unconscious world with separating my desire to be and to have from the rage which I knew I was going to feel if people didn't want me or value me – and then in turn, with separating the rage from the consequent desire to massacre those neglecting me. I didn't expect to succeed in doing this without more sessions on your couch .. but actually, I surprised myself with how I was already able to control at least the external manifestations of my anger. This in itself made me feel that I could do things. But I continued to feel anxious about the monster which I still feared was lurking in the back of my psyche, waiting to take me over. The issue felt like a truly existential one: did I exist or not? If, for example, I decided to be a scholar and to have ideas of my own, did that mean that I was killing everyone else? Or would they be killing me if they didn't agree with me, or wanted to criticise my ideas? I didn't know; all I knew was that I didn't want to get involved in all this killing. So my thoughts became paralysed.

Then a very strange thing happened to me. Some friends had just had a baby, and we went round to visit them. While we were there, she took my thumb and started to suck it. It was a most pleasurable experience .. but every time it got really nice, I found that I had to close my eyes. That seemed most odd. I talked to you about it all.

"Mmm," you said. "The rejection you felt as a baby was real; with a monster mother and a timid father, your exuberance was perpetually nipped in the bud. That is why you HAVE to have; because you feel every second of needing as another total rejection."

I could see that; but what I didn't understand was the feeling of not existing. I felt an anxiety in my whole genital/abdominal region, as if something (me) would fall out, leaving a gap, if I were to stand up to be looked at. It wasn't just having; it was being.

"What is it in front of your eyes when you have to close them?" you asked. But I didn't know.

So you let me lie down.

"Go back to last night," you said, "when the baby's mouth was round your finger. Now look in the blank and tell me what you see there."

I could see my clitoris, elongated into a hard, bird-of-prey, hooked beak. It was awful! I had been very worried when you had told me that my clitoris would have to get longer before my eyes could get longer and I would be able to see .. and now I saw why .. But as I carried on looking, I saw that there was a lovely sucking mouth under the beak — yet because the beak was in the way, nothing could get into it. I *could* use the beak to chop things up .. yet

I didn't want chopped-up things in my mouth. And although I was frustrated at having nothing in my mouth, I was filled with a feeling of enormous pride in myself for resisting the temptation to chop up in order to have.

"See yourself with a beak-face," you told me.

It was dreadful! I could feel my upper lip drawing back and my teeth growing, and my finger-nails tingling and my toes and toenails growing to be 6 feet long and charged with energy .. and I felt a sharpness in my clitoris. And yet, underneath the horror, there was a kind of pleasure – but a pleasure that I felt I had at all costs to hide because I was ashamed and guilty about it.

"Make the face of the pleasure and show it to me," you suggested.

I couldn't. I had visions of it shattering your face to smithereens as you looked at it; then I saw a picture of your face in the same expression .. but this time it wasn't an expression of aggression, but of horror! I felt like a Gorgon. I believed that I would burst if I broke through my defences and showed it – and that was no less terrifying than the idea that harm would come to you. It seemed to me that if I showed it, it would become real, and that I'd then be stuck that way for ever. My muscles were all tight and tingling with fear .. but also with suppressed pleasure. I *wanted* to do it. But I couldn't.

You showed me the face – what it looked like – and I felt the pleasure at last. There was such a sense of relief that you were doing it, but that it didn't make you entirely like that; it was only one part of you. And once I had seen that, my mind filled with memories. I remembered putting my fingers in my mouth as a baby, in a kind of oral masturbation, but instead, chewing them and doing to them all the things I wanted to do to mummy. But my fingers were better than her, because they stayed with me afterwards, for when I wanted to feel comforted and satisfied; they didn't run away like her. And in any case, I realised, I didn't want to attack for its own sake; all I really wanted was to have the pleasure and the libido otherwise denied me.

Then you put your finger in my mouth – really; not just in a picture – and told me to bite it. With some trepidation, I obeyed you .. and you liked it! You sat and smiled and looked pleased .. and suddenly I felt that I could let out all the pleasure because my aggression wasn't destructive. I always knew that I didn't *mean* to destroy – but I couldn't quite believe it. It was such a wonderful feeling; all the channels to the outside world opened up inside me, and the pulsing energy throbbed through my fingers and legs and eyes. I wanted the pleasure of the chewing and biting for its own sake, because in a certain way I felt it was the most delicious and sharp pleasure – one of the best sorts. I felt not like a bird of prey, but like an elephant, stretching out to get things with my upper lip and transferring them to my mouth.

I remembered you saying once that in lovemaking, the woman has a small orgasm in her clitoris first, and that the attention then moves on to her vagina. But because I'd never felt able to acknowledge the pleasures of my teeth, I'd never let my clitoris have an orgasm, and so everything felt somehow wrong. But now I felt I wanted to acknowledge my clitoris in its own right, and not just as an extension of my vagina.

"That's OK," you said.

And I felt my clitoris suddenly lie down and stop screaming; my genital area felt whole and somehow unhysterical – just normal! That was lovely. I felt complete for the first time in my life. What pleasure I was going to have being an intellectual ...

NOT-SEEING AS FEAR OF DESTROYING

Much to my delight, you wanted to do some work on my eyes the next week. I had noticed all kinds of strange things, like the way I closed my eyes when I was being kissed, or kissing; almost as if I couldn't enjoy the good thing unless my eyes were shut. Then I remembered how difficult I used to find sleeping; I was afraid of shutting my eyes if there wasn't a man around. Having a man sleeping in my bed was the single most effective remedy for insomnia that I knew! But what did I think would happen if he wasn't there?

"Keep your eyes shut, and feel what the eyeballs are doing," you told me, once I was ensconced on your couch.

I could feel my lips pulling sideways, and the sides of my eyes stretched. That pulled the eyeball in a little .. but I still had the feeling that it was, in fact, too BIG for the socket, and that the eyelids couldn't close comfortably. Then I looked some more, and I could see, as it were, a channel going through my eye, from the front to the back. But I could feel a big lump in my throat, and in my vagina, blocking them so that I couldn't swallow .. and then there was a lump of gunge in my eye, just behind the pupil. When I looked at it, it turned out to be made of chewed-up flesh.

"Tell it to dissolve away," you told me.

I was afraid; I felt my teeth set together .. but I did make it dissolve. Then I was puzzled; for there was nothing there! I realised that I had been afraid that the stuff only got stuck because there was something there in the way for it to collect on. My teeth, of course! But there were no teeth. There was a just a kind of sucking, and a wonderful clarity like looking out into the sky at night in a country where there are no buildings and no artificial lights, but just the bigness and throbbing silence, and the shining fullness of the cosmos. It was dark inside my eye – but it wasn't blocked. I could see the stars ..

"Why isn't it light inside my eye?" I asked you, puzzled and a little upset despite myself.

"Just enjoy it and stop worrying," you replied.

I felt as if I could now stand at the back of my head and look; I didn't have to be so far forward in order to get in front of the blockage; so everything didn't have to be squashed any more. I began to feel a channel opening from the back of my eyeball to the back of my brain. And the channel was sucking at the front end – drawing things in rather than rushing out to pursue them and grab them and hurt them. Big lips opened up. Yet the back of my head was somehow atrophied. Although the lips knew how to suck, my brain had forgotten how to take in their messages; the area at the back of my brain felt like a dehydrated leaf, rather than the pulsing repository of pleasure that I felt it ought to be.

"Let it take things in," you told me. "Remember how to do it."

I was afraid it would want too much. But I tried anyway; and it worked! There was a wonderful sucking just behind the lens in my eye, where the blockage had been, and I felt as if I was inviting the world in. Then my eyeball was flooded with bright blue light, and the sun came out, and I felt my cheeks sucking all fat and contented against my teeth. Then I realised that my teeth WOULDN'T HURT ANYTHING; they participated in the sucking. The fear of wanting too much was a disguised fear of destructive chewing. And the back of my head relaxed.

As I sucked, images of mummy's breast kept jumping into my mind. Those awful images kept destroying my pleasure and my equilibrium – and even my knowledge of the good.

"Look at the breast and understand it," you said.

I tried to get the nipple in my mouth .. but every time I got my lips to it, it disappeared, only to reappear somewhere slightly different. It wouldn't come to me in response to my wanting it. Then I felt it, hard and cold as steel, rammed into my mouth, choking me .. and again not relating with me, but engaging in a defiant attack. That was why I had felt choked before, and had pulled back my lips and eyes.

"That's a natural physiological reaction to being choked," you observed.

I felt much better after seeing what was going on, and understanding that it wasn't my fault. It also relieved me enormously to know that I wasn't wrong in feeling attacked. Or had I just projected my aggression onto the breast?

"No," you said. "That's not projection; that's fact."

And everything inside me relaxed.

Then you woke me up, and I felt that all visual sensations had an extra depth to them, as if things were rounder. I also had the impression that my eyes, and my face around my eyes, had settled into a different set of positions: more relaxed. On the way home, I took in huge deep breaths through my nose .. and now that I had been released from the suffocation of having too much hard breast in my mouth, I could breathe more easily. Not to speak of walking with greater freedom. It was very nice.

WHAT HAPPENS IF DADDY IS NERVOUS?

Then I had a row with my father. I had written what I considered to be a very fine and rigorous critique of a document which was being promulgated at work, and I was extremely proud of myself. I showed it to him, and left it for him to read. He rang me up a few days later, and suggested that if I wanted to know how to make things less turgid, I should read the thesis of someone he knew, who had a knack of making academic things seem lighthearted and cheeky. I didn't think fast enough to tell him that I found him insulting and down-putting; I was so eager to remain his friend and be respected by him that I made a few rather feeble defensive remarks about my own document, and then agreed to read the other one. But I was furious! How dared he? Catalogues of events from my childhood flooded my memory; there was the time I brought home a report on which every mark except one was an A. He took one look at it and asked what happened to the other mark. I suppose it was his way of complimenting me .. but I didn't feel it like that. And now he was telling me that my document, which was never intended to be light reading, but which certainly knocked home some pro-found truths, didn't match up to this cheeky thing that some other girl had written.

For days afterwards, I was overwhelmed with the feeling that he'd taken my clitoris away, because he only liked little, cheeky clitorises and didn't like them big and serious. Was he jealous? I didn't know. I only knew that I became totally fatigued and lacking in any kind of energy; everything was just too much effort and I couldn't be bothered to be alive any more. I didn't even want to talk to you about it all, because you were a superego figure as well, and in any case, now I was castrated, there was nothing I had to talk to you about. Oh dear, I was sorry for myself! You told me to think positively about my clitoris .. but every time I tried, all I could remember was how it had been hurt. Then I watched it in my preconscious fantasies, and I saw it get big and fat and I loved it .. but someone came and pricked it with a pin, leaving me helpless, but angry.

"Shall we change it all so that it's nice?" you asked me.

Should we? Please! I lay down and you told me to feel my lips and then breathe warmth from them down my body into my clitoris. I could feel it hurting and aching.

"Look at it," you said.

First of all, I could see me as a little girl, at the same time two years old and five years old. Very curious. I was thinking about showing my clitoris and feeling the excitement. But I kept feeling that I ought to shrink back and cover it with my thigh. Then I saw me lying on my back with my legs apart, showing it and laughing and rolling around. But no one looked at it. It became sharp like a beak, and came out from under its hood and pecked at things to show that it was there. Then I felt ashamed; it wasn't surprising that no one wanted to look when it was so horrid. But I knew it wasn't really horrid; it only became horrid when it wasn't acknowledged.

"What would make it feel better?" you asked. "What shall we do?"

I saw a mouth sucking my clitoris, and I quite liked the look of that. But then I felt that, although it would be nice, it would just be another way of avoiding seeing it properly. I decided that what I'd really like was for it to be nicely acknowledged so that it could really be seen.

"I'll count to five," you said, "and then you'll see yourself at a time when you were happy with your own clitoris and played with it yourself."

I expected that I would see me about a year or two old, sitting up playing with my clitoris with my fingers .. but as you counted, I found myself a TINY baby. My fingers were all soft and relaxed, and I was pleased because that meant that I wouldn't scratch or hurt my clitoris. But then I found that I was so young that I actually didn't have the coordination to get my fingers to my clitoris. It was an amazing feeling, being weeks, or days old, feeling again the sensations of almost being like a tadpole, with my arms and legs not at all the focus of my being. It is one of the sensations experienced at your office that has remained ever-vivid in my memory; it was quite extraordinary!

Suffice it to say that I felt my clitoris as a tongue, which I was sucking with my vagina, like a baby sucks its tongue when it's sucking at the breast. I felt as if my clitoris and my vagina were one, like mind and body .. But as I sucked the tongue, I felt it getting fat and excited, and I worried that it would burst. Then I was afraid. I could see myself peeing in mummy's eye, and felt that it was a kind of ejaculation. But I didn't want an aggressive spurting; I was anxious.

"Feel it do it nicely," you said.

And I watched, and I felt the back of my head and the small of my back, and my genital area, all fill up as my clitoris turned into a little fountain which bubbled the water/libido up so gently that it didn't spurt, but fell gently back into me and filled me. Not only that, but it didn't need to get hard, because it could discharge nicely. Then I watched my clitoris turn inwards instead of outwards, to feed my vagina.

"Is that all right?" I asked you. I desperately wanted your approval – but at the same time, I wanted to be able to assert it myself as true.

You didn't answer me directly, but just smiled.

"Now be an adult woman and feel your clitoris nicely," you told me.

I could see it, like the middle of a flower, sucked-in and held, yet at the same time prominent. And I felt such sucking power and such life and energy in my eyes and my clitoris and my fingers. My legs relaxed; it was wonderful. Yet I kept being worried; this business about my clitoris turning in; I couldn't reconcile it with this new picture.

"What's happening?" I asked you.

You explained what was going on: by seeing my clitoris feeding my vagina and being only a communicator with the vagina, I was saying that my clitoris wasn't important in its own right. But I didn't believe that. I wanted to assert my clitoris and show it off.

So why should I see a picture which showed me the opposite of what I really wanted?

Suddenly, there was daddy. He looked at my clitoris and sneered, saying that that wasn't worth anything. Look – he had a big one. And he dropped his trousers. I saw his penis; it was a nice penis – but he was making it quite clear that I was to have a vagina for him, and not a clitoris to compete with him. But I wanted to have both: and the way I had found to achieve this was to make my clitoris serve my vagina. This picture brought great relief to me, because I knew at last what it was that I disagreed with. I knew that clitorises were nice too, and that men ought to like playing with them and not see them as a threat to be dealt with by subordinating them to the vagina – however important the vagina. And that was a real discovery.

When I woke up, I was puffing and panting, letting breath into all the parts of me that had been closed off with all the shrinking back. I felt as if the world was sparkling with life and magic, and was exciting and wonderful; and as if I could suck it all in and have pleasure. But I mean really suck – powerfully and with desire and determination. And that was lovely.

That session had quite a dramatic and immediate effect on my everyday life. I had so much energy that I didn't remember ever feeling so vivid and active. One day I ran for a bus .. and had the distinct impression that I was actually flying. That was quite something. And I was able to engage fully in activities and life generally; it was altogether remarkable. But then came the headaches. Where were they from? I didn't know. I only knew what memories they brought with them.

8
Putting Myself Together

MULTIPLE MOTHER – FRAGMENTED SELF

When I was a child – and indeed, for long after I stopped being a child – I had the impression that my mother's mind was populated by hordes of people telling her what to do and think, and making her life a thorough misery if she didn't do it right. She would often be talking to me about some matter, and I would feel her attention going to the back of her head, rather than coming out towards me, as she looked for ratification of her self from some external – or should I say internal? – source. I never felt properly looked at; she was only able to look out of the sides of her eyes, so that she gave the impression of being sly, or cunning, and I didn't like it. I had the impression that these people in mummy's brain didn't like her very much and gave her a hard time. But they never told her clearly what it was they wanted. So she was never certain what to do or think or feel even when she cast her eyes backwards for instructions.

This meant that everything in her world was only provisional. She was very proud of me for being so clever .. but if my teachers said I wasn't up to scratch, she didn't support me against them, and say that it must be their fault for being boring; she stopped my comics and made me read tedious books that she liked when she was a child. She was very proud of me for being musical – but when I went to an audition which didn't go terribly well, she accepted the view of the auditioner, and didn't let me learn an instrument to a higher level. I don't think I ever forgave her for that. She may even have liked my father once, but as soon as her friends weren't flocking round her telling her how wonderful he was, she began to hate him. She liked our neighbours .. but couldn't ever admit it because they were 'common' and so it wouldn't do to like them. If we went to parties, she was always looking out of the corner of her eye to see who was listening so that she could perform better if it was someone she was trying to impress. Her own judgements and standards were swept brutally away by those of other people, and she made us judge our affairs by this curious yardstick as well. But to a child, all this meant was that she wasn't looking at me and acknowledging me; she was always busy with someone else.

I remember discovering masturbation. I must have been about five years old, and I have the feeling that I found out about the wonderful pleasure of stroking my clitoris almost by accident. Passing my fingers gently over it until it melted was the most extraordinary pleasure, the like of which I didn't remember ever experiencing before. Unfortunately for me, I was so used to submitting my actions to my mother, so that she could ask her censors whether or not it was acceptable, that I told her about it. One part of me just wanted to share the pleasure with her, and tell her about this wonderful discovery. But the other part of me knew that she wouldn't be happy until she'd asked her internal judges about everything I was doing and got their approval. And I wanted to have *her* approval; that would add to the pleasure. I didn't know how just to do things myself and like them; they had to be ratified first. So I explained it all to her.

She was furious! I couldn't believe it – but she took me to the doctor's and asked her whether or not it was healthy for a little girl to do this kind of thing. The doctor laughed and said that of course it was. But the laugh was enough for mummy; it meant that the doctor really despised her and was contemptuous of what I was doing. She was lowered in the eyes of the community because she had a daughter who did these terrible things .. and so it went on. I don't know how much of this was actually said and how much was unspoken .. but it certainly spoiled the pleasure. Instead of stroking, I could only squeeze; and instead of melting, my clitoris began to twitch convulsively. It was one of the real tragedies of my infancy.

And now, as an adult, I began to think about it all again. I had been afraid that I was destroying my clitoris when I stroked it; what other reason could there have been why my mother was so angry? But as I considered it anew, I began to wonder whether stroking and squeezing started out life as a desire to hold things together; after all, my mother didn't appear to me as a whole .. and I wanted to make her into a whole, instead of a collection of parts. Wasn't that nice? But was it, in fact, what I was doing? I asked you what you thought.

"Yes," you said. "You're an integrative sort of person, and have become hysterical that things aren't unified and that you can't unify them."

ANAL INTEGRATION

It also cleared the way for new thoughts. I began to realise that one of the problems I had with studying and reading was that I was not always happy when things were just presented objectively, as 'facts'; I could only understand them within a clearly defined context. *Then* I knew how to interpret things and evaluate them – but I had the most terrible difficulty with them if I had to provide the framework myself. It was as if I had no inner resources to turn to, which might help me interpret reality. It had been a terrible problem while I was a student; I had been all but unable to make sense of scholarly articles and books if I didn't already have an idea of what they were talking about. And if I could see what they were driving at, but disagreed with their framework of reference, then all hell broke loose in my brain. I really didn't know how to cope, because I didn't want to accept what they said, but I couldn't explain why it was that they were wrong. And it didn't seem right to reject someone's argument without being able to say why, and put something better in its place.

One part of me was always rather proud of this ability – or lack of ability! I felt that somewhere in the back of my mind I understood how things worked, and that this was the part of me that led me to reject the bad arguments. Yet not being able to formulate why made me believe that I was terribly open-minded. How we deceive ourselves! But even though I was proud of it, I had to accept that it was annoying and inconvenient, and that it left me at the mercy of theories which I instinctively found repellent.

Now, though, I found myself impatient with this characteristic of my personality. I wanted really to know, and really to be able to evaluate things in a context which I gave them, without having to be dependent on a ready-made, predigested framework of reference. I also wanted to be able to become more confident to believe in my own theories; I sometimes despaired of myself, believing that I would always be the kind of woolly-minded person who believed the last thing that was said to them, even if it contradicted the penultimate thing, which had in turn been accepted as true. Not much room for self-respect there!

We discussed all this at some length, but I felt that we weren't really getting anywhere; my brain obviously wasn't quite ready to understand it. But one day, between sessions, I was walking along the street minding my own business, when a picture just dropped into my mind. There I was, a little girl, with a huge pile of mud in front of me, with which I was playing, putting it in my mouth and feeling its texture and taste with my tongue and my front teeth. I didn't need to be very well schooled in Freudian theory to know what a pile of mud represented .. and, indeed, it turned out to be just the case.

You considered that it was ready to be seen, and you let me lie on your couch to investigate it.

"Go back to the pile of mud and see what you're doing," you suggested.

I was quite surprised to see that I was eating it .. and feeling the texture all round my mouth and palate – not just on my front teeth. I felt my mouth getting bigger and fuller and more sensitive – round rather than tunnel-like. And I could see that if I sang, the sound would resound better in that wonderful round chamber. It was nice. Yet I could also see myself putting mud in my vagina and tasting it there too. As a child, I had been fascinated by putting things in any available orifices .. but mummy had been shocked, horrified and disgusted by this habit .. and I grew up with a disproportionate fear of germs as a result.

"What is the mud symbolic of?" you asked. "See that."

I looked, and I saw a nappy with faeces on it. I was very young

– a baby – and the faeces were yellow and sticky. They had eager, alert eyes and mouths and fingers and were happy and inviting me to play with them. I was happy because I'd made something so nice. But I could see mummy out of the corner of my eye – or, rather, I couldn't see her because she wouldn't look at the nappy and wanted just to wrap it up and throw it away. And so it died. And so did I. It went all hard and lifeless and developed a crust on it, and couldn't play and respond any more. I was sad.

"Be old enough to go on the pot," you told me. "How do you feel?"

Well, there was a battle royal going on! One part of me wanted to do this wonderful thing .. and the other part of me was determined to hang on to it. I was very puzzled, because I really wanted both.

"Be the half that wants to do it," you told me.

I filled the potty absolutely to overflowing! It was all vigorous and luscious and strong and voluptuous. Instead of having just eyes and mouth and fingers, it had the strength of arms and legs too, and the fingers and eyes and mouth were of a more normal proportion. I wanted to play with it, and it was happy and alive and could relate fully. But as I thought about playing with it and making things with it, I got a pain in my clitoris and an anxiety in my fingers. I could see mummy's fingers coming to pick it up and throw it disgustedly away .. and it all shrank away and shrivelled up to be small and bumpy and hard – just one small twig, rather than a big smooth but solid mass.

"Don't mind your mother," you told me. "Just see what you want to make with it."

And .. I made myself a friend! I was so pleased!

"Feel your hands and the pleasure of making," you said.

But I could still only feel the anxiety. Then I saw mummy, smiling with sadistic pleasure, licking her teeth, claws at the ready, eyes shining .. and I felt that she was pretending that everything was nice when in fact it was dreadful. So anything I made with my fingers would also be pretend, but really horrid and sadistic.

"The problem with your mother," you observed, "is that since she really gets pleasure out of being sadistic, her happiness is extremely confusing, and if you go along with it, you feel that you go along with the sadism as well. There is a certain attractiveness to her pleasure, but it conceals a disgust. Why don't you go back to your friend?"

I was so anxious; I was afraid that mummy would smile with her false teeth and fingernails and would seduce my friend and steal him/her – I wasn't sure about the sex. She had always seduced my friends and taken them over and stolen them from me, and I hated her for it, because then they weren't my friends any more .. and I couldn't forgive her this time for stealing what was mine, sucking the blood out of it and then either discarding it or being discarded by it. And now it would be particularly tragic, because I had the best friend ever. I cried and cried; I couldn't bear it.

But, through my tears, I suddenly became aware that this friend wasn't going to let himself be seduced. He was going to stay with me. And we put our arms round each other's shoulders, turned our backs on her, and walked away into our own lovely world. She, meanwhile, deprived of blood, collapsed into a lifeless heap of nails and teeth and bones and hair – dead, gasping. She lay under a black cloud .. as we walked off into the sunshine.

Yet I was still anxious. For a start, had I killed her? After all, I was responsible for her death. But it wasn't my fault if she couldn't survive without blood; if she had known how to share things nicely, we could all have been happy together. So it was *her* fault. Yet even so, I still felt sad. I felt that my friend and my happiness weren't real; that they were just a game to fill the void left by mummy.

"That feeling is because you've regressed again," you commented, "and to protect yourself and your friend, you've taken him back inside yourself again. He's not real because he's not in the outside world. Now, loosen your bottom and your legs and let out lots of friends!"

I was worried; was I really strong enough to do that? You assured me that I was .. so I let out a lovely little friend, and picked him up and kissed him. I looked at him, and found myself thinking that I could even manage a bigger one than that, and it would still be all right. And that thought filled me with such a lovely feeling of pleasure and happiness. We would all be friends, and all play with each other, and be happy ever afterwards!

PEEING AND TIME

Not only was my mother preoccupied when I was a child, but her reactions to me were never constant and so never predictable. I suppose it must have been partly because she had so many people in her head that she was listening to; sometimes she was one person, sometimes she was another .. and sometimes she was so busy paying attention to them that she didn't have a real presence of her own in the outside world at all. However it was, I felt that because she was at the beck and call of lots of different people, what was true today wouldn't be true tomorrow. And that meant there was no continuity in time for me; time was just a series of disconnected episodes. If my mother was cross with me today, it wasn't just a temporary state caused by something I was doing; she really hated and disowned me. That was, for her – and hence for me – eternal as of the present. Tomorrow maybe she'd like me again. And that, too, would be eternal. But there was no continuity between states; my mother took her identity exclusively from the outside world (including that part of it immortalised inside her head), and had no constant persona of her own. No wonder I had problems!

I remember telling you about all this .. and suddenly you had to go for a pee. You came back saying that it all had to do with me, and that you were picking it up from me. I remembered mummy's disgust – eternal disgust – and we discussed it for a while. We didn't do any 'work' that week .. but I certainly had enough food for thought. There was a terrible conflict inside me about peeing. As a child, it was impossible to take me anywhere, because I would need a pee at such regular intervals. Cinema visits, or long journeys, were a nightmare for me. I was 4 or 5 years old before I stopped wetting the bed at night. And even as an adult, I never liked to be more than an hour away from a lavatory, as I was certain to need to use it. I think I must have used every public lavatory in the West End in my time! And as for getting up in the night for a pee .. 6 times was not uncommon. But I didn't know how to be any different, and even though I could see that not everyone was like me, it still didn't occur to me that there might be anything wrong. It was most peculiar.

You soon said we could have a look at it under hypnosis.

"Look in the mirror," you told me. "See your unconscious urethral sensations."

I could see ME, but as soon as I tried to persuade myself to step in front of the mirror, I rebelled; I curled up and crouched over onto the ground, desperate not to be seen.

"Maybe it's not so much that you don't want to show as that you don't want to do it for someone else," you suggested.

That seemed awfully likely ... ! Anyway, eventually, I did persuade myself to look.

I could see my clitoris and its hood enormously enlarged; the hood looked almost like a beak, and the clitoris itself like a little tongue in the middle. The outer edge felt like lips – but lips which could be hard and beak-like; and the clitoris was drawn back as if ready to peck. And yet I was terribly pleased with it when I saw it; I felt as if I could mount the bird and fly. But at the same time it didn't feel quite right. And I thought I peed through my clitoris.

"Go back in time and see what it was that happened," you suggested.

First I felt myself peeing; I made the sea, on which I floated away, to the accompaniment of the most wonderful sensations of pleasure and potency. That was wonderful! Then I felt my vagina sucking.

"Feel your mouth and feel the flowing from your mouth right through into your urethra," you said.

I could feel the sensation you described at both ends, as it were – in my mouth and in my urethra. It was particularly nice in my urethra. But it was blocked up in the middle. Although I wanted to pee and just let it out – because that would be nice – I couldn't, because it was blocked. I felt it in my bladder blocked. And my clitoris hurt. *Did* I pee through it?

Then I felt mummy's breast in my mouth. It was hard .. and it was in at the wrong angle; the nipple was pressing into my palate rather than letting the milk whoosh down my throat. And because it was at the wrong angle, there was a kink in the supply .. and so there was a block in my letting it out. Because the milk should have gone in straight, but was actually being pushed in upwards, so instead of peeing straight out, I was trying to pee upwards! That's why the sensations ended up in my clitoris when they should have been in my urethra. This seemed quite amazing to me even at the time .. and looking back on the session later, I found myself marvelling at the things that can go on without our being aware of them! All kinds of curious things followed from this; I had often felt when I sang that my voice didn't come straight out, but was pushed out through my eyes – too high. And this now made sense ... Extraordinary!

I had to go and have a pee at that point in the session, hypnotised or not, because such a great pressure had built up with all the attention that I couldn't think any more. When I got back, I felt my bladder inflamed, as if it was being scratched away from the inside; as if there were bits of mummy's chewed-up breast in there which wouldn't come out smoothly, but would squirt and spray out in bloody lumps. No wonder I was anxious about peeing!

"Think about your vagina now," you said, "and your clitoris, as you think about sucking the breast."

I felt my shoulders draw back in disgust, and they made a face of disgust. Then I looked .. and it was the same face as my mouth made when it tried to suck the upturned breast. I felt as if I had to scrape it open with my top teeth, and suck with my top lip, and get the milk out in little squirts. Then I became really angry: I saw myself tearing the breast apart and licking the blood which now flowed naturally and freely.

"After your mother stopped feeding you, you would have peed out of a sense of isolation," you told me. "You would have wanted to make things wet instead of dry. But now I think your conflict is whether you are like her or not. The question is: do you pull back like her, and pee in jerks like her and her milk, or not? You would always have wanted to pee nicely, as a whole, but would naturally always have been afraid that it might be like her."

"Now," you went on, "imagine a happy breast."

It was difficult and slow .. but suddenly, the picture came! I was overwhelmed with joy, because I hadn't known about it before. It filled my mouth, and the nipple was soft. And as I sucked, the end of the nipple dilated slightly to let the milk out, instead of pulling back into a hard ball. And that was wonderful. Then I felt my bottom lip pressing the breast .. and the milk flowed out in response. With mummy, the relationship between my bottom lip and her breast had never been established. Yet the pressure of the bottom lip on the underside of the breast was a persuasion, a coaxing, while the relationship that my top lip and gums had had with the upper side of the breast had only been able to be a forcing. So this new relationship was a wonderful change; the world filled with new possibilities and freedoms. And as I contemplated it, I felt the light in my soul change from a steely-blue to a cornfield-yellow .. and that was truly satisfying and contenting.

I wanted to have all this; for it to be a part of me. It was, after all, *my* breast; I'd seen it, I'd made it .. so it was me, and mine.

"Of course you can have it," you told me. "And it will develop more."

I felt that even though it still needed development, with which, I hoped, you would help, it was nonetheless mine and not yours. And that was lovely.

You often talked about the urethral libido being connected with music. It seemed to me, therefore, to be more than coincidence that I so often wanted to talk about singing when we were looking at my urethra. This time, while I was lying down, I was preoccupied by a different aspect of music: I had the impression that I understood the difference between Mozart and Beethoven; Mozart was a tinkling stream, while Beethoven was a big river. I had only ever understood Mozart – the music of the excited natural child. But I became intensely excited as an adult at the idea which suddenly occurred to me – that I might now understand Beethoven. And so it happened. I can't pretend that it happened overnight .. but a new seam of musical understanding opened up inside me, and lay there peacefully, waiting for me to be ready to explore it.

9
Acceptance

LIBERATION-PHILOSOPHIES AND ANALITY

I always loved teaching. It was the only thing in my life that I'd ever really wanted to do. I loved the feeling of being with my students, explaining all the wonderful things about the universe to them, and helping them to understand it all, and to let their souls grow and become full and happy. That, it seemed to me, was the ultimate role of an adult; to pass on the wonders of our civilisation to the next generation. The trouble was that it wasn't as easy as that.

At the time when I started teaching, the progressive education movement held sway. Much of what was propagated didn't affect me directly, as my students were no longer children – but the principles and tenets which were being upheld elsewhere in the educational world could not help but have a knock-on effect throughout its realm. After all, even in teaching adults, one is passing on a valued body of knowledge. But if I was to believe the gurus in the education department, teaching was altogether an authoritarian activity. It stifled the exploring and intuitive capacities of the child, and passed on the values and expectations of a corrupt society. After all, any society which was based on capitalism, bourgeois values, exploitation of underclasses and the rule of the few over the many, must be corrupt. The corruptness, they asserted, seeped through in the very way society organised its teaching: the single, all-powerful teacher passing on closed and non-negotiable 'truths'. Where was the child in all this? they asked.

I was very shocked by this. I felt like Molière's character who is amazed when he finds he's been reading prose all his life and never knew he knew anything about it. Was I deluding myself that I wanted to pass on pleasure and fulfilment and happiness to my students? Was I really just an agent of an authoritarian society? Did I not care about the desires and aspirations of my students, but was I trying to impose my own world-picture on them? Such an idea had quite literally never occurred to me.

"Of course it hasn't," my interlocutors would reply. "That's because you are so brainwashed and indoctrinated with the propaganda of a corrupt and exploiting society that you can't even see it. It just shows how serious the problem is."

When I thought about it, I could see that there was a point in what they were saying. It *was* true that we had a Euro-centric view of things, and that Europeans had done some pretty terrible things over the years, like enslaving other peoples and using them for their own ends. But, it seemed to me, Europeans had done some wonderful things too; they had invented monotheism, Western philosophy, the idea of the individual, personal freedom, democracy, music, art, literature. Could all this be valueless just because the society had also warlike, paranoid, authoritarian tendencies? I couldn't accept this. It must, I felt, be possible to accept the good, reject the bad, and encourage future generations to make saner judgements about the right course of action.

My students were old enough to be making informed and reasoned choices about their futures and their aspirations for society and their role in it. But even they still needed guidance and the support of adults. So the educational theories which held that the only right way ahead was to allow *children* in schools to be the only arbiters of good or bad seemed to me to be thoroughly regressive – a move backwards to a mythical golden age when we were all children and mummy loved us whatever we did .. and so, freed from the shackles of an authoritarian daddy, we would naturally and instinctively make the right choices.

This vision seemed wrong to me for two reason, which were really the same reason seen from two different viewpoints. The first was that the society in which we lived had been made by the people who had made it, and now had problems and issues to face which weren't just going to go away if we ignored them and pretended they'd never happened and weren't there really. If we lived in a world in which other people were paranoid and might attack us, then it seemed just foolish to pretend that they were nice really, and all we had to do was to stop threatening them ourselves. Sure, *we* could endeavour to become less paranoid, so that we knew that our assessment of a situation was more likely to be unbiased .. but that brought me on to my second point. I knew from my experiences with you, that many of the natural drives we have are repressed and perverted in the earliest infancy. It was, therefore, all very well letting children have more freedom .. but we shouldn't delude ourselves that they were going to be any more likely to make natural and innocent and forward-looking decisions than anyone else brought up in our society. The way to help them make better decisions was precisely to teach them, to help them see both the goodness and the contradictions in their ways of seeing things .. and that was not an authoritarian thing to do – far from it. Getting it right would not be easy .. but not to try was just immoral!

When I was at home, sitting in peace, I could hold on to these images and ideas .. but I had some hard times at work, wondering whether I was just a brutal reactionary, thinking that it was a good thing for children to jump through meaningless hoops of learning, just because society told them it would be good for them. My colleagues in the education department were teaching their students to be so child-centred that I often wondered what the point was in having teachers in the classroom at all.

It did occur to me that this might just be another example of totalitarian double-think; teachers tell the child that it can do whatever it likes .. but then make sure that the only things available to do are sanctioned by them .. so it ends up learning what they wanted it to anyway! This seemed to me like an outrageous con-trick which was likely only to confuse the children further.

Suffice it to say that I absorbed much of the confusion and ended up in a frenzy of self-doubt about my own role; was what I wanted to teach my students nice or not? And did I allow them enough freedom to exercise their own minds on what I taught them, and to expand their souls .. or did I repress them and stop them doing what they wanted?

As I was in the middle of all this agonising, I had a dream which explained to me what was going on in my unconscious mind. It was all about needing to defaecate but not knowing whether it was allowed and whether people would like it. I talked to you about it, and we remembered mummy's disgust .. and then her throwing the contents of my potty down the drain. I was so upset. You didn't want to hypnotise me that week – I didn't know whether it was because I'd solved the problem so you didn't need to, or because you thought my conscious mind needed to get to grips with it better on its own .. but we had a very interesting conversation about it all, nonetheless. You asked me what I wanted. And what I wanted was for other people – not just me – to make friends with my faeces. I wanted them to be nice in the outside world as well as in the inside world of being with you.

You told me to imagine us playing mud pies. And even though I was fully conscious, I found that I could see us on the beach, building the most wonderful mud pies. It was good fun, except that I could suddenly see mummy there, spoiling it all with her presence.

"You know," you said, "she thinks we're dirty. But she'd like to like it if only enough people were to persuade her that it's nice. How do you think we can get other people to like it?"

I thought for a moment; these were quite new ideas for me. Imagine people liking it! But then I realised that it wasn't quite such a new idea as I had thought. – that I actually thought that other people already liked it, and that the only thing we needed to do was to help them overcome their fear. I was really surprised to find myself thinking this .. it told me how far I had come with you. I wanted us to have pleasure, so that they could have pleasure. You suggested that I should imagine you and me building a huge mud pie.

"What shall we do with it?" you asked.

I thought that we should call everyone to have a look.

"We don't *need* to do that, you know," you said. "We could just let the tide carry it away. But we will this time."

And everyone flocked to see it, and they were all happy.

"Some people won't like it," you warned me. "What shall we do with them?"

I didn't know. One part of me felt the most immense desire to take a spade and flatten the mud pie; another part of me wanted to use the spade to flatten the people who weren't going to like it. But I didn't really think that either of these was the right course of action.

You agreed; you said that I had a reflex to pull back or try to undo what I'd done as soon as anyone didn't immediately respond, and you thought it was time I tried to conquer this.

"Why don't we persuade the people that it's a lovely mud pie, beautifully made and by a clever girl?" you suggested.

God, I was embarrassed! I could see myself looking around me not knowing what to do with myself. I didn't believe in the power of persuasion, deep down, because mummy couldn't be persuaded .. or even if you could persuade her, she'd have changed her mind in two minutes. But you said it was important to stand by it:

"If people's criticism is sensible, then you can learn something; if it's not, then you can still persuade them."

Well, I really had never thought of that! I was so happy that this possibility existed; the smiling part of me began to believe that it would all be all right. I could stand by my mud pie and not have to destroy it; OK, it would be difficult to do .. but I'd never before even realised that it was possible. That was a wonderful liberation.

DOING IT ACCEPTABLY

One morning, as I stood on the station platform waiting to go in to college, I felt quite broken up. This happened to me often, and caused me the greatest depression; the feeling didn't usually last once I arrived at work, but it filled me with the most enormous terror as I anticipated my arrival in the building. On this particular morning, I looked around the platform at the people there – especially those students on their way to the college at which I worked – and I was filled by such a profound hatred for them that I thought I'd kill them. This both shocked and upset me, and I wanted only to go home and go back to bed for the day. I didn't, of course, but the desire was there. But why? I had no idea.

I talked to you about it, and this time you let me lie down to look at it in more detail. You told me to see a crystal ball; then you made it move a long way away, and then right back near me again. As it receded, I hoped that it was going right away for ever .. and as it came back, I felt myself becoming more and more anxious.

"Look in it," you told me, "and see what it is that makes you feel trapped."

I saw myself in my cot, standing holding the bars, wearing striped dungarees and a huge nappy. I thought I was just about a year old, as I couldn't stand confidently without support .. but there was something that made me feel that maybe I was somewhat older. Either way, I was bashing my head against the wall of the cot until it moved across the room, trying desperately to reach oblivion. That was an interesting picture, because even as an adult, I had a tendency to knock my head against the wall when I became upset, in a desire to knock myself out and dull the pain of existence.

"Why should you want to do that?" you asked.

I went back to the baby picture, and looked at her mouth. It was nice, with a big pink tongue. Then I felt mummy's breast running away, and I didn't feel my mouth nice any more. And then I didn't want to eat, because I would fill my nappy and mummy would be cross and I'd feel disgusting. Yet I couldn't not eat, and I couldn't not pee and defaecate; it just wasn't possible .. so I was trapped, and the only thing I could do to get rid of the problem and the pain was to obliterate myself.

"What is it in your head that you are trying to knock out?" you asked.

I could only think of faeces. That seemed ridiculous – and yet I could feel my brains, and they seemed to have the same texture as faeces, and I certainly felt that the pleasure of making thoughts and making things were the same pleasure. That cast quite a light on my extraordinary reactions of hot sweating whenever I expressed a controversial opinion! The taboos were the same, because the libidos were related. Amazing.

"I think that you made a mental representation of the pleasure and the creation when the physical representation wasn't liked," you commented. "But then you still had difficulty in showing it."

My mind filled with images: I had tried so hard; I had shouted and sung, and called mummy's attention to what I made – but she had overruled my games for her 'better' ones, and contradicted my opinions on the most precious subjects .. and I was sad. I didn't even want her to touch me in case she squashed the faeces in my nappy up my back and then thought I was disgusting. There was nothing.

"What is it about the people's faces on the station platform that you found so upsetting and which jumped so violently at you?" you asked.

 ˙I could see only their teeth .. then I saw mummy's teeth, gritted and bared in pain-pleasure. I returned to the baby picture and saw her shaking me and baring her teeth in disgust .. but it was libidinised disgust, as if she liked the very horridness of it all. I hated it! I tried to show her what a nice pleasure-look was like; I used my eyes to express my pleasure and my appeal for her to like it. My eyes shone .. but they were ignored.

"Why don't we see the scene of grief in slow motion?" you suggested. "Stand in your cot and do what you want to do."

I saw myself standing there and doing two big plonks in my nappy. And then I realised that I liked it – that the scene *didn't* have to roll on to the horror. Yet .. what should I do with it instead of the horror? Could I act upon it, do things with it?

"I'll come in and just watch you," you said.

On rolled the picture .. but this time you were there. I stood in my cot, my eyes gleaming with pleasure, and did it while you watched. And you didn't *do* anything; you were just pleased. I was so thrilled. I felt all my body warm, and I made lots of noise and jumped up and down.

But I was still nervous. We talked about it for a while .. and suddenly, I realised that if I allowed myself to really believe that you loved me, I would be so excited that I'd lose control and smother you. I saw myself letting the cot side down, and quite literally flying across the room to envelop your face with my body. But surely that would be too much? I waited for you to blench and move back. But you didn't; you smiled and waited to meet me! You *liked* it!

I was SO happy; I didn't have to do anything with the faeces just now; I could just wait until I was ready, and in the meantime I could enjoy the pleasure of having made them and having them acceptable. And my unbridled passion acceptable too ...

"I'm going to wake you up now," you told me. "And your eyes will feel nice."

And they did; they felt beautiful and they smiled .. and I felt a deep but quiet sense of pleasure and relaxation through my whole body. Very nice .. a kind of quiet confidence.

BEING ACCEPTED

I was still worried, though, about the disproportionate effect that my mother seemed to have on my life, even though I rarely saw her and didn't live with her any more. I could always hear her voice in the back of my head .. and on the rare occasions when I did speak to her, she was always either frightened by what I was doing – was I defying authority too much? – or trying to take it over and make it hers. It was as if she and I competed for her attention, and I always lost .. then in the end I felt that I had no right to exist, but should surrender everything to her – or else should be Prime Minister (at the very least) so that she could share in my really big penis.

"How can one cope with a monomaniac, megalomaniac mother?" you asked.

It was always a relief to me when you asked such questions, because you took the issue onto another level. There I was worrying about whether I was right, or she was right, or who was right .. and you just cut through it all by showing me that there was another way of seeing it. Not that I was able to think of a sensible answer! In fact, I couldn't think at all. I just sat in my chair and cried and cried in fear.

"Let's have a look at what's going on here," you said. "Would you like to lie down?"

So I lay down and you asked me to feel how mummy held my bottom when I was a baby; how her hands felt under me. But I had no memories of any such feelings; in fact, all I could see was her try-ing to *avoid* my bottom. She held her arm under my thighs so that my bottom hung over it .. or she held me by my body. Very occa-sionally she would touch my buttocks – but only touch, not hold.

Then, quite suddenly, she went into a total frenzy. Her teeth clenched and she spat out the words through them. She was thrusting her finger hard and repeatedly up my anus, saying,

"You dirty girl, I'll kill it, this is what you deserve!" and scratching it and tearing it.

Even as I experienced this violation, I was quite sure that mummy had never actually done that .. but the feelings were there; she had *wanted* to do it. And there was a sexual element in it – a sadistic pleasure. But then she felt guilty and went to wash her dirty hand – but only because she was guilty. Yet she looked disgusted. I could see her looking at my vagina in the same way, desiring to violate it and tear it. I felt *such* a shock .. and yet, at the same time, it was such a relief just to have seen it clearly at last, and to have expressed it. It was almost like a thought which had become con-stipated, held in, and that I'd not talked to anyone about .. so the recoiling fear and horror remained with me without my being fully aware of what was causing it. I tried to say,

"Hey, mummy, why are you doing that?"

But her eyes wobbled away from mine, evading contact, and she was gone before I had a chance.

You intervened at this point.

"I'd like you to imagine *my* hand holding you," you told me.

I could feel the palm all receptive and soft, so that my bottom and vagina wanted to relax into it. Then I found that I could feel my bottom all soft and round and contented. Then I saw my vagina kiss-ing your hand and wanting to take it in, sucking at it and exploring it, asking it to come and visit me. And it was lovely. I wasn't just a producing machine, but also a receiving organism. And now that I didn't have to protect myself against violation, I could stop using my teeth as a portcullis, and then having to fear that they'd be broken, or that they'd be vicious .. or whatever. I could just relax and be relieved and exist. More than that – I could have a right to exist!

RESOLVING THE MASOCHISTIC SYNDROME

I still didn't understand, though, why my mother sacrificed herself all the time; only it was worse than that, really, since she caused other people the pain in the first place, and then took it on herself .. and then made them feel guilty for the pain they were causing *her*!

"Your mother's mind rejects logic, and the categories of space and time," you told me. "You find that confusing, but aren't prepared to capitulate to her."

That certainly made sense of all the curious feelings I'd had over the years that space and time didn't really make sense. By this time in the analysis, I was finding it very much easier to hold on to them and understand things through them .. but she was still able to break through my defences if she really tried. I wanted not to have to have defences, so that there was nothing to break .. but it was difficult. And the other problem was that one part of me wanted a man to sort it all out for me, while another part wanted to be so together that he didn't need to. This put me in the difficult situation of asking the man to do what I didn't really want him to do .. and then being angry with him when he didn't do it. Yet I hated being angry all the time.

"I think you should lie down for a while," you suggested. "Now, think of yourself as nice, and strong."

Easier said than done. I started to shake, and my eyes twitched. I could see the sun out and me standing naked and proud. Then I saw mummy. She was after my clitoris. She wanted to tear it out, bite it off. I put my hand over it to protect it, and ran like hell! Every time I stopped, she was still there; and if I showed her that I still had my clitoris (which I wanted to do to reassure myself) it redoubled her fury to have it, and she chased all the harder! So I covered it again and ran.

I couldn't think, though, why she wanted it. Then I heard her saying it was because I'd had her nipple and bitten it away .. so she wanted her revenge. But I didn't bite her nipple away! I was hopping mad to think that that was what she thought sucking was all about. But then I saw a huge, pale blue swollen breast with an enormous blue-brown nipple .. and she gave it to me in such a way that I *had* to bite it; she actually invited me to bite it .. and now she had the cheek to be angry with me!

My clitoris felt large and important. I wanted to have it in safety, and to be able to show it to her in a way that wasn't defiant – because defiance isn't pleasure.

"Just stand and feel your own self," you told me. "Then I'll come in my straw hat, and you can show it to me if you want to."

I saw myself standing there, still and proud and pleased. And as soon as I wasn't hysterical and running away, mummy couldn't hurt me. She actually couldn't. Her arms wouldn't move towards me, and she hopped up and down in frustration .. but could DO nothing. I was safe. And I could enjoy myself in safety because she was at a distance; it was like seeing her held back by an imaginary fence. I could just smile at her and do my own thing! My clitoris was big, and it was real.

Then I realised that I hadn't made any pictures of showing it to you. That was because I wanted it to be mine; then I would show it to you. I didn't want to exist *because* you'd looked at it.

"That's right," you said. "I'm pleased you've come to that decision; I was only offering to help if you needed it."

It made me very happy that you weren't offended, but were pleased at what I was doing for myself. For today, I wanted to think just about myself .. and it was lovely that you were prepared to let me and not feel left out or neglected.

When I woke up, it was like being a different person. As I walked down the street, I could sway my hips because I could show and like my clitoris. On the way home, I sat in a very crowded train. Opposite me was a little boy who stared into my eyes in the way small children do. And I looked back into his eyes without flinching, and we smiled at each other. I think that was the first time such a thing had ever happened to me.

LEARNING TO SHOW MYSELF NICELY

Soon after this, I became aware of a desire to go shopping and buy myself some sexy clothes. Yet I didn't know how to do this. Why not? I had a clear picture of what I wanted to look like and what kind of clothes would create the right image .. but I was totally inhibited about doing it. Buying clothes had always been a trial for me; I always ended up with plain and ordinary things, because I felt that it was somehow wrong to have nice clothes. It was almost as if there was a moral principle attached: if you don't like me for what I am, why should I deceive you by dressing up in beautiful clothes, pretending to be something I'm not; either I am acceptable in whatever I wear, or it is clear that you don't like me; so the plainer clothes I buy, the more I put to the test my essential acceptability. It never occurred to me until I met you that what I wore might be an expression of how I felt about myself, so that if I wore nice clothes, it showed I liked myself – and that was nice. Yet, I suppose, I must have known that wearing plain clothes said that I was afraid I wasn't nice .. otherwise why would I have been afraid of deceiving people?

I talked to you about all this, and you said that I still thought I was my mother, and that until I distinguished myself from her, I wouldn't think that what I did was nice, and I wouldn't want to buy myself sexy dresses and be seen. I started to cry at this point; although I knew that I was different from mummy, I didn't have any positive concept of what it was that I was; a concept of me without her. It was like an empty set. So what could I do? I wanted to believe it, but I also wanted a positive thing to believe in, rather than a negative thing.

So I lay down, and you told me to see the mirror.

"Step in front of it as just what you want to look like," you encouraged me.

Well ... I cried and cried. I heaved for breath; I felt as if the world was coming to an end. It was terrible. Eventually, though, feeling half dead, I stopped crying and was able to tell you what I'd seen. The problem was that before I could step in front of the mirror, the 'other' me jumped in. Snakes swayed from her pubic hair, and gathered everything up and swallowed it. The nice me was there, but further back from the mirror; she smiled and wanted to be my friend .. but I could only see bits of her at a time because of the snaky one being in the way. And she receded further and further until she stopped smiling and started crying because she felt lonely. Then I felt terrible!

"Look at the snakes," you told me. "You've got to face them."

And .. there were the nice snakes and the not-nice snakes. The nice ones slithered round things and embraced them and held them, but were able to hiss and sting and be assertive if they needed to. I liked them. I liked being assertive. I didn't want to be just passive like the other girl in the mirror. Yet as I told you about this, I saw her come forward and kneel down in front of the snakes and stroke them and be nice to them. And they liked it. Then once she'd done what they wanted, they would do what she wanted, and go purring off to rest and to give her pleasure. They were now her slave, after she'd been theirs. And that was nice. Then she could let go fully and be passive and relaxed .. but she liked and acknowledged the snakes.

"Do penises like the snakes, too?" I asked you.

"Of course," you replied.

"Are all women like me?"

You told me that fundamentally they were, but that some were more passionate and assertive than others. You explained to me that first I needed and wanted to be accepted as a partner and be listened to; then I'd be submissive and accepting. After this, you woke me up. Then you explained things to me some more. You said that snakes were not just phallic symbols, but also the symbols of life, and that under patriarchy, the penis had taken on that role. I found that extremely interesting. And the pleasure of being able to assert myself was quite wonderful; I felt my whole body tingle with it .. it was like a dream come true.

INTEGRATING THE PENIS

We saw the snakes again, quite soon, but in a completely different context. This time, I was angry with you because I wanted you to hypnotise me .. but you wouldn't. I felt foolish and humiliated because I'd shown you what I wanted and you wouldn't listen .. but also because I felt that I wanted to look truly at myself and you wouldn't either let me or look yourself. I felt myself growing hugely large – you told me it was manic compensation – and pleased with myself; this happened to me often, but the largeness was always followed by the most terrible crash as I realised that actually, I wasn't big and important after all, but only little and feeble – far littler and feebler than I really was .. I suppose it must have been a kind of depressive interlude, as in manic-depressive syndromes. Anyway, suffice it to say that I was livid with you. I hated it when you wouldn't put me in touch with myself, because I still felt that the Self I had access to wasn't nice, but only my unconscious knew what was what really. I suppose it would fit with not-seeing; I had hidden my nice self, so it wasn't visible or accessible. But it was no good if even I couldn't get to it.

I talked to you about the anger, and you asked me to tell you all about it. But I couldn't think of anything to tell you!

"You're indulging in a bad habit and paralysing your brain," you told me.

"Well," I retorted, "it's a better habit than exploding with inarticulate rage, which is the alternative."

Yet even I could see that some middle path would be better. Some path where I could be angry properly, but didn't have to explode. Or, even, where I didn't have to get so angry in the first place ..

You let me lie down after all, to see what was going on.

"Look at yourself in the mirror," you told me.

I could see myself crouching down, teeth gnashing and fists clenched, trying desperately to push myself out of my bottom, or to throw myself away. I felt that I was horrid and disgusting .. and yet at the same time, I was in despair because I liked myself and didn't want to have to throw myself away.

"Where are the monsters?" you asked.

I hadn't mentioned any monsters .. but you were right; I could feel them in my genital region, and there was a pain in the muscle behind my pubic hair.

"Stand in front of the mirror again and look," you said.

I saw nothing! Only snakes and tongues laughing at me. I was confused. Did I exist? I tried to tell the snakes I did exist .. but they just sneered from a different direction as I went towards them.

"Let's try again," you suggested. "Look at yourself properly."

This time I saw myself – not a little me, but a me my present age – but in back view. I was trying to get rid of something at the front. Then I realised that it was a penis! I found myself terribly reluctant to tell you about this, in case you said I didn't really have one – because I knew I did. But I told you anyway .. and you said that was very nice! Not only that, but you asked me about it.

"What is it like, and how does it feel?"

It felt like a little flame, all hot and pleasurably excited .. but it was very nervous and that inhibited the pleasure.

Then I thought that if I was allowed to have it, I'd show it to people. It was a big, erect penis .. but when I tried to show it, it fell down like a felled tree. It wasn't like a penis that stops being erect and becomes little and soft; it just keeled over and fell forward. I was very upset. What was the point of having a penis if I couldn't show it to anyone? In any case, I didn't know what to do with it. Feeling it erect made me feel my vagina .. so I knew that I was still a woman .. but if I tried making love with my vagina, my penis would get in the way.

"Men would like you to have both, you know," you told me. "That would excite them."

Suddenly, I started to remember how fascinated I had been by frogs when I was a little girl. It was because their tongues were hinged at the front so that they could jump out and get things. As a child, I had become quite an expert at throwing raisins, sultanas, peanuts – anything small like a fly – into the air and catching them on my tongue like I imagined frogs caught insects. But as I thought about it now, I realised that I didn't want my tongue – or my penis – to be hinged at the front any more; I wanted it to be hinged at the back. The reason the muscle behind my pubic hair hurt was because everything was trying to strain too far forward .. I didn't want to poke forward and fall over any more.

"Relax the muscle," you said. "Then see what happens."

I felt my penis right high up near that muscle .. and then I felt it melt into me. The testicles ended up in the labia majora, and the shaft of the penis down the mons veneris, so that just the end protruded as my clitoris. It hadn't GONE; it had melted into me. So although I didn't have the physical form, I still had all its feelings and all its strength. Yet I didn't need to poke it out at people for it to be seen, because I could feel it.

"What do you look like?" you asked.

I could see myself glowing, as if the sun was behind me .. only it wasn't behind me; it was *in* me. And yet the glow wasn't of light, but of energy. I said to you that I thought this must be libido.

"How clever your unconscious is," you remarked.

God, I was pleased with myself!

Then I felt everything oozing out of me like it oozes out of lovely music. I could see my teeth glowing – not flashing, but glowing – and my cheeks shining red. I felt a shimmering aliveness about my skin. This caused me a momentary anxiety; would it be so receptive that other people would exploit it and clog it up – soot it up? And would I then just have to accept this? I hoped not. Would it be possible to brush away their soot and continue to be alive?

"Of course," you answered. "Indeed, you must do so."

That was wonderful; now that the sun was so strong inside me, I felt my fingers and toes filling out and becoming libidinised; they had been so cold .. and suddenly they were warm.

It wasn't until you tried to wake me up that I realised how deep these pictures were. I felt as if I was coming back to the world from a distance of endless miles .. the roundness ebbed gently and throbbingly back into my body .... and I was contented.

UNITING MYSELF WITH MY REAL VAGINA

Over the years, we worked many times on a profound fear which caused me a great deal of anxiety: did my vagina poke at things or not? One week, I felt as if my vagina was separated from me; as if I was afraid of losing it. It felt almost as if it was in two layers, an inner and an outer vagina, whose two parts were themselves not connected properly either with themselves or with one another. I spent that week keeping myself frantically busy; doing nice concrete things was the only way I could find to hold myself together .. and it did cross my mind to wonder whether some of the people I knew whose diaries were always fully booked for weeks and months ahead were perhaps sufferers from the same syndrome – but without being aware of it. I really had a nice time rushing around keeping busy .. but there was always a nagging thought in the back of my mind that this wasn't how things ought to be; I ought to have been able to produce activity from within myself – my own natural reserves, as it were. I was always rather envious of people who seemed so relaxed within themselves that the atmosphere around them was full yet peaceful, even if they weren't actually doing anything. I felt that I wanted to create something from inside me .. yet I didn't really know who I was. It was most baffling.

I talked with you about it, and you observed that a woman needed a penis; either to have for herself or to have from a man. I could see what you meant, but at that moment, I was more interested in vaginas than penises; I felt that if mine was more confident, it would be less hysterical about wanting a penis, and I would be able to be less hyperactive. So you let me lie down and see what was going on.

"Tell me whatever comes into your head," you said.

I felt as if I had ants crawling in my vagina. Then I felt my lips very thin and pursed .. and my vagina the same. It was as if I was keeping the energy out of it .. and it was having to find other places to go – tingling in my fingers, laying down fat deposits on my bottom and thighs – anywhere but where it ought to go. Then I felt a cushion in my brain which seemed to be the same shape as my vagina .. and I watched myself having lots of wonderful thoughts, yet being unable to deposit them in my brain; they just rushed around and got lost.

That was a good picture; it was just how things were in real life. I would often sit down to read, or to think, or to listen to music .. and a wonderful, brilliant thought would occur to me. I would be so proud of myself, and jump around inside, thinking what a profound genius I was. Then I would think: well, that's all very well, but what now? I quite literally didn't know what to do next. Occasionally, I would write down my profound thought in a book .. but then I didn't know what to do with that either, and it would just sit in a drawer of my desk, rotting. But there would be no connection with the outside world, or with productive activity.

"What does your vagina want to make it feel happy?" you asked.

It wanted a penis! Yet it had to be a nice, soft, alive, giving penis that wanted to be inside me and wanted to give itself to me. I didn't feel that I knew very much about that kind of penis; that I only knew about penises that wanted to enjoy themselves, so that essentially they withdrew from me rather than came towards me; that they related not with me, but with themselves. I wanted a nice penis, so that I could show my desire to suck and it would be loved and appreciated.

"What happens when you suck your mother?" you asked.

I felt her breast go hard, so that the nipple pulled up, away from me. Then I realised that the double vagina which had been bothering me was a false vagina! My fear of losing it was actually a *desire* to lose the one nearer the surface .. and underneath it were teeth in the deeper one. Teeth to try and get the warmth out of mummy. And I was ashamed of them; I didn't want to have them. Perhaps that's why I covered them up with the second layer of vagina. She didn't know, though, how to be soft and just let it flow, so that I wouldn't need to use my teeth; she only knew how to poke herself at me, and I didn't like it.

"You're not united with your real vagina," you observed. "Ask it what it wants."

It was angry with me! It was annoyed because I didn't show it and be proud of it; and its anger was justified. I felt that before I could talk to it any more, I needed to say I was sorry to it. I felt so guilty and so terrible!

"That's all right," you reassured me. "Just say you're sorry and then ask it again what it wants"

It wanted to hang lower. It wanted its tip to protrude further out so that it could be seen.

"Let it do that," you told me.

I felt a muscle relax inside me .. and my vagina fell .. and I realised that I'd been holding it in all these years because I was afraid that letting it fall would be the same as poking it out, like mummy would. And rather than be like her, I'd held it in and not had it even for myself. But in fact, letting it fall wasn't like poking it out. It was relaxed and soft, not tense and hard. And that was lovely.

But we weren't finished yet. My vagina felt emaciated. I had starved it of energy for so long that it was all thin and didn't meet in the middle. I had often been puzzled about why I walked with my legs apart at the top, as if there was a gap, and had noticed that a lot of the people I knew also walked nervously, as if they had a horse between their legs. It always made me feel rather uncomfortable, watching them, as if my vagina was drying up .. and now I understood why. But I now felt that if my vagina was fat, it would be able to feel itself and have contact with itself, and then I'd believe in it even if there wasn't a penis inside it. I'd always felt that it was all very well for penises, because they were solid .. but that all I had was a tense hole.

"OK, then, fill it up," you told me.

My first thought was what a wicked pleasure this was! Then I realised why; mummy would see me .. and she wouldn't be able to bear that; she'd have heart failure. I had been protecting her all these years by hiding myself. But now I thought, "Blow that, stupid old bag," and just let it fill up. It was a curious feeling; I had imagined somehow that letting myself be full would be somehow not nice; I couldn't explain how I meant .. but I felt now that I had been worried about nothing. Being full up wasn't a bit like I had imagined.

It was all very curious. I could feel new thoughts and feelings, and yet I couldn't see them or even think them. It was as if I was creating new concepts out of a primaeval chaos – or at least, a primaeval something – for which I had as yet no words and no pictures. It was wonderfully exciting, because there was a rightness about it all which somehow didn't need words. And gradually, I began to see pictures of a vagina from the outside, so full and fat that it was almost closed .. and yet it wasn't closed; it had the same molten metal, hot, excited, yet heavy and calm feeling about it as the nice penis. It was able to let go without being afraid, because that was its natural self .. and yet it was letting go and not erupting, so it remained calm and melting rather than thrusting and assertive. So I felt the same power as the penis – but without needing to have a penis. It was wonderful.

"Is this real?" I asked you. Can I really show it without it being taken away?"

I was anxious: if I showed it, it would get bigger with the pleasure, and then it would be all the more terrible if it was taken away.

"Yes, it's real," you said. "And it's yours, and it's nice to look at it; and no, it won't be taken away."

I was so happy. I too was potent. The session left me quietly tired, like a happy baby who has had what she wanted and now wants to sleep. But that kind of peaceful sleep was almost new for me; it was a most wonderful discovery ..

10
Banishing the Forces of Darkness

Unfortunately, I was still subject to the occasional 'timeout' from reality. One day, I found myself precipitated again into a formless anxiety-state. The most sensible thing for me to have done would have been to ring you up and reestablish contact with normality .. but such was the anxiety I felt that I actually didn't dare to risk it; I was afraid that if you were busy, and didn't talk to me nicely, I would be even more shattered. So I came to your office and put a note through the front door telling you what a bad way I was in and asking if you would ring me up when you were free, sometime that afternoon. Then I waited. But the phone didn't ring.

At this point, with my last hope gone, I lost all control; I went completely out of my mind with grief and anxiety. Obviously, I thought, I was such a monster that you had had enough of me; you didn't want to talk to me; I was making such demands on you that you couldn't cope; you were showing me that you didn't just jump to attention when people ordered you to .. there wasn't a terrible thought that didn't pass through my mind that afternoon.

I had the most dreadful evening, and barely slept a wink all night, worrying about how I'd alienated you too .. and what a tragedy it was for me that you had allowed yourself to be alienated when you'd encouraged me to trust you .. and so on. It was dreadful. I squeezed myself all night, trying to make myself real, and only feeling wretched afterwards because reality was all a figment of my imagination.

So imagine my surprise the next day when the phone rang .. and it was you! You'd just got my note and you were sorry to hear that I was upset. Was there anything you could do to make me feel better? You could have knocked me down with a feather. It transpired that you hadn't seen the note the day before, but had only just picked it up, and, of course, were ringing to cheer me up, as I had asked if you would. I felt most odd. Why had I not trusted you? Why had I immediately assumed the worst? Why had the idea that you might not have seen the note not even crossed my mind as a possibility? It seemed terribly wrong .. and I decided that I couldn't go on behaving like this; I should discuss it with you as a clinical issue as soon as I had the opportunity.

You let me lie down to look at it properly.

"Squeeze yourself and tell me what you feel," you told me.

I felt that the squeezing started out life as a sucking, and that that was nice .. but that it very quickly turned into a sensation more in the teeth and in the clitoris. It was as if I had said:

"You like me sucking, don't you? Nice, isn't it?" and the answer had been "no". I felt as if I was going to explode through two little points just beneath the inner tips of my eyebrows .. and then my brain detached itself altogether. It couldn't cope! It went into 'cotton-wool' mode.

"Let's look for the experience that set all this off, shall we?" you suggested. "Suck and feel the nipple there. Suck nicely."

So I sucked nicely .. and for just an instant, everything was lovely and the breast was soft and responsive .. then suddenly, it spat me out! That was most curious; on the one hand, it was clearly the sensation I had. On the other hand, how could it spit me out? I thought about this problem for a moment. It seemed that the breast had become erect, almost like a phallic penis .. and in extending and becoming hard, it had left my mouth stranded way away from the position it would have really liked to be in! So I felt spat out, pushed away.

I put the hard breast back into my mouth and tried to get my lips back to their desired position. But then the nipple was so far down my throat that it was practically touching my soft palate, and I felt that I would choke. I pulled my throat back but that was definitely not nice. Eventually, I realised that by sucking my own cheeks, and pulling them in between my jaws, I could preserve the sense of having my mouth full, yet at the same time have the nipple far enough forward in my mouth for it not to choke me. The nipple then landed up just behind my front teeth, and to suck, I squeezed it between my tongue and my teeth.

Well, that was all very well, but now I wasn't relating to mummy any more, but only to myself. And I felt in my teeth, which I was now using to help me get the milk out, that on the one hand, I was terribly clever, but that on the other hand I wanted to destroy this hard nipple which had deprived me of the pleasure of relating with it. And this confusion between cleverness and destructiveness had been one of the bugbears of my life. I suppose that's why I was always so ambivalent about being at university at all, and why I was always prepared to accept from mummy that if I was clever, boys wouldn't love me. If there hadn't been a predisposition in me to believe it, I'd just have dismissed it for the nonsense it is.

But back to the pictures. There was another problem: although I did at least get milk this way, it didn't feel right. For a start, it came in spurts. Because my lips weren't properly positioned just to press in the right place and have it fall out - like out of the neck of a balloon filled with water when you press the pool upwards – and because in any case the breast wasn't relaxed enough to allow that – I had to squeeze at it and get the milk out in little spurts. My teeth and my clitoris hurt.

THEN I realised that not only did the milk go into my mouth through my teeth, but that it also came out of the nipple through its teeth! I was pleased that I was at last succeeding in relating to mummy in terms that she understood and was happy about .. but at the same time I also felt terribly sad and ashamed that I'd had to compromise in this way. Yet when I did it, I hadn't known that I'd get stuck in that position; I thought I was just doing it to relate to her, and had never considered that it might have consequences for my own character. But now I had to pee through the teeth in my own clitoris. That was how I was. Yet I had never wanted to end up like her; I had hoped it would all be all right.

"That's right," you said. "You knew even as a baby that you would solve the problem one day."

I had really known even then that one day I would meet someone like you who would help me to put it right. I said to you that it had been such a difficult moral decision; if I didn't enter her world, then I would have starved to death – and I didn't want to commit suicide.

"Just so," you commented.

We talked about the way I had masturbated, squeezing myself .. and you told me that I had reenacted the whole scenario with myself in that way: that my hands had become my teeth and my clitoris like the nipple. That certainly explained how it was that masturbating always seemed so necessary, and so pleasurable - yet was followed by pain and guilt. And now I wanted not to have to do it any more.

"OK," you said. "Make yourself the nipple your instincts have always wanted. I'll count to five, and then you can feel it in your mouth. It is happy, and you can feel its libido."

I saw it smiling at me and saying it was pleased to see me! I felt that my tongue could relate to it without being bitten by its teeth. It wouldn't spit me out. But I was still afraid it wouldn't like me, and would pull away.

"Tell it you like it and see what happens," you suggested.

What happened was that it came into my mouth! I felt it all soft and big – so big that my mouth couldn't be small and polite and hold in the dribble; it just all fell out down the outside of the breast. Then I found that because the milk came out properly, I didn't have to suck so hard, and I didn't have to suck so often; everything slowed down and there was time and pleasure. And although I could feel the nipple, because the breast lay big and fat on my tongue, it didn't bare its teeth at me in face-to-face combat.

"Feel the nipple with renewed and expanded sensitivity," you told me.

And I suddenly felt it just lying there, calm and happy, giving itself to me and not pulling back. That was quite a revolutionary feeling for me; it was wonderful. Then I felt it all wet and almost covered in liquid jelly – not hard and dry and sandpaperlike, like the old one.

Then I became aware that my eyes were looking back anxiously, worried that mummy was there and was going to upset my relationship with this lovely new breast. And she was .. yet I felt strong enough to bring my eyes forward and declare that I had new friends now. But I still felt that this would kill her. I was afraid to be happy!

"It won't kill her," you said, "although she will be hopping mad. Tell her you've joined the happy ones."

I was afraid that the new breast wouldn't want me any more if I severed my ties with mummy and so gave myself fully and unconditionally. I was afraid that it was my fault that mummy hadn't liked me, so that if I offered my absolute friendship to the new breast, it wouldn't like me either.

"On the contrary," you said. "It will be delighted; that's just what it wants you to do."

As you spoke, I felt myself with a body that rubbed on my new mummy's soft tummy, and she grew a tummy as well as a breast, and then a face .. and it smiled serenely and proudly down at me, and I was happy and quiet. It was the feeling that I had always yearned for, and which I felt I had never before had. It was like coming home.

"The changes in the inner geography of your mouth will be reflected in your vagina," you told me.

I hadn't quite realised until that point how many changes had taken place to make all those new pictures, how my tongue was more relaxed, and my lips bigger, and the whole oral cavity less tense and held-back. It was very nice indeed. But it was a lot to digest, and I felt that my brain wouldn't comprehend all the implications for a little while. But there was such a feeling of relief that I didn't have to kill mummy, and that I could look at her and say that I was different – and then not capitulate, but *stay* different. It was lovely to be able to relax, because I wasn't having to defend myself against imminent attack any more. I felt my whole body softer and more yielding. It was nice.

ORGASM AS REALITY

But I still felt that I didn't know how to have proper orgasms. It wasn't clear quite what I mean by that; it was just a feeling that everything wasn't quite right inside. And I was truly desperate about it. Before I knew about orgasms, I didn't mind if I didn't have one; the undischarged excitement just made me more eagerly expectant for the next love-making session. But once I did know, I was absolutely despairing if it didn't work. I used to look round at people I knew and wonder about their sex lives. Did they have orgasms or not? And if they did, was I less psychologically healthy than they were, or was this just something I wasn't prepared to compromise about, while they were? My whole life became a big obsession with orgasms. I didn't know how to be a real woman. And until I did, I felt that I wasn't worthy to exist.

"Women are vessels," you told me.

I knew that already; what I didn't know was how to be a vessel.

You thought this one was worth investigating under hypnosis. First of all, my brain pulled up a whole gamut of dreadful pictures of mummy and daddy in bed again, and both of them experiencing a vast range of sadistic pleasures together. Then I saw daddy jumping out of mummy in case she bit him. He believed that at orgasm, he lost his penis.

"It sounds to me like you saw your parents practising coitus interruptus," you commented. "Then you interpreted him jumping out at the point of orgasm in what the sadistic circumstances rendered a natural way – that is, that your mother was going to bite him."

That made sense – but I'd never thought of it as a possibility. My mind explored it: I felt mummy excited and nearly having an orgasm, and beginning to lose control .. and him jumping out .. and her biting herself in shock .. and then wanting to bite his penis off for not satisfying her. And I realised something I'd never been conscious of in the outside world – that during lovemaking, I was always waiting for the moment when Eddie would jump out, and that that inhibited my responses .. but by the time I found out that he wasn't going to jump out, it was too late. Then I was angry with myself and felt worthless because he'd had an orgasm and I hadn't. I felt that he had a penis which could do things and give things out, and that I didn't.

But there were surprises afoot for me!

"It's been difficult for you," you said," because even though you knew it wasn't right the way your parents did it, you have no model for the way to do it really. I'd like you to bring up from the depths of your instincts the picture of a nice woman having an orgasm."

Well, I lay on your couch .. and felt totally stupid. It was as if I was going to do something ridiculous.

"It's good that you've noticed that," you said, "but there isn't anything stupid about it."

And I realised that knowing something to be true wasn't the same as fantasising about it in the fear that it might be false. I knew that this was true.

"Lie her down and put her finger in her vagina and let her masturbate," you told me.

I felt all my face and body relax. Then you said,

"Women also ejaculate, you know. Feel the convulsion and feel her ejaculate."

One part of me already knew this .. but another part of me was overwhelmed with joy. I felt the lining of my vagina become firm and thick .. and then it was as if all the pores opened and let a wetness out – like a colander or a sprinkler .. inside my vagina! And by doing this, I sucked the orgasm out of the man; that was very nice.

"How does she look now?" you asked.

She was smiling .. and she was all limp and relaxed, like a rag doll. Yet it was all deep inside me; not out of my clitoris. It was different in kind from the orgasm of a man. It felt bigger and further-reaching. And that surprised me .. after all, women are supposed to be inferior and passive!

"Yes," you said, "women do feel orgasms at a deeper level than men do."

I asked you if men liked women having orgasms .. and you said of course they did. That was really nice; I don't know in retrospect why I should have been worried. But I continued to feel surprise, not just at how different it was from a penis-orgasm, but how different it was from the almost Platonic Ideal Orgasm that I'd imagined – a kind of other-worldly orgasm. This one was nothing to be afraid of, because I didn't have to leave my Self to have it; it was part of me.

I was puzzled by what I meant by the last bit. My hypnotised brain didn't have enough energy for external generalisations to cope with it properly. But when I woke up, I realised that because I thought only penises had orgasms, I had invented myself an Ideal penis which had Dionysiac orgasms, ecstatic orgasms – literally 'standing outside' me. And so I couldn't fully comprehend it because it wasn't part of me.

RECIPROCITY AS REALITY

We continued this story the next time I saw you. I felt that there was more to it than I had seen yet. You let me lie down, and told me to feel myself. I felt all sharp, like a bolt of lightning. I wanted to make myself smooth, but I didn't know how. Then I wanted to take my contact lenses out so that I shouldn't see,

"You must look," you told me.

I hated you for making me look .. but it was only because I really wanted to look, but was afraid that I'd feel pleasure and then feel ashamed. Yet I felt that the pleasure of the sharpness had started out nice, even if it had been corrupted. I was afraid. But you said we should see everything from a different perspective.

"I'd like you to see an ideal couple," you said. "Watch them making love, and draw the images out of your deepest instincts again."

I cried with pleasure, because last time you'd only let me see myself.

"That was so that you should have a proper image of yourself," you told me.

But the job was only half-done .. and I was delighted to be able to finish it. I saw my ideal couple making love, stroking one another, so that they drew pleasure from each other. They were smiling just because they were joyful .. it wasn't a grating teeth-baring smile trying to pretend that they were happy – and they looked and felt quite natural, as if this was the only way to be. I watched her vagina and his penis shining like the sun, sending rays pulsing warmly right through their bodies.

And they weren't afraid! They weren't looking over their shoulders to see if anyone was coming to attack them; such a possibility just never entered their minds! They were like an unfortified town. I was particularly struck by the passivity of the woman. She was being stroked and giving things out and getting things back .. but she wasn't herself doing the stroking.

"That's right," you said. "By the passionate stage, the woman is passive."

I had always felt it my job to get things soft .. but from the position of sharpness, it was extremely difficult to know what to do. It made all my thoughts sharp, and so wrong. Then I couldn't trust my own judgements.

"See the passion hotting up," you told me.

And I saw them – I saw him stroking her breast .. but although everything was faster and firmer, it was still smooth and rhythmic, not sharp and jabbing. And it was MORE pleasure to ask for more.

"Watch them have an orgasm," you said.

Actually, that was the first picture I'd seen; it was obviously the one I wanted to see most. But now I saw it in proper detail; I watched the fires join and become one. Then they just melted into one another. It was like two small pools becoming one large one. No shooting or squirting .. just melting.

"See and feel how time stands still," you said, "and becomes a part of eternity. It is dying that the armoured ones are afraid of."

That was a wonderful thought, the idea of eternity .. but as you said "dying", I felt myself drawn back into the old sharpness, so that already I couldn't even remember, except as a memory-picture, the pleasures of the soft world. Then I realised that this had been the story of my life.

"I'll count to five," you said, "and then you'll get back to the soft world .. and from that perspective, I'd like you to look at your parents."

Very slowly, I felt my confidence in the new world ebbing back.

"Feel it as well as see it," you told me.

I felt all full and warm inside. Then I looked at mummy and daddy in bed .. and, to my amazement, I saw that their primary feeling in bed was not sharpness, but desperation! I felt "poor things"; they couldn't feel themselves at all and were crying and stretching out and squeezing and pulling in a desperate desire to feel something. Their brains were all dessicated and shrunk to the size of dried peas, and cowering inside the tops of their skulls. And there actually wasn't enough room in their brains for them to feel the feelings – the big feelings.

I was puzzled about why I should only ever have seen the sharpness; it all looked so different from this angle. But then I started to see .. there wasn't enough room in the channels for the libido to flow; it was like furred arteries .. and orgasms had to be like bursting and not melting because for the libido to get out, it had to shoot out through the little hole. And that felt sharp. Then, in the pain – or pleasure – of the shooting, they had to pull back their lips and their skin, to show their teeth .. and the sharpness.

I began to be afraid that I had to be drawn into all this again .. that in order to understand mummy and daddy and to relate to them, I had, as it were, to become them. But you told me that that was just a misplaced loyalty.

"You can be nice to them and help them from your position of difference," you said.

As you said that, I saw myself standing there in front of them .. and they stopped sawing at one another and lifted their heads and turned them towards me and smiled with relief. That was wonderful. I could change things, and didn't have to be a slave to what they wanted. And the feeling stayed with me after I woke up, too; I felt my brain expanding and getting softer, and stopped feeling that I was going to be attacked. And there was room and time for everything .. the world, in addition, had a remarkable clarity, as if it had been washed ..

BANISHING THE FORCES OF DARKNESS

What hadn't been washed, though was my moral sense. I still felt terribly that I had to engage with the forces of darkness in order to conquer them. If I was arguing with someone at work about the meaning or nature of equal opportunities, for example, I always felt that I had to understand what they were saying before I could be fully confident to assail their position. Then I would try to show them ways in which I thought their position was inconsistent, or contradictory, or whatever. But first of all I would be polite to them and do them the honour, or however one might see it, of listening to what they said. Even if I knew before I started that it was going to be rubbish.

You were very angry with me about this. You said that I was a moral coward and that I compromised with the forces of darkness.

"By entering into their world and their arguments, you already weaken your case, and in circumstances where you understand that they are on the side of evil, you should condemn them first and acknowledge any small points they might have later," you stormed at me.

I didn't like this at all; there I was, convinced that I was doing the right thing – morally – and here you were, telling me that my moral sense was not just a little astray, but completely beyond the pale. Yet, when I thought about what you said, I could see that it was a different dimension of thinking from any I had previously experienced. I explained to you that I would like to be able to do what you suggested, but that I always felt swept away by the force of these people, and felt that I didn't have any ground of my own to stand on. So I had to stand on theirs. Now that I thought about it, I could see that I didn't like it, but it was better to fight from their territory than not to fight at all.

You were not convinced. I felt that we were not friends. You were totally disgusted with me, and I was such a moral worm that there was no hope for me ever. I watched myself time after time making a decision about what path to take, in my routes through practical situations .. and it didn't matter what path I took, the other would have been the right one. Eddie and I had a dispute with my mother one day, and I had to leave him to sort it out, because although I could think clearly about how to handle it for as long as I didn't have to talk to her, I was afraid that as soon as I got on the phone, she would bamboozle me and I'd lose my sense of what was right and what was wrong. I was certain that I would be unable to resist entering into her arguments, that I would spend a short while believing that I had succeeded in making my point .. and that I would put the phone down, only to realise that I had unwittingly capitulated to her.

The problem was that a part of me felt that she was entitled to her position, but that I wasn't entitled to mine; in practice, this meant that if we disagreed about something, I was always on the defensive, trying to justify myself, while she took up the attack. That, as I can now see, put her in a much stronger position than me! But I couldn't see it then.

I had the most wretched week, during which I passed through rage with you, to rage with myself, to total and absolute contempt for myself, mingled with the most vicious self-hatred.

"Your mother casts doubt on your own perceptions," you told me, when I finally (as it seemed) saw you again. "She tells you that they are false, and that only she knows the truth. Then she invades you, gobbles you up and leaves no space for you. Not only that, but she conceives any desire on your part for a separate identity as a total rejection of her. You don't love her. So you are torn between being her – which you don't want – or being yourself, but without a mother – which is unacceptable."

What a choice! I was sure that both of these positions were so unacceptable that whichever one I'd chosen, you could never possibly want to look at me again .. but fortunately, I was wrong in this judgement too, and you wanted to hypnotise me to make it all better.

"See the mirror and see your real self," you told me.

I could see myself with my feet on the floor, feeling the ground with my heels as well as my toes. My shoulders were pulled back, rather than pulled forward in fear; my thighs were firm and strong and round, yet not fat, and they shone with libido. I could bounce on the ground and the rhythms could go through me properly – not with shock-waves as had been the case in the old me. My legs were somehow set further back in my hips, leaving my bottom and my haunches more relaxed and able to hang better. I suddenly realised that I was poised for stability and not for flight! And that made a lot of difference.

"You can see clearly now," you said.

And suddenly a white mist lifted from behind the windows (as it were), and a world of bright red, blue and green appeared. I hadn't even known it existed! And I smiled with joy. I felt that I had never known what people smiled for; it was a reflex of politeness which had nothing to do with Life. But here I was smiling.

11
The Good Self

ON BEING POLITE

By this time, the fear and anxiety which had characterised my life before I knew you had receded to a degree which was nothing short of miraculous. There were still things I wanted to discuss with you, but the desperate urgency to change things overnight because the NOW was intolerable had all but vanished. I became free to look more deeply at things, because there was more time in my soul. And it was in this context that I became aware of occasional outbreaks of a generalised, low-level anxiety which, while not being debilitating, nonetheless detracted from the quality of my life.

The solution to this problem also came gently, introduced by a dream which fascinated me: I was on the beach, where I saw lots of little girls in bikinis. They were about 4 or 5 years old and they looked very pleased with themselves. But when I looked to see why, I noticed that in fact they had no bikini bottoms .. and that they all had little penises! And the more pleased with themselves they became, the bigger the little penises grew. I didn't know what to think. I didn't have a penis. Was this good or bad?

"What happened to your penis?" you asked me when I next saw you. This wasn't the first time you'd asked me this question; but I was still puzzled as to what the answer was. After all, I didn't have one .. yet the question made sense .. and that meant that my brain was so scrambled that I couldn't even address the issue properly and evaluate the evidence.

"Lie down then," you suggested. "Now, tell me anything that comes into your mind."

I was afraid that I would be attacked; that anyone who touched me would be attacking me. I especially felt it in my breasts and behind my pubic hair. But I couldn't see who it was who was going to attack me. Then my clitoris stood up to protect me. I didn't feel that it was going to be attacked; it wasn't protecting itself, but protecting me. My teeth and nails became aggressive and clenched, too.

Then .. I saw little me with a penis, not knowing whether to show it or to cringe back. I wanted to show it, but I was afraid that it would be attacked. Then I felt it all warm and wet, as if it was bleeding. On the one hand it wasn't unpleasant, but on the other hand it made me feel devastatingly sad. Yet I didn't know why. I felt guilty for not feeling that it was unpleasant. It was all very strange.

"I'll count to five, and then you will see a blank, and see what it's all about," you told me.

Suddenly I saw the dining room of the house where I had spent my childhood. It was as clear as yesterday; I could see the colour and texture of the curtains, and the shape and feel of the dining room table which used to provide me with shelter as a house, or a ship, or whatever I needed for the games I was playing that day. I must have been about four or five. And I was sitting on daddy's lap. We had a special game that we used to play, where each of us had to get the other's ear lobe in our mouth before our own ear lobe was caught by the other's mouth. It was enormous fun.

Well, in this picture, we were playing this game, and having a marvellous time .. but suddenly, he got an erection. And he threw me off his lap and stood up. I was really shocked – literally. Then I saw that inside his trousers he still had an erection. But he turned away so that I shouldn't see it. And I quite literally didn't know what to do; there was nothing I could do to make it better now that we had reached this point. I wanted to take his penis and look at it .. but it was clear that he wouldn't like that. And then I found myself wanting to squeeze it until the pips squeaked, and *force* it to give me what it had .. but for a start, this wasn't a nice thing to do, and secondly, it would have tasted like apple pips – all bitter and revolting – even if I had. So I could do nothing. I was quite paralysed.

It was interesting seeing all this again and reliving the memories.

Now that I saw it, I remembered it happening the first time .. but I had retained no conscious memory of it at all. I knew that we used to play the ear-lobe game, and that we had enjoyed it – but this episode had completely been obliterated from consciousness. Yet it had really happened; it wasn't a fantasy-picture, or an interpretation of a happening – it was a real part of my history.

"What *ought* to have happened?" you asked me.

I saw myself again on daddy's lap, feeling his penis all warm and big, and playing with it. And it was nice and we shared it. And then I *didn't* take it away, or eat it up, or have sex with it; after I'd felt it nice and been pleased, all I wanted to do was to go and play Wendy houses under the table. Yet I had felt daddy imply that I'd do all sorts of terrible things to him. Nothing to do with him; I was the one who was going to take his penis. No pleasure for him – just my desire.

Then I realised that I'd always felt that men expected me to take their penises, whether or not I wanted to, and whether or not it was appropriate. And I hadn't always wanted to, and had terminated some very pleasant friendships as a result of my feeling that I was letting the men down. And all because daddy made me feel that he *expected* me to take his penis .. and then didn't like it! In addition, I often felt that anything I did was by definition wrong. Then I recoiled in shock .. then followed the guilt .. then the terrible lassitude which could take hours or even days to dissipate. Yet now I saw that the little girl *did* know how to do it, *did* do it nicely, and – most important of all – *did* know when enough was enough!

That was wonderful. After waking up, I felt my eyes deeper in their sockets because my face at the cheeks had become wider and left the eyes more room. And I had lost the feeling that I needed to mind my ps and qs and protect myself against unseen attackers. And that was very nice.

HOW TO BE SEPARATE – BUT NOT ALONE

Although I was always worrying about whether or not people liked and respected me, the evidence was that they did. For as long as I could remember, I had been coopted onto committees. No sooner did I walk into a meeting than someone would ask me to join the committee! Or that's what it felt like, anyway. It was very nice, being wanted so much; the trouble, though, was that I found it so difficult to say no.

I liked most of my committee work very much, and was fascinated by the practical and political business of writing papers, lobbying MPs, attending meetings, and so on. But it became ridiculous; the phone never stopped ringing, and I was totally exhausted by all the demands being made on my time and energy. The problem was exacerbated by the fact that almost all my committees seemed to elect me to their Chair – and I quite literally didn't know how to refuse! It was bizarre; I used sometimes to feel that I was living in one of Ionesco's plays. I particularly identified with the circumstances of one in which furniture removers keep bringing more and more furniture to a house until there isn't any room for anyone to live in it, and the whole play reaches a crisis of absurdity. Well, my life was so cluttered by committees that I didn't have room to move, either. Yet I didn't altogether like living in the theatre of the absurd. But why couldn't I get out of it? I felt like a victim, not a participant – and that didn't seem right.

One day, it dawned on me that I could ask you to help; it *wasn't* inevitable that things should happen like this. I began to wonder whether my inability to say no resulted from narcissistic deprivation. I felt that I couldn't refuse people who wanted me to join their committees, because I was desperately dependent on their looking at me and liking me. Even when I became overwhelmed by work, I couldn't resign because I was afraid I would let them down, and they would be angry with me, and I would then lose the sense of narcissistic gratification with which they provided me. My eyeballs became very hard, as if pulled back, and I felt two corresponding spots of tension at the base of my back, just above my buttocks.

You let me lie down to look at this.

"See your real self in the mirror, and relax the part of your brain concerned with vision," you told me.

A vision of the self I *didn't* like flashed through my brain. Then there was the mirror .. but I wasn't in it. Nor was I standing in front of it. Gradually, I saw a foot poke its toe in .. and then run away! Then the whole of me flitted across. Eventually, I saw all of me; I liked this lady, but I didn't really believe she was me. And I hated the other me .. but I didn't really believe that she wasn't me. So I was neither of them.

"Look at the nice one," you said.

Her skin was shining almost as if someone had oiled it. And it glowed yellow, or golden; it picked up all the light and had wonderful deep contrasts of light and shadow. She was round without being fat, and her belly was connected to her clitoris. She didn't get cut off at the legs .. and that meant that her legs were alive and had her in them. And her clitoris was part of her .. so it didn't have to poke out. It felt supported .. but by the rest of her, not by something external. It fitted well.

Then I could feel her bottom and her vagina sucking – but also pushing and letting things bubble gently out.

"Relax her back," you told me.

I felt my pelvic girdle fall forward at the back. This disconnected it from my backbone; and that was wonderful. I hadn't ever been aware that I was so tense that my pelvis was almost squeezed onto my backbone, so that it was stuck to it from the pressure. It was really nice to feel it released! My legs and hips could move better; they could swing because there was space. And things didn't spurt out of me; they flowed. It was like lava from a volcano, but in the gentle pulsing phase, not in the explosive, pushing-everything-up-into-the-air phase. It was very nice.

"How does your vagina feel?" you asked me.

There was space in there. It was as if it had become a whole room after only being a corridor; so there was space for things to happen. It wasn't that there wasn't a corridor any more – there was; but it led somewhere, and it was deeper inside me and somehow lower down. It was like not having my tongue stuck to the roof of my mouth.

"Look at her top half now," you suggested.

Her face was smiling .. but it smiled from the lower jaw and not

from the upper jaw, so the teeth didn't have to bite. And now it was
more relaxed, the cheeks could stay fat and the skin above my cheeks
didn't have to tense up, baring my upper teeth. I could still bite if I
wanted to .. but now I could choose. Then I saw her shoulders relax
and pull further back, so that her breasts were more prominent and
more visible .. and yet they didn't POKE out because their position
was natural.

"Can I leave the not-nice one and become the nice one?" I asked
you, hopefully.

"It's not quite as simple as that," you told me. "Be the not-nice
one."

Instantly, I felt my cheeks pucker and my clitoris hurt.

"You're hiding something," you said. "Look at yourself and tell
yourself to stand up and that it's all right."

But as I looked, I saw myself wanting to kill mummy. That was
what I was hiding .. and I still wanted to do it. I still wanted to
experience that pleasure.

"You have become fixated on the desire to kill your mother,"
you told me. "You have to give it up. You can achieve the same
freedom for yourself – or even a better freedom – by differentiating
yourself from her and doing something else."

And as I watched, the not-nice me shed her skin, and mummy
lay on the ground lifeless as I stepped out of her. I emerged looking
like the nice me, but not knowing quite what to do. The nice me
came towards me and invited me to come to her. Then she took me
in her arms and hugged me and told me she'd teach me how to do
things. And we both shone. Then we took each other's hands and
danced around together – both naked and both quite natural and
unselfconscious and without covering our genitals with our thighs.
We weren't *stopping* ourselves from doing so .. we just didn't want
or need to.

It was so wonderful, the feeling of being close to 'another'
woman, and feeling enveloped by her warmth and trusted by her and
trusting in her. I'd often felt that pleasure in being with men – but
this lady was showing me how to be a nice woman .. and how could
I be friends with men if I didn't know what being a woman was like?
We stroked each other all over, feeling each other and drawing each

other out. And I felt that eventually, when I'd learnt all about it, we would become one.

I felt my whole world-view change. My universe was populated by people onto whom I projected a concept of love and womanhood. But all my assumptions were now changing, and I could see quite different things in people; new qualities I'd never even have dreamed of. I felt that now I had a friend, and standards to judge by, and someone who would always love me and understand me, so I was now in a position to discriminate. I didn't *have* to be grateful all the time; I could appreciate things that were good, but could refuse to grovel in gratitude to every little crumb that came my way. And that made me proud of myself; the idea that I didn't have to accept garbage but was worthy of better and able to produce better for myself was very nice indeed.

I asked you, would she and I become one just by letting them.

"Yes," you said. "Now lie down on the grass together and go to sleep."

And we did. Then you woke me up .. and I felt the waters lapping gently into my brain and up my body. The wave-motion was less forceful than it had been upon waking up on previous occasions – but it was no less deep. It was like floating away.

My brain was all in a different place! There seemed to be more of it over my eyes, and my sense of balance was slightly upset. I could FEEL the bits moving inside my head. Then I felt you, and I felt you moving in the depths of your soul, and I felt you in the depth of my soul, and I felt that we met and understood each other. And I realised that I wasn't afraid of the dark any more; the dark underworld had finally been cleared of monsters and I could see. I was free of the fixation of killing mummy.

"It occupied a large part of your brain," you told me. "A lot of libido was diverted to it .. and then diverted to hiding it. I am pleased that you have stepped out of her skin."

And as you spoke, even though I was fully conscious, I saw the nice me beckoning me to come and play with her and be with her and do my thing with her. And I wanted to go with her and be her and do her thing, which would be *my* thing, and be proud of it.

Then I found that I could see you and acknowledge your world,

and separate myself from it. This meant that I was now in a position
to enjoy your world and to be your friend. I realised that I didn't
have to take you inside me in order to know you; that people have
to be separate as well as together .. and that differentiation as to
which person is which makes all the difference to the pleasure. It was
all very interesting; I suddenly saw that there were more people in
the world than just me projected into many bodies! And that was
fascinating. I was free to look.

*   *   *

But what was there to look at? It was amazing the way the solution
of one problem cleared the way for some other difficulty to bring
itself to the surface to be investigated. I had honestly never realised
how complex the human soul was. Or, rather, I had realised that it
was, but had no idea what all the ramifications looked like. But I
found myself very pleased with myself, because even before I knew
you, I had rejected simplistic, sloganised views of the universe; I had
known that it was all more complicated than some of our political
ideologues would have us think. I suppose that some of them made
things seem very complicated, and wrote huge and wide-ranging
treatises on the world and its evils .. yet even most of those who
acknowledged the complexity couldn't see what it consisted in, and
obfuscated the real issues by embroiling themselves in ever-
increasing detail about things which either didn't matter or were
only trivial aspects of important truths.

For example, take the campaign for unilateral nuclear disarma-
ment. This correctly identified the fact that it is crazy to have so many
such dangerous weapons lying around the world, and that it's crazy
for superpowers (and others) to spend all their time defending
themselves against an enemy. Of course. Who wouldn't agree with
that? But the real question, it seemed to me, was WHY this happened.
Until that question was answered, the problem could never be finally
solved. Maybe it would be sensible to get rid of nuclear weapons
unilaterally, if that reduced the total number of weapons and also
gave a superpower the confidence that it wasn't going to be attacked.
But it didn't seem that the conclusion that the campaigners drew was

the inevitable one. They felt that if we gave up nuclear weapons, then other people would follow suit, as they realised they didn't need them either. But it seemed to me that the whole desire to have nuclear weapons in the first place wasn't as rational as the anti-weapons campaigners were alleging. So if we gave them up, *nothing* followed logically about what other people might do. For their reasons for having such weapons went far deeper than the practicalities of having to have the same arms as their potential opponents. Perhaps it would *still* be a good and moral thing for us to give up our nuclear armaments .. but not for the reasons given. The issue was far more complex than CND would have us believe.

Or take Marxist ideology. Of course it is true that some people are exploited by other people, and that people have become alienated from their products and their labour. But to interpret the whole world as if it was an economic equation, without asking WHY people allow this to happen to them, and why the oppressors feel the need to oppress them, seemed to me also to be looking at the problem from the wrong point of view. The important question had to do with motivation and desire, not statistics and mathematics. People are more than fractions of a populace. So they could write the most supremely scholarly books about Marxist ideology and practice; all I could see was that most of it missed the fundamental point.

ON HAVING A CLITORIS AND HAVING IDEAS

The trouble was that I still had difficulty in uniting all these thoughts and feelings with my Self. I still didn't know what it was I was able to see and able to understand. Nor did I know why I couldn't see, and couldn't understand. I had some vague feeling that it had something to do with penises – but what that thing was, heaven alone knew! I could see how much more beautiful and slim and relaxed I'd become since the session when we freed me from my fixation on killing mummy .. but I didn't know how to live as my free self.

"Why don't you lie down?" you suggested. "Look in the mirror.."

And before you could say any more, my unconscious leapt in front of it. No more cowering in the corner! I could see her jumping up and down. And she had such a lot of energy. But it was all a bit hysterical; she wouldn't calm down and be looked at properly.

"Tell her to calm down, and to listen," you told me.

She turned to me with big, alert, interested eyes and shining big cheeks. She really looked at me. It was lovely. She drew me to her by her look and acknowledged my existence as an important person.

"We're going to ask her to show us what she's always wanted to do, but repressed," you said.

I saw her go and sit down at a table covered with books for reading and writing. But she was uneasy because her clitoris hurt and she needed a pee. And she couldn't do what she wanted with unadulterated pleasure because her clitoris kept tweaking at her. Then I found myself thinking that mummy regarded passing exams and other such things as ways in which I could be better than men .. and then steal their penises from them. That was why she wanted me to go to university in the first place. But her attitude had made me rather ambivalent about it .. which was a pity, as I really liked learning things!

"Perhaps you could be a little girl and see yourself peeing," you suggested.

I saw myself about 4 years old.

"Pee like you've always wanted to," you told me.

I could see the picture: I was on the lawn and just letting the pee well up out of me and envelop the ground. It was like stroking the ground and the grass, and acknowledging it, and taking it into myself and making it mine, part of me. I hadn't realised that peeing, too, was a taking-in sensation. And I felt that the sensation was enormous, universal, as if I encompassed the whole of the heavens. It was lovely. But my clitoris was still hurting too much for me really to experience the feeling fully.

"Pull the face of the nice clitoris," you suggested, "and then of the hurting clitoris."

I could see the face of the nice clitoris, all soft and sucking. I could feel the sensations of it all soft and responsive and oceanic ..

but again, the hurting got in the way. My brain couldn't quite cope. Yet, as I thought about it, I found myself feeling that there wasn't really anything the matter with my clitoris except that it had a grievance that it wanted to tell us about and have us acknowledge and be nice about, rather than tell it that it was its own fault or whatever. And I felt terribly that I had let it down, because I had internalised the poker-faced mummy, and not been nice to it myself.

"I'll come along and help," you said. "I'll be there and you can tell me."

I saw little me standing on the lawn, spreading my labia majora with my fingers and showing you my clitoris. And you looked and smiled. I opened my mouth to say: "It hurts because mummy's stolen my penis." But then I realised that that actually *wasn't* what I wanted to say, even though I'd always represented it to myself that way. What I really wanted to say was: "Look. Isn't it nice? But mummy says there's nothing there." And I was so pleased that I'd realised what was the matter, and then I could also acknowledge it because I knew what it was I was arguing against. I felt everything relax with pleasure between my legs. I had something. And it wasn't a penis.

"Will you show it to Uncle George?" you asked me. "I'd like to see it."

That was a problem; the only ways I knew to show it assumed that it was really a penis. For clitorises aren't visible when you're standing up. And I was trying to show it standing up. So I had to get my body (and my brain) into a whole new position. And it took some working out how to do it!

Suddenly, though, I saw myself naked on your lap. You were naked as well. And my clitoris was up against your penis, and your penis was stroking it, nuzzling it, and telling me how it liked me and liked my clitoris, and that we were mates, you and I, and that we understood one another. It was like licking or sucking each other; it was lovely. Then .. you were lying down, and I was sitting on your tummy – and that made my clitoris visible to you. I was showing it to you and you were pleased and liked it. You told me how delighted you were and how much you liked looking at it and how much trust it showed in you that I could do that, and how nice it was for you. And it was all wonderful; I felt so acknowledged and happy. It was as if I didn't have to TRY any more, but could just BE.

But at this point, I started to feel rather nervous. What would happen if .. And yes, there was mummy at the door, looking at us. I expected that she would spoil it all, by being angry or making some fatuous sneering remark. But in fact, she gazed at us in total non-comprehension. She actually didn't have the brain-cells to understand what was going on. And she went away again!

Then I saw big me at the table of books again. My clitoris was taking them all in and feeling them and sniffing at them like an elephant's trunk. Then .. I'd had enough. I didn't need to be an obsessive intellectual; I could just do it because I enjoyed it, and then stop and do something else. I didn't have to prove myself to you. You would love me anyway, just because I had a big brain that knew how to enjoy itself. So I went out for a walk in the country – still in the picture-world. It all felt like the universe I'd created by peeing, or acknowledged and taken in by peeing. So I felt part of it, and felt that all the trees and flowers were part of me. It was much nicer looking at something which I had a relationship with than something that had nothing to do with me. It was lovely.

When I woke up, it was like the gentle lapping of the waves again. I felt like an elastic band that had been stretched and that could suddenly boingg into relaxation. And then .. I felt the universe in my clitoris, and could see the vault of heaven in my mons veneris. It was extraordinary!

ON ACCEPTING THE INSTINCTS

After all this, I found myself wanting to have opinions and express myself more than I could remember doing for a long time. As a child, and even as an adolescent and a young adult, I had retained an enormous enthusiasm for things, and wanted always to talk and chew ideas over, and get excited about them. But as I became a proper adult – and especially after going to university – I had become less alive. It wasn't going to be worth getting excited or having an opinion; after all, what was the point? What was it all for? And what would it change anyway? I had become totally lethargic about matters of the spirit – except in exceptional circumstances; I knew that underneath, I was still passionately interested, but the real-world obstacles seemed too great. This, it occurred to me, must be why people settle for boring lives; they lose their sense of wonder. But now I found mine coming back!

It wasn't altogether as simple as that, however. With the desire came a new awareness of all the feelings and obstacles which had prevented me from realising it the first time round. Yet this time there was you to help. And it was in relation to you that I found the drama played itself out. You would often talk to me about things – politics, philosophy, and so on .. and I would feel that I didn't quite take in what you said. It was very exciting and I wanted to respond .. but it was difficult for me. It was even more problematic if I disagreed with you. Was it allowed to disagree with you, or did I have to say yes all the time? Was I allowed to express an opinion about something in my own right; could I introduce a new topic of conversation, or was that forward or aggressive? I didn't know. But what shocked me was how my head would fill with terrible fantasies of people dying .. and it being my fault. What on earth was going on in my head?

We talked about this for some time; you didn't want to hypnotise me too early in the realisation process, as you wanted my ego to take on the challenge itself first. We discussed my relationship with penises, and how I wasn't sure whether the part of me that thought they liked me was telling the truth or whether it was just a crazy, optimistic fantasy which would only delude and mislead me, leading to more let-down and misery in the long run.

It was very difficult for my ego to get to grips with all this. I felt that you were asking me to replay all the tragedies of my youth, with their disappointments and feelings of meaninglessness – and I had an enormous vested interest in the protection mechanisms of not looking at it, not acknowledging it, not having to feel the pain. So it was a hard few weeks. But at the end of them, I felt that I had isolated the feeling of pain and anguish from my Self, so that even if it was there, it wasn't essential to my being. Life was still hard, because the

process of keeping the pain at bay used up a lot of my energy, so the
Self I had now separated from the pain still couldn't do very much
.. but it was a great deal better than thinking it was all a fundamental
part of my being.

You were not really impressed, unfortunately. You said I was
having a tantrum and that I needed to be spanked. I told you that if
you spanked me, I'd bite your hand.

"I couldn't care less," you said. "You have lost control of her,
and she needs spanking."

Part of me was glad you were going to spank her. But part of
me, when it came to the crunch, was afraid that maybe I hadn't
separated my Self from her .. and that you were going to spank me.
That made me very angry.

You let me lie down and told me to look at my unconscious as
it had been behaving over the past few weeks. God, it was furious!
It was barely human, it was so livid! Its teeth were bare and pointed,
and its hair stood on end and sparkled like lightning with static electricity. Its hands were clenched and it was almost on all fours with
primitive emotion. She was shitting and peeing all over the floor in
fury. All that energy! And all locked up in tantrumming .. when it
should have been mine to use constructively. What a waste! She was
starving me of energy.

But as I looked at her, I found, to my amazement, that I liked
her! I had expected to find her contemptible and unpleasant .. but actually, I had enormous affection for her. And as soon as she saw me
liking her, she grinned at me. I'd taken notice of her, and that was
all she wanted. She had no shame, no embarrassment; she was completely amoral! She came up to me and climbed up my leg; then she
rubbed her bottom and her urethra against my tummy. And it was
soft and lovely. And that was all she wanted. No more defaecating
or peeing on the floor.

Yet I found myself worried. It was very nice, having her there
– but I wasn't sure which of us was me. I could feel my neck getting
all tight. She was only a bundle of uncontrolled instincts and I didn't
want her to take me over.

"You're afraid of her," you observed. "You don't know how to handle her because you haven't got a model of how to do it. I'll show you if you like. Here I come, in my straw hat."

In you came. I was jealous; she was going to like you more than she liked me.

"Watch me," you said.

And I saw you standing there .. and your penis didn't pull back. You weren't afraid. You looked at her, and your look didn't condemn.

She looked at you. And she thought: "This man will kick me in the behind if I misbehave. So I'd better not." And she went to you and climbed up your leg and nestled in the hair on your chest and put her arms trustingly round your neck, just taking it for granted that she was your friend. Then she went to sleep, perfectly content.

I was puzzled. Did I approve? What about morality? Was it right that this unthinking world should hold sway? After all, she wasn't grateful for being accepted after being a bad girl; she wasn't even sorry she'd been a bad girl. She just knew that things with you were nice if she was good .. so she'd be good. I might calculate that and think of it as immoral expediency; SHE didn't .. she just did it. But what were my 'morals'? Were they my ego, my superego, or what?

"I'll count to 5 and we'll have a look," you said.

I was terrified. But .. into view came a bent little old lady with a long nose and a stick – a dessicated old maid, thin and stick-like. Then I found myself thinking that, despite everything, I *still* believed that I had to give up my clitoris in order to have a vagina; that being a woman meant having a vagina. But I didn't *want* to give up my clitoris. Therefore, I thought, I couldn't have a vagina. And I erected my clitoris as the moral standard protecting my decision. But then there were no deep instinctual pleasures, so the only ones left were killjoy ones: thou shalt not have a vagina. But the little wild creature had a vagina and wasn't prepared to be controlled by the over-dominant clitoris. So her development had been arrested by the old lady with the stick – the personification of the over-developed clitoris. It was truly fascinating, seeing all this.

But the trouble was that as I *did* have a vagina, my anxiety that I had to give up my clitoris if I wanted to keep it made them both angry. My vagina got angry because it was deprived of its clitoris, and my clitoris got angry because it was always under threat of my choosing to have a vagina instead .. and so on. I wanted to have both.

"Of course you have to have both," you said.

You shook the old lady by the nose. And as you acknowledged her nose – her clitoris again – it got smaller, and she stood upright and supple and threw away the stick. She was me! And the little one looked at me from the vantage-point of your chest .. and stretched out her arm to her new friend!

I was worried, though. I asked you, won't men be upset if I have a clitoris? Won't they feel threatened? Don't I have to give it up to please them?

"Of course you don't" you said. "Men like clitorises because their penises can then have real companionship. As for being threatened, happy vaginas and clitorises don't attack men, so there is nothing for men to feel threatened by."

And, do you know, I had quite literally never thought of that as a possibility. I had thought that the way I behaved, protecting men from my clitoris, was 'moral' – but in fact it was all based on a contorted logic. That was such a relief. Imagine it being moral to like sex and to expect men to like it as well!!

When I woke up, I found myself thinking what a funny thing reason is, and how important it is to get the major emotional premises right in order that proper value-judgements may be made. Indeed – *all* judgement is affected. The idea that the whole arena of argument in which I had been operating was life-denying and invalid was a new and wonderful feeling. How nice it was to be freed from the compulsion to think – but just to be allowed to get on with feeling, without censorship!

HAVING MY SOUL BACK

One wonderful day, I woke up and decided that I'd like to ask you for my soul back. When I first came to see you, I was a complete wreck, not knowing who I was or what I wanted. But now I felt strong and valiant; I wanted to step out into the world and do things for myself. It wasn't that I wanted to stop coming to see you; there seemed to be far too many interesting things left in my soul that I'd still like to explore. It was more that I wanted it to be me coming to see you rather than you giving me access to myself.

I had been very pleased to give you my soul to look after. It was safe with you, and well cared-for. I knew that mummy wouldn't be able to get at it for as long as you had it – and at the beginning of our friendship, that was my major concern. Now, though, I often found myself irrationally angry with you because I was afraid that you wouldn't hypnotise me. And when I asked myself why I should be angry with you when the only things you ever did for me were wonderful, the answer that rose inxorably from the depths of my soul was that I wanted to be me at all times; I didn't want my appointment with you to be the only time I ever met myself properly; I didn't want you and not me to decide when it was appropriate for me to meet myself. I wanted to be your equal.

This was a most extraordinary feeling of liberation; I was big enough to defend my soul against my mother all on my own .. and if there were still problems (and I didn't delude myself!), then we would *both* sort them out, you and I. I was so excited when I realised that this was what I wanted. Never before had I had the courage to acknowledge myself and own myself. I throbbed with joy.

You were delighted; you didn't say – not that I had expected you to, but my mother would have – that I was abandoning you and that you were hurt and rejected, and was this all I was giving you in return for all the care and attention you had lavished on me. No – you let me lie down straightaway.

"Feel your body," you told me.

I could feel it like a mountain stream, all rippling through me. And it was gleaming golden in the sunlight. I liked it.

"Now," you went on, "we're going to have a big, solemn, soul-handing-over ceremony. It is a big responsibility, taking charge of a soul. You must assume it with due care and attention." You sounded like Sarastro, and we both laughed. But you were right, and I appreciated the seriousness with which you were taking it.

"I'll count to five, and you'll feel your soul re-enter your body," you said.

I was swept by a wonderful feeling. My soul took up residence in a part of my brain – and in my chest. I could feel it warm and vibrant and alive and life-giving. Then it popped out and told you how grateful it was for all the love and attention you'd given it, and how much it had enjoyed living with you .. but goodbye now, George .. it was so pleased to be coming home. And it waved good-bye to you, and hoped it and you would still be friends. I wept a little; it was a quite overwhelming experience.

Then I became aware of something rather curious; the part of my brain which had housed my superego just faded away. It wasn't dead .. it was just not there. It was like milk teeth after you've lost them.

"You have an ego-ideal now, not a superego," you told me.

And as you spoke, I realised that my superego had always lived in my jaw, stopping things getting past, while my ego-ideal lived INSIDE me .. I had taken it in .. past the erstwhile garrison manned by my superego.

I was still rather anxious, though. There were going to be so many new things to learn. For example, in the old regime, the only way I ever had of telling anyone I loved them was to give them my soul. I was just a bit nervous, therefore, that you would feel that the fact that I wanted it back meant that I didn't love you any more.

"Of course not," you said. "It is nice for me that we are two people who can have the pleasure of being ourselves *and* the pleasure of responding to the other being him- or herself."

I had often felt while I lived inside you that it was a bit cramped.

"That's right," you agreed. "Now you'll be free to ask me what I think about things and to share your thoughts with me, rather than just asking me what you should do."

And that was nice.

"How does your vagina feel now?" you asked.

It felt very nice .. except that my pubic bone ached a bit; it was nervous.

"What about?"

It was afraid that if it relaxed, and my vagina wasn't armoured and held up from within either, then my vagina would fall out! And that would be most particularly a tragedy now that it was full of me and not full of mummy.

"Relax it and see what happens," you suggested.

You pulled yourself into all kinds of strange positions so that I could see what it felt like and how it looked when it was pulled back, and how my bottom tightened and my pelvis tipped slightly forward to hold it in.

"Relax your bottom and feel the pubic bone come forward and feel your back relax," you said.

Well .. I could! And then I became aware, as if for the first time,. of the 'back' wall of my vagina. It was so deep; there was such a lot of room going way back, in my vagina. Then I felt that the back wall of my vagina was shared with my bottom. They were somehow related with each other through the wall. And I felt a pleasant and agreeable pressure from my rectum into my vagina. They were, in a certain respect, a single system. But the feelings weren't all squashed up at the front .. they were all over. In my clitoris too – a lovely relaxation. And my legs were free; they too had been crushed by the pulling on the pubic bone. Yet as I lay and relaxed and sucked, I became anxious that mummy and daddy would see me like this and I worried about how I would be, as it were, impelled to react. Would I seize up again?

"Stop worrying about them looking at you," you told me, "and look at yourself. That's what counts; you're the judge now."

You told me to stand in front of the mirror. I saw a huge round shining ball. I was really pleased.

"That's the infantile picture," you said, "the round happy baby."

Then I watched it grow up .. but all I could see was the genital area. It had big sparkling alert eyes, and a nose which sniffed around, and a mouth which tasted everything. It participated in the world; it didn't just have things happen to it. But nor did it suffer from the infantile delusion that it made everything happen. The world was there, and it could have an effect on it – but it didn't MAKE it; it interrelated with it. And that was lovely. I could *do* things.

The next thing I saw was myself grown-up, sitting on the ground, with my legs out in front and my knees bent and feet flat on the ground. My vagina was relating with the ground, coming out, as it were, to meet it .. and my arms were stretched out as if to embrace things, in a kind of round, ready to absorb and take in way – even if there was nothing there at the moment. And my belly was round, and my skin glowed golden and warm. And I felt hungry .. yet I knew that, for the first time ever, I would know when I'd eaten enough. I related with and respected myself. And that was lovely.

Then I watched her stand up and lift her leg as if to dance like a ballerina. I could see all her genitals as she faced me full on. And her vagina didn't fall out! Now that it was active and participated in the world, rather than just passively experiencing the world when it was lucky enough, it was alive. And because it was alive, it was a part of me, and the question of it falling out just never occurred. It just didn't make sense. Of course it wasn't going to fall out! It was part of me, and connected to me; it didn't have to be held on by some external means, which then might fail me.

"What does it feel like, having your soul?" you asked.

I had to think about that .. but the answer, when it emerged, filled me with a warm, flowing pleasure. I felt that wherever I was, that would now be home; home would be inside me rather than outside. And that was wonderful; I was pleased. You said you'd wake me up now .. and instead of feeling sad as I often did, I felt such a sense of excitement and adventure – because my soul was going to stay with ME now, and not go back to its 'safe house' with you. It was safe with me, and we were going to be buddies in the adventure of my life. I felt a quiet thrill as you brought me back to full consciousness; I felt full up and solid. My bones were heavy and warm inside me, and I was relaxed and serene, confident that I would be strong enough to meet the world face to face. I was so grateful to you .. we were separate people now – and I loved us both.

After this, life had so much time in it, that I had never imagined it could all be so full and so interesting. I would catch myself thinking that although I liked nice things – like soft duvets on the bed to snuggle into – I didn't need them any more because I carried the softness and comfort around with me now. I had always known that life had another dimension; and now I had begun to discover its depths.

GIVING DADDY'S PENIS BACK

Now that I was myself again, I wanted to start my new life with a clean slate. And, I felt, there was something I needed to do before I would be fully at peace. But what was it? I didn't know; all I was aware of was a curious sense of generalised anxiety. Accompanying this came all my old preoccupation and guilt about religion. It took me a long time to realise what was going on – but one day, I understood that I was still anxious that maybe I had torn off daddy's penis – or God's penis – and I wanted to give it back to him, so that we could start again with him and me being separate people too. You thought this was a good idea, and you hypnotised me again to let me do it.

You held my head.

"It can expand into my hand," you told me, "and your brain can grow and become flexible and un-rigid. Now, look at God."

Well, I couldn't see God. But I could see a wide-open sea shore with the sea and the sand stretching to the horizon. Daddy was on the beach. Two mes were walking towards him: a little me, about 3 or 4, and a big me, my present age. We were all naked. Little me was holding daddy's penis aloft in her hand, like a fish she had caught, and she was saying: "Here you are, daddy. I'm sorry I took it. Now I've got her (big me) as my mentor, I don't need it any more. I am me without it. Please have it back for yourself."

Daddy was pleased to have it back. He took it and looked at it. It was almost as if he hadn't registered that he didn't have it. He was contented. Then he put it against himself where it should go. And his body sucked nicely to hold it back on .. and then it was his again. I wept with relief and pleasure. We all looked at one another and were pleased with ourselves. Then the little me went head-first up the vagina of the big me, and was absorbed into her. I didn't need little me any more, because she'd paid her debt and so her *raison d'être* as a separate being was over. She could come home .. and I could become integrated.

Then I saw daddy become small and me become huge. But now I was me in my own right, I wasn't angry with him any more for being small – and that was nice.

Then .. I saw God. He was on the horizon, smiling. And he embraced the sea and the land; he wasn't sucking them in or overwhelming them .. he was just being there, protecting and loving them. He was big and, as it were, lay over everything. I couldn't see his penis because it was below the horizon, but I didn't become anxious or worry that I'd steal it or anything like that, because I could just see from his demeanour and the way he was that he had a penis and that it was nice. And he looked at me and I was happy.

At that point, I wanted to wake up; I was content with what I'd seen. But while I was relaxing before you woke me, I saw God become the sun setting over the horizon .. and although it – or do I mean he? – was going to sink out of sight, I knew that he was still there and that he would rise again in the morning .. and I felt quiet and full and blissfully, relaxedly happy. There was a foundation for life – at last!